B+T

MESSAGES TO THE WORLD

MESSAGES TO THE WORLD

THE STATEMENTS OF OSAMA BIN LADEN

Edited and Introduced by
BRUCE LAWRENCE

Translated by
JAMES HOWARTH

VERSO
London • New York

First published by Verso 2005
Introduction © Bruce Lawrence 2005

1 3 5 7 9 10 8 6 4 2

Verso
UK: 6 Meard Street, London W1F 0EG
USA: 180 Varick Street, New York, NY 10014-4606
www.versobooks.com

Verso is the imprint of New Left Books

ISBN 1-84467-045-7

British Library Cataloguing in Publication Data
A catalogue record for this book is available from the British Library

Library of Congress Cataloging-in-Publication Data
A catalog record for this book is available from the Library of Congress

Typeset in Bembo
Printed in the USA by Quebecor World, Fairfield

953.805

958.104

650 TERRORISTS - 600 20 Bin Laden, U
SA - Biog

CONTENTS

EDITOR'S ACKNOWLEDGMENTS

The labor of many went into the making of this volume. Dr Miriam Cooke read through most of the longer statements with me and offered invaluable insight into the rhetorical nuances of Osama bin Laden's often archaic Arabic. Also providing help tracking down the cascade of Qur'anic and *hadith* references in the messages was Kevin Fogg, a recent graduate of Duke University. Another Duke resource was Dr Ebrahim Moosa. A trained religious scholar and an authority on Islamic law, he commented on juridical aspects of bin Laden's persona, and also read drafts of the Introduction. Finally, Dr Flagg Miller, a linguistic anthropologist, gave permission to cite his unpublished talk on Osama bin Laden's use of Arabic speech forms in audiocassettes.

Dr Khaled Hamid and Tammy Elmansoury provided invaluable help in tracking down Arabic transcripts of bin Laden's speeches, as did the staff at the Institute of Arab and Islamic Studies, University of Exeter. Statement 5 is reproduced by kind permission of CNN.

To all of these individuals I am grateful, though none of them bears responsibility for the final form of these statements, the headnotes introducing them, or the Introduction to the book as a whole. I remain the person of record in the challenging but critical endeavor to bring Osama bin Laden's actual statements into the conversations and considerations of a wider English-speaking public.

TRANSLATOR'S NOTE

The publication of these translations—rendered directly from the Arabic—requires some brief contextualization. Although Osama bin Laden enjoys global notoriety (and a considerable virtual presence), the primary material has often been surprisingly difficult to track down, and has been obtained from numerous different sources: transcripts of video and audio tapes, newspapers and the internet; the latter complicated by the fact that many of the websites on which the statements were first posted have subsequently been shut down. In certain cases, various different versions of an "original" text appear to be in circulation. Nevertheless, although the question of authenticity inevitably arises when ever a message is released in bin Laden's name, the 24 statements in this collection, issued over a ten-year period, have all been accepted as genuine by a majority of the experts and officials who have examined them. In the case of four statements (Messages 4, 5, 16, and 21), Arabic texts could not be sourced, and existing English translations have therefore been used; where appropriate, the syntax has been altered for consistency and clarity of meaning.

All due effort has been made to overcome the syntactical and stylistic difficulties of rendering bin Laden's distinctive style into English. For clarity and flow of language, religious formulae that normally follow the invocation of God or the Prophet Muhammad (in particular the customary "Peace be Upon Him") have been omitted. For the most part, key Arabic terms have been translated into English; those of particular significance are glossed in the footnotes on first usage. A handful of terms, including *umma* and *jihad*, have been retained in the original Arabic throughout the text, due to their intrinsically untranslatable nature.

Bin Laden's citations from the Qur'anic and the *hadith* have been referenced in the footnotes wherever possible. *Hadith*, the "traditions" conveying the words and actions of the Prophet Muhammad that were accumulated by scholars after his death, are seen as critically important within Islamic jurisprudence. For Sunni Muslims, there are six canonical collections of hadith, of which two in particular (those by al-Bukhari and Muslim) are seen as the most authoritative. While every attempt has been made to identify all those cited by bin Laden, given that hundreds of thousands of hadith exist some have inevitably proved impossible to track down; it is to be hoped that future scholarship will identify them. All dates are given in the Western calendar (AD), unless where indicated by AD (*anno hegirae*, the year of the Prophet Muhammad's hijra, or migration, from Mecca to Medina in 622 AD, which denotes the first year of the Islamic calendar).

It hardly needs to be emphasized that the opinions conveyed in these statements in no way reflect the personal views of the translator, nor of any of those who assisted. This book is intended to provide a better understanding of the dynamics of political Islam, not an endorsement of bin Laden's ideas.

Besides the editors, whose valuable comments and suggestions helped to ensure the rapid completion of the project, the following people are also owed thanks: Muhammad and Harfiyah Abdel Haleem, Esma al-Samarai, Kevin Fogg, Geert Ruardij, Dominique Zarbhanelian, Koen Strous, Massimo Fusato, Amani al-Souqi, and Sama al-Souqi.

James Howarth
Amman, August 2005

INTRODUCTION

Bruce Lawrence

Although Osama bin Laden has become a legendary figure in the West, not to speak of the Arab world, the body of his statements has till now never been available to the public. Occasional fragments are cited, and—much more rarely —a few speeches have been reproduced here and there in the press. Yet official pressures have ensured that, for the most part, his voice has been tacitly censored, as if to hear it clearly and without cuts or interruption would be too dangerous. This does not mean that bin Laden's messages have reached no audience. But they have done so by flying below the radar screen of official— government and media—discourse about the war on terror, and entering an alternative sphere, till now largely confined to Arabic-speakers. Although his addresses are typically scriptural in mode, his rise to prominence mirrors the latest phase in the Information Age, the techniques of which he has in his own way proved a master. In a period of ten years that coincide with the emergence of a virtual universe, moving from print to internet, from wired to wireless communication around the globe, bin Laden and his associates have crafted a series of carefully staged statements designed for the new media. These include interviews with Western and Arab journalists, handwritten letters scanned onto discs, faxes, and audiotapes, and above all video recordings distributed via the first independent Arabic-language news outlet, the Qatari satellite television network al-Jazeera. These are the texts that make up this volume. For the first time they make possible informed critical discussion of bin Laden's outlook; they are no longer limited to the scrutiny of secretive government agencies and counter-terrorism experts.

To understand them, it is necessary to know something of the biography of their author. Osama bin Muhammad bin Laden was born in 1957 in Saudi

Arabia. His father was an illiterate Yemeni laborer from the Hadhramaut whose business acumen enabled him to secure building contracts for the Holy Sanctuaries, and to become a trusted confidant of the al-Saud family. When he died suddenly in 1968, Muhammad bin Laden left a fortune of $11 billion to his 54 children, by twenty or more different women. Bin Laden's mother, who was Syrian, was quickly divorced by his father, and remarried to another Yemeni. His father died when he was ten. The young bin Laden attended the Management and Economics School at King Abd al-Aziz University in Jeddah. Though he was an indifferent business student, he took courses in Islamic studies taught by Abdallah Azzam and Muhammad Qutb that seem to have influenced him deeply. Azzam (1941–89) was a Muslim Brother from Palestine. He had studied at al-Azhar University in Cairo in the early 1970s, before moving to Jeddah in 1978. Muhammad Qutb was the younger brother of Sayyid Qutb, the Egyptian thinker who became the most powerful voice of radical Islamic protest against both Arab nationalism and Western hegemony in the time of Nasser, and who was executed in 1966. Bin Laden dates his own political awakening from 1973, when an American airlift ensured Israeli victory over Egypt and Syria in the Yom Kippur War, and King Faisal of Saudi Arabia imposed a temporary oil embargo on the West.

After leaving university without having completed his degree, bin Laden entered his father's construction empire. He proved himself a successful manager of several of its businesses, and seems to have accumulated a sizeable personal fortune, though not as much as is often attributed to him. While still a very young man, he seems to have either volunteered or been picked by Riyadh to help organize the flow of Saudi funds and equipment to the *mujahidin* who had taken up arms against the Russian-backed regime in Afghanistan. He first arrived in Peshawar in 1980, on the border between Afghanistan and Pakistan, when he was only 23. There he worked with Azzam, contributing to his free circular *al-Jihad*, while also setting up his own operation in Peshawar, a guesthouse for Arab recruits to *jihad* against the Soviet Union. Called *Sijill al-Qaeda* or "Register of the Base," it was later known simply as *al-Qaeda* or "the Base." At this time, he cooperated closely with the Pakistani secret service or ISI (Inter-Service Intelligence Agency), and the CIA, the two other external patrons of the *mujahidin*. He may have been uneasy about his connection with the CIA—later he denied it altogether—but there is no contemporary evidence of his moral dilemma. With American and Saudi funds, and his own construction experience, he helped build mountain bases, including at the cave complex called Tora Bora, and training camps in the border regions. Later he seems to have fought courageously in battles around Jalalabad, as one of the many thousands of Arab volunteers in the war against the Soviet occupation of Afghanistan.

When Russian troops pulled out of Afghanistan in 1989, US funds were abruptly withdrawn. The battle-hardened Arab Afghans, largely split into national groups, were left orphaned and warring amongst each other in Peshawar. Only the training camps were to remain, used throughout the next decade by the ISI for Afghan and Kashmiri *jihadi*. In 1990 bin Laden returned to Saudi Arabia. There, when Saddam Hussein invaded Kuwait some months later, he offered to organize a fighting force of Arab Afghan veterans to defend the Kingdom against the threat from Iraq. The Saudi royal family not only rejected his proposal, but also invited half a million American and other foreign troops into the country to protect the dynasty. It was these "infidel" forces that launched Operation Desert Storm against Iraq. Their presence in the Land of the Two Holy Sanctuaries was blessed by leading Saudi *ulema*, including Sheikh Abd al-Aziz bin Baz, Chief *Mufti* of the Kingdom, as well as the sheikh of al-Azhar in Cairo. Religious scholars and others who protested were harassed or jailed by the Saudi authorities. Bin Laden was among them. Under house arrest for a spell, he was able to leave the country for Sudan in 1991. He was still only 34.

For the next five years, bin Laden settled in a large, well-guarded compound outside Khartoum, under the protection of a Sudanese military regime which at that time was linked to the radical Islamist leader Hassan al-Turabi. Other Arab Afghans, including the Egyptian who was henceforward to be his most important associate, Ayman al-Zawahiri, joined bin Laden there. Although remaining active as a businessman in Sudan, bin Laden seems to have organized the arrival in Somalia of Arab Afghan veterans. He would later claim that it was they, the "true" *mujahidin*, who had delivered decisive blows against US forces that had arrived there under UN auspices in 1993, but were soon withdrawn after suffering humiliating setbacks. It is virtually certain that bin Laden was also attempting to organize underground opposition to the regime in Riyadh. The Saudi authorities tried to assassinate him several times, without success. In 1994 they stripped him of his citizenship. At the end of the year he responded with his first major public statement: an attack on the Grand

Mufti bin Baz's blessing of the Oslo Accords (Statement 1), released in London by the newly established Advice and Reform Committee, an expression of the indignation felt by radical Muslims at the "apostasy" of Arab rulers who were cooperating with the West.

Six months later, the Egyptian president Hosni Mubarak narrowly escaped death in an ambush during a state visit to Ethiopia. When the organizers were traced to Sudan, Washington and Cairo added to the pressure already on Khartoum from Riyadh to expel bin Laden from the country. In May 1996, he and his entourage returned to Afghanistan, taking refuge in the Tora Bora mountains, north of Jalalabad. In September, the Taliban captured Kabul and over the next two years imposed, with Pakistani support, the most unified rule the country had known since the fall of Afghan Communism. Enjoying mutually respectful, if not always warm relations, with the Taliban regime, bin Laden set about organizing the resources, finance, training, and safe havens needed in which to reassemble young fighters for the defense of Islam, as he saw it. At the same time he sought to project his aims to a wider audience, conceding interviews and proclaiming the creation of a World Islamic Front in conjunction with al-Zawahiri and two leading Pakistani Islamists in early 1998 (Statement 6). Six months later, simultaneous bombing of American embassies in Kenya and Tanzania left more than 200 dead and many more injured, with massive loss of life. This was the first major terrorist action indisputably traceable to bin Laden. The Clinton Administration dismissed proposals to have him extradited from Afghanistan. Instead, they launched a cruise missile attack on one of his bases in Khost in August 1998, seeking but failing to kill him. He was now world-famous. Three years later, al-Qaeda activists hijacked four planes in the United States and in suicide missions destroyed the World Trade Center, and severely damaged the Pentagon, killing 3,000 people, most of them Americans.

It was not until 2004 that bin Laden publicly acknowledged his role in planning and organizing the attacks of 9/11 (Statement 23), but from the start few doubted that he was the author of this epochal act of terrorism. The Bush Administration's response was not long in coming. A month later, Operation Enduring Freedom unleashed the heaviest bombing assault on any country since World War Two, flattening Taliban resistance and facilitating the conquest of Afghanistan by US proxies. Bin Laden, the prime target of the campaign, escaped capture, as did the Taliban leader Mullah Omar. In places of deep hiding somewhere along the Pakistani–Afghan border, he has continued to defy all attempts to find him, despite a $50 million bounty on his head and massive sweeps by Pakistani and US forces. The capacity of the loose network of affiliates emanating from al-Qaeda to act outside the Arab world has been greatly weakened, but not extinguished, as the bombings in Madrid of February 2004 and in London of July 2005 have shown. Within the Middle East, on the other hand, the Anglo-American invasion of Iraq has created a fertile recruitment ground for bin Laden's conception of *jihad* against the West. Though physically cut off from the battlefields of Mesopotamia, his voice resounds across them through audiocassettes and satellite TV, apparently inspiring many of the most ferocious attacks on the occupiers and their local allies. Still a fugitive somewhere in the Hindu Kush, he has released a series of messages to the people of Iraq, the nations of Europe, and the citizens of the United States. Many of them are reproduced and freshly translated in this volume. Collectively they underscore that Osama bin Laden remains a force to be reckoned with.

But what kind of a force? We have only glimpses of bin Laden's personality, and much remains mysterious about the man. It is clear that few of his early associates saw him as a potential leader. The newly appointed Saudi ambassador to Washington recalls him as "a very shy person, very self-effacing, extremely sparse in his words and generally a do-gooder."[1] But is it possible that something of the spirit of his father moved him from the start? Muhammad bin Laden had risen from nothing to untold wealth in the shadow of the newly petro-rich Saudis, in a career that must have involved many a gamble. Bin Laden would prove himself as much a risk-taker as his father, but in another way. Coming out of the shadow of docile Muslims, within a world order dominated by the West, he rallied fellow-believers in the pursuit not of fortune but of *jihad*, beyond all the allures of prosperity, professionalism, or familial comfort. In that cause, he must have inherited some of his father's practical gifts. Already in his twenties he seems to have been a capable manager, at the head of a large construction complex, applying natural organizational skills he would later use to channel Saudi money and matériel to Afghanistan. The creation of an international network of sacrificial activists and the complex logistical planning of 9/11, in conjunction with his small group of associates, can be regarded as the culminating achievements of this side of bin Laden.

1 "Questions for Prince Turki al-Faisal," *The New York Times Magazine*, August 28 2005, p. 11.

But these organizational gifts alone, magnified as they were by the ample financial resources at his disposal, would never have given him the position he now enjoys in the Muslim world. That is due to other human qualities. Bin Laden is not an original thinker. Most of his ideas stem from writings by early mentors, in particular Abdallah Azzam's *Defending the Land of the Muslims is Each Man's Most Important Duty*, which, published in Peshawar in 1985, laid down a comprehensive case for individual *jihad* against the West. Nor is bin Laden an outstanding Qur'anic scholar: he lacks the command of textual subtleties that mark Wahhabi exegetes in Arabia, or their Azhari counterparts in Cairo. Yet he is well versed in the classical scriptures and traditions of Islam, and uses them to great advantage. He moves easily in the Qur'an as a book of day-to-day guidance, a source from which even the illiterate can draw strength both as pious Muslims and as advocates of radical change within the world they uneasily inhabit with other, less committed believers. This level of learning, real if not exceptional, provides the basis of religious authority for his pronouncements. What gives these their unique force, however, are his literary gifts. Bin Laden has earned many labels by now—fanatic, nihilist, fundamentalist, terrorist—but what actually distinguishes him, among a host of those described in these ways, is that he is first and foremost a *polemicist*. The many different statements collected in this book are nearly all constructed as arguments with real or imagined opponents and interlocutors.

Polemical arguments are tactical—"talking for victory," as Boswell put it of Johnson. They will cut corners with logic or evidence, as bin Laden frequently does, though they cannot go too far without risking loss of their power to move or persuade. Bin Laden's polemics, moreover, have to be understood within a set of Islamic genres unfamiliar in the West. They draw, as the linguistic anthropologist Flagg Miller has remarked, on at least five types of Muslim public discourse: the declaration, the juridical decree, the lecture, the written reminder, and the epistle. Bin Laden is not concerned to obey the rules of each genre, but weaves fluently back and forth between them. It is this capacity for rhetorical manoeuvre, argues Miller, that "enables bin Laden to legitimate himself in relation to different traditions of religious authority."[2] If his decrees

---

2 W Flagg Miller, "'On the summit of the Hindu Kush': Osama bin Laden's Declaration of War reconsidered," talk delivered at the University of Michigan in March 2005; cited by permission of the author.

are more formulaic and general in tone, his declarations and epistles address specific groups—not only followers or foes in the Muslim world, but Europeans or Americans as well, as will be found below. In each case, there is an adjustment of the polemical register to the particular audience for whom the message is intended. Common to all these messages is the literary skill with which they are composed. Not everything in them has necessarily been written by bin Laden himself: there is reason to believe that in some cases other hands may have contributed to the final text. But what is crystal-clear is that these messages are not ghostwritten tracts of the kind supplied by professional speechwriters to many politicians in the West, whether American Presidents, European Prime Ministers, or their Middle-Eastern counterparts. They speak in the authentic, compelling voice of a visionary, with what can only be called a powerful lyricism. Bernard Lewis, no friend of radical Islam, describes a typical message published below as "a magnificent piece of eloquent, at times even poetic Arabic prose."[3] Bin Laden's standing in the Muslim world is inseparable from these literary gifts.

Beyond the organizer and the polemicist lies, finally, the hero. To Westerners for whom bin Laden is the incarnation of villainy, this may seem the last word in perversity. But for millions of Muslims around the world, including many who have no sympathy with terrorism, bin Laden is an heroic figure. His worldwide charisma is based not just on his success in so far eluding Americans and their allies, exhilarating as that may be for many ordinary Muslims. It is because his personal reputation for probity, austerity, dignity, and courage contrasts so starkly with the mismanagement, bordering on incompetence, of most Arab regimes. Unlike the latter, bin Laden has demonstrated that he can forego the temptations of wealth, that he dares to strike powerful wrongdoers, and that he refuses to bend before superior might. "Bin Laden is seen by millions of his co-religionists—because of his defense of Islam, personal piety, physical bravery, integrity and generosity—as an Islamic hero, as that faith's ideal type, and almost as a modern-day Saladin," reports Michael Scheuer, head of the CIA unit charged with hunting bin Laden. "For nearly a decade now," observes Scheuer, "bin Laden has demonstrated patience, brilliant planning, managerial expertise, sound strategic and tactical sense, admirable character traits, eloquence, and focused, limited war aims. He has never, to my knowledge, behaved or spoken

3 Bernard Lewis, "License to Kill," *Foreign Affairs*, November–December 1998.

in a way that could be described as 'irrational in the extreme'." Indeed, for all the terror sown by his actions, concludes Scheuer, "there is no reason, based on the information at hand, to believe bin Laden is anything other than what he appears: a pious, charismatic, gentle, generous, talented, and personally courageous Muslim. As a historical figure, viewed from any angle, Osama bin Laden is a great man, one who smashed the expected unfolding of universal post-cold war peace."[4] These encomia express, no doubt, the not uncommon admiration felt by a professional for a particularly skilled enemy—with the kind of overstatement to be found, for example, in writings of the British military historian Liddell Hart about German generals in World War Two. Yet even discounting their hyperbole, such CIA tributes are striking; they provoke further reflection on the man behind the many personae.

How are such eulogies, from friend and foe alike, to be reconciled with the actions for which bin Laden has been responsible? Is the West wrong to call him a terrorist? His messages make it clear that, by his own admission, the answer is no. Bin Laden freely concedes that he has practised terror. What the messages invariably go on to say, however, is that this is a reactive terror—a response to what he perceives as the much greater terror exercised by the West over an incomparably longer period of time. Definitions of terrorism vary widely: it is well known that many who are now hailed as freedom fighters in their own communities, and accepted as respectable statesmen by the powers that be, were once denounced as terrorists, responsible for killing innocent civilians—Israeli leaders like Begin and Sharon prominent among them. In this sense, bin Laden's principal innovation has been to organize terrorist actions thousands of miles away from the territories he seeking to liberate. But this, he insists, is itself only retaliation for innumerable prior acts of aggression by the West in the Muslim world, thousands of miles away from Christian homelands. For 200 years now, the *umma* (Islamic global community, or supernation), has been under attack, from the first French invasion of Egypt in the last years of the 18th century and the seizure of the Maghreb in the 19th century, the British grab for Egypt and the Italian for Libya, the carve-up of the whole Middle East by Britain and France at the end of World War One, the sponsorship of Jewish colonization of Palestine, the suborning of nominally independent rulers in the Arabian peninsula, down to contemporary American control of the entire region.

4 Anonymous (Michael Scheuer), *Imperial Hubris* (Potomac, 2004), pp. 104, 114, 168, 103.

Is this an exaggerated description of the unbalanced relationship between the West and the Muslim world? There are no Arab military bases in Texas or California, no Arab contract mercenaries stationed in Britain or France, no Arab fleets in the Gulf of Mexico, no Arab-sponsored schemes of forcible settlement in the Mid-West. All the lines of intrusion and violence historically run in one direction. Yet such aggression does not condone bin Laden's acts of terror; they are abhorrent not only to Westerners, but also to many Arabs. Yet in the Middle East, few can forget the much heavier loss of life caused by centuries of Western domination. Bin Laden's victims number perhaps 5,000— about half as many as the number of civilians said to have died under American bombs in Afghanistan. As he never ceases to point out, the West has killed far larger numbers in the region within living memory. The liberal use of poison gas and aerial strafing of Iraqi villages by Winston Churchill in the 1920s, the crushing of the Palestinian uprising of the 1930s, France's colonial war in Algeria in the 1950s and 1960s, have been followed now by deaths through malnutrition and disease inflicted on the children of Iraq in the 1990s, due to UN sanctions. Bin Laden, ever alert to the principle of reciprocity, dwells insistently on the enormity of Iraq's suffering. He exaggerates its size: starting with 600,000 victims, he ends with 1.5 million, while the real figure was nearer 300,000. Yet he is correct about the staggering disproportion in the numbers of those killed on both sides. "Because you have killed," he warns Westerners, "we must kill. Your innocents are not less innocent than ours." Few things he has said are as chilling as Madeleine Albright's statement that this massacre of the innocents was "worth it" to the West. Even though nothing can ever justify bin Laden's own retaliatory killing of innocents, the indifference of Western leaders to the atrocities committed against Muslims helps explain why, despite widespread revulsion at his use of terror, he continues to be so admired and even trusted by ordinary people in the Middle East.[5]

Should bin Laden then be described as a contemporary anti-imperialist fighter adaptive to the Information Age? This is the view of one of the most level-headed of sociologists, Michael Mann. He writes: "Despite the religious

5 The Pew Trust Global Attitudes survey released on June 23 2005 found that while Muslims are worried about the consequences for themselves of the war on terror, a surprising number still have confidence in bin Laden's conduct in world affairs. The sixteen nations covered in the survey included neither Saudi Arabia nor Iraq, where the extent of support for him was likely to be much greater than in the countries surveyed.

rhetoric and the bloody means, bin Laden is a rational man. There is a simple *reason* why he attacked the US: American imperialism. As long as America seeks to control the Middle East, he and people like him will be its enemy."[6] The kernel of good sense in this judgment is plain. Objectively speaking, bin Laden is waging a war against what many—admirers as well as critics—now call the American empire. But it is crucial to note that he himself never uses this vocabulary. The word "imperialism" does not occur once in any of the messages he has sent out. He defines the enemy differently. For him, *jihad* is aimed not at an imperium, but at "global unbelief". Again and again, his texts return to this fundamental dichotomy. The war is a religious war. It subsumes a political war, which he can wage with terms appropriate to it, as he demonstrates in his addresses to the peoples of Europe or of America. Yet the battle in the end is one of faith.

Does this matter, or is it just a question of vocabulary? For some, bin Laden's use of Qur'anic authority for his struggle is little more than a convenient mask, disguising the reality that al-Qaeda is actually an Arab version of the Red Brigades or the ultra-left groups that practised terrorism in Europe in the 1970s—their lineal successor, so to speak. This view is not convincing. Of the intensity of bin Laden's piety there can be no doubt. What is more controversial is his orthodoxy. His critics have from the beginning charged him with selective use of the Qur'an and Traditions, for purposes incompatible with the intention of God's Word or the teaching of His Prophet. Certainly, it is difficult to find in his writings any hint of the traditional Islamic values of generosity, hospitality, and tolerance. But it is also true that everything he has written falls within the framework of a reaction against aggression, for which he has strong scriptural support. Islamic jurisprudence distinguishes between offensive war (*harb*), a campaign of conquest launched under official leadership against the land of the impious, and defensive struggle (*jihad*), to be waged as a matter of individual obligation by all Muslims when the *umma* has come under attack. In the latter case it is the *dicta* of the 14th-century Syrian jurist ibn Taimiyya, who rallied the faithful against the terrifying scourge of the Mongol invasions, which provide the most authoritative guide for conduct. His *fatwa* reads: "the first obligation after the (profession of) Faith is to repel the enemy aggressors who assault both sanctity and security."

6 Michael Mann, *Incoherent Empire* (Verso, 2003), p. 169.

Taking this injunction seriously, bin Laden points to passages in the Qur'an that he reads as authorizing a generalized *lex talionis*, one capable of covering even the killing of innocent infidels in revenge for the killing of innocent believers. In much the same way, he invokes a lethal Prophetic Tradition against the Jews, and less ferocious but still hostile passages in the Qur'an, when dealing with modern Israel. It would be wrong either to dismiss these references as imaginary, or to take them as representative of contemporary Muslim opinion. From everything we know about the best Muslim political theorists, it is conceivable that some of them might also have called for a *jihad* to expel infidels from the Land of the Holy Places. Yet such a select reading of scriptural sources and extra-scriptural authority sits ill with the conscience of the great majority of contemporary Muslims: for all but a few, implacable warfare in the name of *jihad* is not the sole or the best measure of Islamic loyalty.

What then are the prospects of the cause for which bin Laden is prepared to lay down his own life? It is clear that what originally launched him on his hugely ambitious undertaking was the confidence instilled by the victory of the *mujahidin* over the Red Army in Afghanistan, followed by the withdrawal of American forces from Somalia in 1993. If one superpower could be defeated, and even ultimately destroyed, by warriors for the faith, why should not the other, which had proved much less resilient in Mogadishu? This dream was based on two great miscalculations. Like many revolutionaries—the Russians after 1917, the Cubans after 1959—bin Laden and his associates ignored the special conditions that had given them victory in one society, imagining it could be reproduced with the same tactics in other societies. But Afghanistan was like no other country of the Middle East: it was economically and culturally much less developed, ethnically more divided, geographically much more inaccessible, with unique traditions of mountain warfare and resistance to the invader. Even so, it required massive amounts of US finance and weaponry, and the full backing of the Pakistani state, for the *mujahidin* to prevail. Bin Laden's reluctance to admit the scale of this assistance, visible in the interviews below, meant that he later overestimated the ability of the Taliban, isolated from any external support, to withstand the subsequent American assault. The Afghan experience could not be mechanically repeated elsewhere; it was more vulnerable in itself than he had imagined. As for Somalia, the inconsequential American landings there, more a public relations than strategic operation, were no gauge of the powers of the Pentagon. The effect of both Afghanistan and Somalia seems to have been simply to lure him into illusions of US fickleness and weakness.

Connected to these miscalculations is the nature of his religious vision itself. One of its most striking features, displayed throughout the texts in this book, is the absence of any social dimension. Bin Laden was barred from the kind of analysis that would have allowed him to distinguish the different structural features of the various Muslim societies in which *jihad* was to be awakened, and made him hesitate in inflecting the notion of "One, Two, Three, Many Afghanistans." Morally, he does denounce a host of evils. Some of them— unemployment, inflation, and corruption—are social. But no alternative conception of the ideal society is ever offered. There is an almost complete lack of any social program. This alone makes it clear how distinctive al-Qaeda is as a phenomenon. The lack of any set of social proposals separates it not just from the Red Army Faction or the Red Brigades, with which it has some-times mistakenly been compared, but—more significantly—from the earlier wave of radical Islamism, whose leading thinker was the great iconoclast Sayyid Qutb. In place of the social, there is a hypertrophy of the sacrificial. Bin Laden's messages rarely hold out radiant visions of final triumph. His emphasis falls far more on the glories of martyrdom than the spoils of victory. Rewards belong essentially to the hereafter. This is a creed of great purity and intensity, capable of inspiring its followers with a degree of passion and prin-cipled conviction that no secular movement in the Arab world has ever matched. At the same time, it is obviously also a narrow and self-limiting one: it can have little appeal for the great mass of believers, who need more than scriptural dictates, poetic transports, or binary prescriptions to chart their everyday lives, whether as individuals or as collective members of a commu-nity, local or national. Above all, there is no rush to restore a Caliphate today. Bin Laden seems at some level to recognize the futility of a quest for restitu-tion. He sets no positive political horizon for his struggle. Instead, he vows that *jihad* will continue until "we meet God and get his blessing!"

Despite these crippling weaknesses, the force of bin Laden's appeal is far from spent. The reason for that is very clear. Not only has the West's long-term abuse of the Middle East, which gives his movement its moral power, not been in any way amended since he began his struggle. It has now been viru-lently aggravated by the Anglo-American occupation of Iraq, visiting biblical humiliation, destruction, and chaos on the third most hallowed land of the *umma* (after Mecca/Medina and Jerusalem). If ordinary Muslims doubted the designs ascribed to the West by bin Laden before the invasion of March 2003, and all that has followed, considerably fewer are likely to do so today. In the infernal landscape created by the shattering of Iraq, dedicated fighters inspired by his summons proliferate to carry out deadly suicide missions, alongside a nationalist resistance which has learnt to cooperate with them. The ranks of *jihadi* are being replenished with every week that American forces and their allies remain. Can the carnage cease until they are driven out or devise a face-saving way to retreat?

Bin Laden's own fate remains uncertain. Unless he dies a natural death in hiding, it seems inevitable that sooner or later his hunter will catch him. If captured alive, he will doubtless be killed on the spot, as Che Guevara was forty years ago. His captors will know that it would be useless to torture him for information, as they have his lieutenants; while to put him on trial would risk huge embarrassment for those attempting to judge him, given his powers of eloquence and their own record. He is not troubled by the predictability of this end:

> So let me be a martyr,
> dwelling in a high mountain pass
> among a band of knights who,
> united in devotion to God,
> descend to face armies.

This poem, which concludes his Sermon for the Feast of the Sacrifice (Statement 19), could be bin Laden's epitaph.

His posthumous legend will live on, like that of Guevara, to inspire other such knights, until such time as different, more humane heroes can attract the idealism of Muslim youth, and find a better way not only to liberate their homelands but also to forge a brighter future for those liberated.

I

FROM SUDAN 1994–1995

1

THE BETRAYAL OF PALESTINE

December 29 1994

Although Osama bin Laden released other statements prior to 1994, this is the first of his public pronouncements intended for a wider audience. It is addressed as a letter to the Chief Mufti, the foremost juridical authority, in the kingdom of Saudi Arabia, bin Baz. Appointed Head of the Council of ulema in the early 1950s, bin Baz continued to enjoy official authority in Riyadh until his death at the age of 87 in May 1999. When Iraq invaded Kuwait in 1990, King Fahd had required the ulema to endorse the arrival of American and other foreign troops on Saudi soil, and bin Baz complied with two decrees, the first on August 14 1990, authorizing US deployment (Operation Desert Shield), and the second in January 1991, permitting Muslim troops to join in the attack on Iraq (Operation Desert Storm). These edicts outraged Islamic purists, leading to a moral gulf between the sahwa *(dissident theologians) and the* ulema *that widened throughout the 1990s.[1]*

Thus in May 1991 a group of dissenters addressed petitions to bin Baz, arguing that the kingdom's apparent inability to defend itself without reliance on foreign troops was a consequence of the House of Saud's renunciation of Islam. The result had been the intrusion of Western values at the expense of Muslim principles, the corruption of Saudi princes and officials, and dependence on the United States, to the point of a sell-out of Palestinian rights to gratify Washington. Another major expression of growing discontent at the direction of the regime was the "Memorandum of Advice", a 46-page document sent to King Fahd by a group of 107 wahhabi clerics in July 1992, which criticized the government for corruption and human-rights abuses and for permitting US troops on Saudi soil. King Fahd dismissed seven of the seventeen members of the Council of ulema *for refusing to denounce the Memorandum. In 1994 authorities cracked down hard on the* sahwa, *throwing its chief activists into jail, including Safar al-Hawali and Salman al-Auda, its two main leaders.*

1 For the *sahwa* (religious awakening) in Saudi Arabia, see Gilles Kepel, *The War for Muslim Minds* (Belknap Press, 2004), pp. 176–93.

Bin Laden, who had been living in exile in Sudan since 1991, was stripped of his Saudi citizenship in the spring of 1994. According to his own account, the repression of the sahwa was the chief motive for the creation of the "Advice and Reform Committee" (ARC) that he set up in the summer of 1994, based in north London.[2] His open letter to bin Baz was issued through the London office of ARC five months later, establishing his credentials as a scholar of the moral intent of Islamic law, one able to speak on behalf of the spirit and not just the letter of the law. The background to the letter is a repudiation of the corruption of the Saudi dynasty, and the collusion of bin Baz with the degeneration of its rule—illustrated by the spread of usury in the kingdom, the failure to uproot communism in Yemen, the imprisonment of devout scholars. But the specific object of bin Laden's protest, in his first major public declaration, is bin Baz's endorsement of the Oslo accords of August 1993 between Israel and the Palestine Liberation Organization (PLO)—"your latest astonishing juridical decree", a betrayal of the word of God and of the community of the faithful, "clearly a response to the political wishes of the regime". The letter makes it plain that Palestine, far from being a late addition to bin Laden's agenda, was at the centre of it from the start.

"The best *jihad* against a despotic sultan is the word of truth."[3]

You are well aware what a great status the scholars, the men of knowledge, have been given by God. It is no wonder that He has given them this distinguished standing, since theirs is the legacy of the Prophets, from whom they have inherited this religion. They protect it from the corruption of fanatics, from the false ascriptions of liars, from the interpretations of the ignorant, and from the dilutions of profligate oppressors. They represent the model exemplars of our *umma*[4] in promoting the victory of truth, despite all its burdens and preferring it to a worldly life.

The virtuous scholars who were the forefathers of our *umma*, and their successors, undertook these missions admirably. Sa'id bin Jubayr's stance in the

---

2 Located in Dollis Hill, and nominally established "to promote peaceful and constructive reform with regard to the way Arabia is governed, using only legitimate means", the London office of ARC issued numerous communiqués. Its director, Khaled al-Fawwaz, appointed by bin Laden in July 1994, would claim that "The Advice and Reformation Committee ... is simply a continuation of those reformers who have been working for decades": Peter Bergen, *Holy War Inc: Inside the Secret World of Osama bin Laden* (Phoenix, 2001), pp. 91–2.

3 From the *hadith* collection of ibn Hanbal, vol. 3, no. 11,127. For ibn Hanbal, see n. 6 below.

4 *Umma* is the global Islamic community, or Islamic supernation.

face of al-Hajjaj's tyranny,[5] when he stood up for the truth, Imam Ahmad bin Hanbal's challenge to the power of the sultan and his patience in the struggle over the nature of the Qur'an,[6] and ibn Taymiyya's[7] heroic endurance of prison for the victory of the traditions of the Prophet—all these are examples of people who embraced their duty to help the truth and its people. These eminent leaders undertook this duty so that truth would be victorious and out of zeal for their religion. May God bless them all.

Honorable sheikh, by mentioning all this we wanted to remind you of your duty to your religion and to our *umma*, and to bring your attention back to your enormous responsibility. For recalling this will be of benefit to the believers. We wanted to remind you at this time, an age in which falsehood has spread, in which corrupt and wayward people have caused controversy, and in which the truth has been buried, preachers have been imprisoned and reformists silenced. What is even more curious is that this has not only happened in your knowledge and with your silence, but as a result of your juridical decrees[8] and

5   An Iraqi from the town of Kufa, Sa'id bin Jubayr (d.714) was one of the leading jurists in the generation immediately succeeding the Prophet Muhammad. Bin Laden here refers to bin Jabayr's doctrinal dispute with al-Hajjaj ("the bone crusher"), governor of Iraq during the Ummayad caliphate of al-Walid I. Outdone, al-Hajjaj ordered bin Jubayr to be beheaded; however, al-Hajjaj reportedly lost his senses on committing this atrocious act and died within a month.

6   The Baghdadi Imam Ahmad ibn Hanbal (780–855) was a theologian and jurist, and is revered as one of the fathers of Islam. He compiled a collection of the traditions of Muhammad and founded the Hanbali school, the most traditional of the four orthodox schools of Islamic jurisprudence; he also opposed codification of the law, believing that jurists should be able to derive legal solutions directly from the Qur'an and *sunna* (the traditions of the Prophet). Bin Laden here refers to a period between 833–35, when ibn Hanbal was tortured and imprisoned for refusing to adhere to the Mu'tazili doctrine of a created—as opposed to eternal—Qur'an, which was briefly dominant at the caliphal court in Baghdad during the 9th century.

7   Born in Mesopotamia and educated in Damascus, ibn Taymiyya (1263–1328), the "Sheikh of Islam," was a reforming jurist, preacher, and scholar of Islam. He sought to return Islam to a strict interpretation of its sources, as laid down in the Qur'an and *sunna* by the Prophet Muhammad, his companions and early descendents, the *al-salaf al-salih* or "righteous predecessors", stipulating that any decision or practice that deviated from that of the *salaf*—such as the worship of saints—constituted *bida* (religious innovation) or *shirk* (idolatry). He was imprisoned for his beliefs and died in a Cairene prison. His writings are a major source for the *wahhabi/salafi* movements in Islam, which reject modernity and advocate that society should emulate that of Muhammad and the early believers, as literally described by the Qur'an and the *hadith*. Ibn Taymiyya advised the strictest possible application of *sharia* in the most detailed aspects of everyday life, and the use of coercion on those who did not conform to it. Although it incorporates many other elements of preceding ideologues, bin Laden's discourse is rooted in *wahhabi/salafi* thought; here, bin Laden describes how ibn Taymiyya was found guilty of heretical thinking and imprisoned for his defense of traditional thought.

8   "Juridical decree" throughout this volume represents the Arabic word *fatwa*.

opinions. We would remind you, honorable sheikh, of some of these juridical decrees and opinions to which you may not be giving your full attention, even though our *umma* might fall into seventy years of error because of these decrees. We do this in order that you might appreciate along with us even a fraction of the serious consequences that follow from them. Here are some examples:

1. No one can be unaware of the tremendous spread of corruption, which has penetrated all aspects of life. It can no longer be a secret to anyone that various evils have spread, as detailed in the advisory memo submitted by a select group of scholars and reformists.[9] Among the most serious things the scholars highlighted in this memo was the setting-up of rival authority to God. This can be seen in the enactment of man-made laws that deem illegal acts to be permissible, the worst of which is the practice of usury,[10] which is now widespread in the country thanks to the usurious state institutions and banks, whose towers are competing with the minarets of the two Holy Sanctuaries.[11] The length and breadth of the country is positively teeming with them. It is surely well known that the usurious regimes and laws with which these banks and institutions are working are legitimate in the eyes of the ruling regime and officially certified by it. We have heard from you only to the effect that practising usury is absolutely prohibited, although this position ignores the fact that your words deceive people because you do not distinguish in your judgment between those who merely practise usury and those who legitimize it and make it legal. In fact, the distinction between these two issues is very clear: he who practises usury is committing a serious and grave offence—but as for he who makes usury legal, in doing so he becomes an apostate and an infidel who has placed himself outside the religious community, because he has considered himself an equal and a partner to God in deciding what is permissible and

9 Bin Laden here refers to the "Memorandum of Advice", a letter signed by 107 prominent Saudi Islamists in July 1992, for which see the Headnote to this text.

10 Usury is forbidden throughout the Qur'an and *sunna*; see for example Qur'an, 2:275; 2:276–80; 3:130; 4:161; and 30:39. See also the *hadith* of Sahih Muslim, book 10, no. 3,880.

11 The Two Holy Sanctuaries (*al-haramain*) are Mecca, the holiest city in Islam, the site of the Haram Mosque (containing the Ka'ba, the most sacred Muslim shrine); and Medina, "the radiant", Islam's second holiest city, where the shrine of the Prophet Muhammad, and the first mosque of Islam, the Quba mosque, are located. Throughout his statements, bin Laden refers to the "Land of the Two Holy Sanctuaries" in place of Saudi Arabia, as an indication of his loathing for the "apostate" Saudi royal family.

what is not. (This is something we have detailed in an independent study, which will be published soon, God willing.)

Although he who practises usury to the utmost degree has declared war on God and on His Prophet, yet still we hear you expressing praise and commendation for this regime, which is not satisfied merely with its addiction to usury, but has also legalized and justified it. The Prophet has said, as related by al-Hakim, "There are 73 easier ways to offend God than usury, such as to marry your own mother."[12]

And ibn Abbas said, as related by ibn Jarir: "Committing usury is a serious offence, so the leader of the Muslims should call the offender to repent, and punish him if he fails to do so."[13] This is just for those who practise usury, so what about those who legalize it?

The political and economic crises that the country is suffering, and the crimes of all varieties that have spread through it like wildfire, are a punishment from God. They are part of the war that God Almighty has declared on those who have not ceased to practise usury and similar evils, and of the eradication of usury that He has ordained: "God blights usury, but blesses charitable deeds with multiple increase."[14]

2. When the king hung the cross around his neck and showed it to the world, happy and smiling, you excused his deed and justified this terrible act, despite the fact that it clearly constitutes unbelief and that it shows pleasure and preference for the perpetrator of the deed, rather than for knowledge.

3. When the forces of the aggressive Crusader-Jewish alliance decided during the Gulf War—in connivance with the regime—to occupy the country in the name of liberating Kuwait, you justified this with an arbitrary juridical decree excusing this terrible act, which insulted the pride of our *umma* and sullied its honor, as well as polluting its holy places. You considered this to be a way of seeking help from the infidels in your time of need, neglecting the curbs and restrictions such a call for help necessarily imposed.[15]

12 Al-Mataqi al-Hindi, *Kanz al-Amal*, p. 507.
13 Al-Qurtubi, *Tafsir al-Qurtubi*, p. 650. Abdullah ibn Abbas was a cousin of the Prophet Muhammad; he was an expert in Qur'anic exegesis, and an authority on the traditions of the Prophet. Muhammad knew him from infancy.
14 Qur'an, 2:276.
15 A reference to the decree issued on August 14 1990 by Sheikh bin Baz and the *ulema*, approving King Fahd's decision to authorize the deployment of foreign troops in Saudi Arabia.

4. When the ruling Saudi regime undertook to help and support the leaders of apostasy, the Communist Socialists in Yemen, against the Muslim Yemeni people in the last war there, you kept a committed silence. But when the tide turned against these Communists you issued—no doubt under pressure from this regime—advice calling on everyone to agree to peace and reconciliation on the basis that they are all Muslims![16] It is ludicrous to suggest that Communists are Muslims whose blood should be spared. Since when were they Muslims? Wasn't it you who previously issued a juridical decree calling them apostates and making it a duty to fight them in Afghanistan, or is there a difference between Yemeni Communists and Afghan Communists?[17] Have doctrinal concepts and the meaning of God's unity become so confused? The regime is still sheltering some of these leaders of unbelief in a number of cities in the country, and yet we have heard no disapproval from you. The Prophet said, as related by Muslim: "God cursed him who accommodates an innovator."[18]

5. When the regime decided to attack Sheikhs Salman al-Auda and Safar al-Hawali,[19] who had stood up for the truth and suffered much harm, you issued a juridical decree condoning everything suffered by the two sheikhs, as well as justifying the attacks and punishments suffered by the preachers, sheikhs, and youth of our *umma* who were with them. May God break their fetters and relieve them of the oppressors' injustice.

---

16 When a war broke out in 1994, between Islamic, conservative north Yemen and the Marxist south, the Saudi government, alarmed by the prospect of a populous, unified state on its borders, provided substantial resources in secret backing to the Marxist forces. Afghan veterans and Islamic groups supported the north, which took Aden in July 1994, when an amnesty was declared.

17 Bin Laden is referring to the People's Democratic Republic of Afghanistan, in power from 1978 to 1992. The USSR invaded Afghanistan in December 1979, installing Babrak Karmal as Afghanistan's new President. In response, bin Baz declared the fight against Soviet occupation, which lasted for ten years until the Soviet withdrawal from Afghanistan in 1989, to be a legitimate *jihad*. The last Communist president of Afghanistan, Muhammad Najibullah, stepped down in 1992, and remained in sanctuary in the UN compound in Kabul until September 1996, when Kabul fell to the Taliban. Najibullah was tortured, killed, and hanged from a traffic light.

18 From the *hadith* of Sahih Muslim, book 22, no. 4,876.

19 Salman al-Auda (1955–) and Safar al-Hawali (1950–), Islamic scholars, were the two most prominent activists of the religious "awakening" inspired by the insurgent attack on the Great Mosque in 1979, which mingled radical wahhabism with the ideas of the Egyptian Sayyid Qutb, prominent writer and member of the Muslim Brotherhood. The two were imprisoned in 1994, not long before bin Laden's letter was written. They were released in 1999, at which point they began to go their separate ways. Both, however, condemned terrorism in the wake of the 9/11 attacks.

These are only some—by no means all—examples. It has become necessary to mention them in light of your latest astonishing juridical decree justifying peace with the Jews, which is a disaster for Muslims. This was clearly a response to the political wishes of the regime, which decided to reveal what it previously had in mind and enter into this farce of capitulation to the Jews. You issued a juridical decree wholly endorsing this peace, which was praised and lauded by the prime minister of the Zionist enemy and his parliament, after which the Saudi regime announced its intent for more normalization with the Jews.

And it seemed as if you were not satisfied with abandoning Saudi Arabia, home of the two Holy Sanctuaries, to the Crusader-Jewish forces of occupation, until you had brought another disaster upon Jerusalem, the third of the Sanctuaries,[20] by conferring legitimacy on the contracts of surrender to the Jews that were signed by the traitorous and cowardly Arab tyrants.[21] These contracts constitute a serious and dangerous calamity containing deceit and deception from a number of different perspectives. We raise the following points:

1. The current Jewish enemy is not an enemy settled in his own original country fighting in its defense until he gains a peace agreement, but an attacking enemy and a corrupter of religion and the world, for whom the words of the Sheikh of Islam ibn Taymiyya apply: "There is no greater duty after faith than unconditionally fighting the attacking enemy who corrupts religion and the world. He must be resisted as hard as possible, as stipulated by our companions the scholars and others."[22]

The legal duty regarding Palestine and our brothers there—these poor men, women, and children who have nowhere to go—is to wage *jihad* for the sake of God, and to motivate our *umma* to *jihad* so that Palestine may be completely liberated and returned to Islamic sovereignty. Palestine could do without this

20 Jerusalem (in Arabic, al-Quds) is the third holiest place in Islam after Mecca and Medina. The Temple Mount (known to Muslims as al-Haram al-Sharif, or the "noble sanctuary") is the site of two major Muslim shrines, the Dome of the Rock, whence Muhammad is believed to have ascended to heaven and the al-Aqsa mosque, the largest mosque in Jerusalem. The Israeli Prime Minister Ariel Sharon's visit to the Temple Mount in September 2000 is generally held to have sparked the beginning of the beginning of the second Palestinian *intifada*, or "uprising", also known as the "al-Aqsa *intifada*".
21 The Oslo Accords were signed on September 13 1993 between Israel and the Palestine Liberation Organization.
22 From ibn Taymiyya's book, *al-Ikhtiyarat al-Faqahiyya*, p. 309.

kind of juridical decree, which abandons the *jihad* and lets things be, which accepts the enemy's occupation of the holiest of the Muslims' holy places after the two Holy Sanctuaries, and which confers legitimacy on this occupation. The kind of decree that fully supports the enemy's attempts to face down the zealous Islamic efforts to liberate Palestine by means of *jihad*, which the operations of the heroes and the youth of Muslim *jihad* in Palestine have shown to be the only useful way to confront the enemy and guarantee the country's liberation, God willing.

We might remind you at this point of your previous juridical decree on this issue. When you were asked how to liberate Palestine, you said that it was impossible to reach a solution unless this was considered an Islamic issue, and unless we stand shoulder to shoulder in solidarity with Muslims in order to save them, and unless we wage an Islamic *jihad* against the Jews until the land is returned to its people and these deviant Jews return to their country.[23]

2. Given that this false place with the Jewish enemy, to which defeatist Arab tyrannies and regimes are committing themselves, comes full of conditions, can it really be allowed to happen? Everyone knows that is not the case. For this alleged peace that the rulers and tyrants are falling over themselves to make with the Jews is nothing but a massive betrayal, epitomized by their signing of the documents of capitulation and surrender of the Holy City of Jerusalem and all of Palestine to the Jews, and their acknowledgment of Jewish sovereignty over Palestine for ever.

3. These apostate rulers who are fighting against God and His Messenger have no legitimacy or authority over Muslims, and they are not acting in the interests of our *umma*. But through these juridical decrees of yours you are giving legitimacy to these secular regimes and acknowledging their authority over Muslims, in contradiction of the fact that you have previously pronounced them to be infidels. This has been made clear to you by a select group of scholars and preachers in their appeal to you to refrain from issuing such juridical decrees. We enclose a copy of this appeal to remind you and bring it to your attention once again.[24]

23 *Fatawi bin Baz*, 1/281.
24 Here, bin Laden is probably referring to the Memorandum of Advice, sent to bin Baz; see Headnote, p. 3.

This juridical decree of yours was deceitful, as it contained shamefully misleading generalizations. It is not even valid as a juridical decree on the authority of a just peace, let alone this fake peace with the Jews, which is a huge betrayal of Islam and Muslims. No normal Muslim would accept it, let alone a scholar like you who is obliged to show zeal for our religious community and our *umma*.

Anyone who undertakes to issue a juridical decree concerning the serious issues of our *umma* has a duty to be knowledgeable about all its dimensions, and the dangers and detrimental effects that might ensue from it. Such knowledge is one of the indispensable conditions of becoming a jurist.[25] The Imam ibn al-Qayyim says: "Neither the jurist nor the ruler can issue a juridical decree and rule in truth without two kinds of knowledge: first, material, tangible knowledge and true understanding of the surrounding context, and secondly, the duty of understanding God's judgment that he has laid down in His book and on the tongue of His Messenger. He then has to apply the one to the other."[26]

If these are the general conditions necessary for a juridical decree to be issued, then they are certainly necessary for any juridical decree pertaining to *jihad* and making peace and the like. The Imam ibn Taymiyya says: "When it comes to *jihad*, we must take into consideration the correct opinion of religious scholars who have experienced what is confronting the worldly men, except for those who focus solely on the ritual aspects of religion; their opinion should not be taken, nor should the opinion of religious scholars who have no experience in the world."[27]

The falsehood in previous juridical decrees, even if not issued by you, were knowingly uttered by their authors and had dangerous consequences, but when they come from you, it is certain that the fault in them should not be ascribed to a lack of legal knowledge on your part, but rather to a lack of understanding of the truth of reality. The necessary conditions of such juridicial decrees cannot be fulfilled, so they are therefore unfit to be issued in the first place. This makes it necessary for the issuer to stop issuing juridical decrees, and to leave it to the specialists who can bring together knowledge of legal judgments and knowledge

---

25 "Jurist" throughout this volume represents the Arabic word *mufti*.
26 From the book of ibn al-Qayyim, p. 38. The Syrian Imam ibn al-Qayyim (691–751 AH) was a Sunni scholar of Islamic jurisprudence. A student of ibn Taymiyya, collected *hadith* and was an expert in Qur'anic exegesis.
27 From ibn Taymiyya's book, *al-Ikhtiyarat al-Faqahiyya*, p. 311.

of reality. For example, when the Imam Malik ibn Anas was asked about different readings he deferred to the Imam Nafi, may God bless them both.[28]

Honourable Sheikh, our considerable concern at the state of our *umma* and of scholars such as you is what motivated us to remind you of all this. For we esteem you and those like you too highly to think that the ruling regime could exploit you in such a terrible way and throw you in the face of every preacher and reformist, or that every word of truth and call to honesty would fall silent at your juridical decrees and opinions, as happened with your response to the Memorandum of Advice and the Committee for the Defence of Legal Rights, and others.

Honorable Sheikh, you have reached a good age, and you have achieved much in the service of Islam, so fear God and distance yourself from these tyrants and oppressors who have declared war on God and His Messenger, and stand with the righteous men. The forefathers of our *umma* and their successors have set a good example, and one of the most prominent characteristics of these righteous scholars was the way they disassociated themselves from the sultans. The Imam Abu Hanifa[29] and others, with their great integrity in matters of religion, avoided working with the rulers of their age, even though those sultans cannot be compared to the rulers of today, whose degeneracy and corruption of religion is no secret. And in our time, when Sheikh Abdallah bin Hamid[30] has realized the danger of the course that the ruling Saudi regime is taking, and the damaging consequences for those who participate or are

28 Imam Malik ibn Anas (714–96) was a celebrated Sunni scholar of Islamic jurisprudence (*fiqh*), which comprises the ruling of Islamic jurists to direct the lives of Muslims. Born and raised in Medina, Imam Malik's outspokenness against the ruling Caliph led to his flogging. He went on to found the "*Maliki madhhab*", one of the four Sunni schools of jurisprudence (*madhhab*). Each is named after a classical jurist, and reflects the unique culture of the time of the jurist in question, when the rulings were made. Bin Laden is here referring to the respect and deference that Imam Malik showed to his teacher, Imam Nafi, even though the former turned out to be by far the greater scholar.

29 Imam abu Hanifa (699–795) was born in Kufa, Iraq. He was an important Islamic scholar of jurisprudence, and is the founder of the Hanafi school of jurisprudence. Bin Laden is referring here to Abu Hanifa's refusal of the title of Chief Judge of the State, a post offered him in 763 by al-Mansur, the Abbasid ruler of Baghdad. His refusal led to a dispute with al-Mansur, and to his arrest and imprisonment. He died in jail.

30 Sheikh Abdallah bin Hamid was a member of the *mufti* in Saudi Arabia under bin Baz, and head of the supreme council of judges. He issued a number of statements regarding the Saudi government's adoption of laws that ran contrary to Islamic law, and tendered his resignation under growing pressure.

implicated in it and desert their religion, he resigned from the Supreme Council of Judges. The Imam al-Khattabi warned of getting involved with these rulers: "I wish I knew who is getting involved with them today but does not believe their lies and who is speaking justly when he sees their councils, and who is advising them and who is taking advice from them."[31]

And the Prophetic saying is true: "Whoever enters the sultan's door has been led astray."[32] So beware, honorable sheikh, of relying on these men, whether in word or in deed, "and do not rely on those who have been oppressive or else the fire will befall you—for what other protectors do you have than God?—and you will not be victorious."[33]

He who is unable to proclaim the truth can at least refuse to proclaim what is not true. The Prophet said, as related by al-Bukhari: "He who believes in God, let him say something good on the Last Day or be silent."[34]

And finally, we pray that you do not take these words out of turn or consider them to overstep the limits of etiquette. We could not be silent or fail to speak out, for the matter is too serious to justify turning a blind eye.

What we have mentioned is known by the men of knowledge, and a select group of our *umma*'s scholars and preachers has previously brought it to your attention, presenting to you several appeals in this regard. They included the one made a while back asking you to refrain from the juridical decree justifying this alleged peace with the Jews, which is no more than capitulation. They showed that this juridical decree did not meet the necessary conditions of legality and they warned of the many dangers—both religious and worldly—that would follow from it. The signatories of this appeal included the honorable Sheikhs ibn Jabrin, Abdallah al-Qa'ud, Hammud al-Tuwijri,

---

31 Quoted in ibn al-Azraq, *Bid'a al-Sulk Taba'a al-Mulk*, p. 176. Ahmed ibn Muhammad al-Khattabi was a 10th-century Afghani poet and traditionalist renowned for his piety.

32 Al-Mataqi al-Hindi, *Kanz al-Amal*, p. 2,312.

33 Qur'an, 11:113.

34 From the *hadith* collection of al-Bukhari, vol. 8, book 73, no. 160. Born in Bukhara, Persia (in modern-day Uzbekistan), Muhammad al-Bukhari (810–70) devoted himself to the collection and authentication of *hadiths* from an early age, and in so doing travelled throughout the Islamic world. He reputedly learned over 600,000 traditions, true and false. A conservative, he was a friend of ibn Hanbal (see above, n. 6). Al-Bukhari returned to Bukhara, where he compiled the *al-Jami al-Sahih*, a collection of 7,275 tested traditions. His book is highly regarded among Sunni Muslims, and considered the most authentic collection of *hadith*; many Sunni scholars consider its authenticity to be second only to the Qur'an.

Hammud al-Shu'aibi, al-Barrak, al-Auda, al-Khudairi, al-Tariri, al-Dabyan, 'Abdallah al-Tuwijri, Abdallah al-Jalali, A'id al-Qarni, and many others.[35]

In conclusion, we ask God Almighty to respond to our striving for truth and provide for us, his followers. We ask Him to show the liar his lies, and help us avoid them, and to establish an order of guidance for our *umma* in which those who obey Him will be proud and those who disobey him will be humbled, and in which good is enjoined and evil rejected, and in which justice is done and the truth is spoken, in which the banner of *jihad* is raised up high to restore to our *umma* its pride and honor, and in which the banner of God's unity is raised once again over every stolen Islamic land, from Palestine to al-Andalus and other Islamic lands that were lost because of the betrayals of rulers and the feebleness of Muslims. We ask Him to direct our affairs for the best and to take away our sins. We ask Him to help us to say and to do the right things, and for success in what He loves and what pleases Him in life, and for the best outcome when we die. He is our protector and enabler. Our final prayer is praise be to God, Lord of the worlds.

> The Reform and Advice Committee, London Office
> Osama bin Muhammad bin Laden

---

35 Bin Laden here refers to a document petitioning bin Baz not to give juridical approval to the signing of the Oslo accords. The signatories include Salman al-Auda (see above, p. 8, n. 19).

2

THE INVASION OF ARABIA

(c. 1995/1996)

This message, dating from the mid-1990s, and addressed to the "honorable scholars of the Arabian peninsula and Saudi Arabia in particular", can be regarded as a complement to bin Laden's letter to bin Baz. It is an appeal to dissenting Wahhabi clerics, such as those who had signed the 1992 "Memorandum of Advice to King Fahd". Unlike the letter to bin Baz, no return address is indicated in this document, though it may be assumed that it too came from the London office of the Advice and Reform Committee. In it, bin Laden's principal object of attack is the stationing of American and other foreign troops in the Arabian peninsula, 'a calamity unpredecented in the history of the umma*', which he denounces with concentrated scriptural support. Responsible for the disaster are—still unspecified—rulers and scholars who have become apostate collaborators with Western powers. Aggression against the* umma *extends more widely still: Bosnia and Chechnya are already listed as further cases. Believers must be called to battle against it, in a* jihad *that "will go on until the Day of Judgment."*

To the honorable scholars of our Islamic *umma* in general and to the scholars of the Arabian peninsula and Saudi Arabia in particular, may God keep them.

Peace, and all God's mercy and blessings be upon you.

You are all aware of the degree of degradation and corruption to which our Islamic *umma* has sunk, in its government and in the feebleness and cowardice of many of its scholars in the face of its enemies, as well as in its internal divisions. This is because of their neglect of religion and weakness of faith, which allowed the enemy to attack. The enemy invaded the land of our *umma*, violated her honor, shed her blood, and occupied her sanctuaries.

This aggression has reached such a catastrophic and disastrous point as to have brought about a calamity unprecedented in the history of our *umma*, namely the invasion by the American and western Crusader forces of the Arabian peninsula and Saudi Arabia, the home of the Noble Ka'ba, the Sacred House of God, the Muslim's direction of prayer,[1] the Noble Sanctuary of the Prophet, and the city of God's Messenger, where the Prophetic revelation was received.[2]

This momentous event is unprecedented both in pagan[3] and Islamic history. For the first time, the Crusaders have managed to achieve their historic ambitions and dreams against our Islamic *umma*, gaining control over the Islamic holy places and the Holy Sanctuaries, and hegemony over the wealth and riches of our *umma*, turning the Arabian peninsula into the biggest air, land, and sea base in the region.

> There is usually consolation for events,
> But there is no solace for what has happened to Islam.
> The Peninsula's fate cannot be mourned.[4]

All this happened on the watch of the region's rulers, and with their active participation—in fact, these are the people actually implementing the plans of our *umma*'s enemies. This invasion was financed by these rulers using our *umma*'s wealth and savings.

1 Throughout this volume, "direction of prayer" refers to the Arabic *qibla*. For any reference point on earth, the focal point for prayer is the Ka'ba, located inside the al-Haram mosque in Mecca. Originally toward Jerusalem, the *qibla* was changed in the year 624 to point towards the Ka'ba during Muhammad's exile in Medina, and has remained the direction of prayer ever since.

2 The Noble Sanctuary of the Prophet and the city of God's Messenger denote Medina "the radiant", the second holiest city of Islam after Mecca. It is the city to which Muhammad and his followers emigrated in 622, whereupon it became the seat of Muhammad's burgeoning government.

3 Throughout this volume, the terms "pagan" and "paganism" denote the Arabic *jahili* and *jahiliyya*, an Islamic concept describing both a historical period (Arabian society before the coming of Islam) and a general state of ignorance of Islam. In some radical Islamic thought, *jahiliyya* has come to denote a function analogous to the Marxist concept of false consciousness. The Egyptian writer, theoretician, and member of the Muslim brotherhood Sayyid Qutb reformulated the term, applying it to modern-day Muslim societies. He believed that the influence of European imperialism had left the Muslim world in a condition of debased ignorance similar to that of the pre-Islamic era. Following Qutb, some radical Islamic movements see *jahiliyya* as an active force, emanating particularly from permissive American society, and seducing Muslims away from the laws of God. Participation in modern liberal capitalist social and political institutions is seen as a symptom of *jahiliyya*. This concept substantially informs bin Laden's discourse.

4 Bin Laden does not give a source for these two lines of poetry; it may be assumed that he composed them himself.

Honorable and righteous scholars, this is the first, the biggest, and the most dangerous Crusader invasion of Saudi Arabia, and the leaders that some were counting on to defend our *umma* from aggression appear in fact to be the tools of that same aggression. And many scholars who were supposed to stand up for the truth, support their people and motivate our *umma* towards their duty of preparing for *jihad*, have forsaken our *umma* and pandered to the rulers.

Honourable and righteous scholars, we remind you of the covenant that you made with God, to show people the truth without fear or apprehension: "God took a pledge from those who were given the Scripture—'Make it known to people; do not conceal it.' "[5] And we remind you of the words of God Almighty: "As for those who hide the proofs and guidance We send down, after We have made them clear to people in the Scripture, God rejects them, and so do others."[6]

Honorable and righteous scholars, this is your role. Today is your day. Our Islamic *umma* is confronting a very grave challenge and being subjected to terrible aggression, and her rulers and many of her scholars have forsaken her. Who will lead and direct her, if not you?

Would you give the reins of our *umma* to secular, apostate opportunists?

Our *umma* has despaired of all those politically and militarily bankrupt leaders, who have lost all credibility. She is looking to the divine scholars who lead her with inspiration and drive her on the right path and fight with her in the theatres and battlefields of *jihad* for the sake of God Almighty. If you do not dedicate yourselves to this task now, then what are you waiting for?

After the Crusaders' occupation of Saudi Arabia, the Jews' violation of Palestine and the first of the two directions of prayer,[7] and the destruction and slaughter being meted out to Muslims in Chechnya[8] today and Bosnia[9] yesterday and throughout the world everyday, can matters get any worse?

---

5 Qur'an, 3:187.

6 Qur'an, 2:159.

7 This refers to Jerusalem, the original point towards which Muslims prayed. See n. 1 above.

8 Bin Laden is referring to the first Chechen war (1994–96), when Russian forces invaded the breakaway separatist republic of Chechnya, and in which an estimated 80,000–100,000 Chechens died. Since 2001, President Putin has placed the Chechen conflict under the umbrella of the "War on Terrorism". Attacks by Chechen separatists have continued to take place, notably the mass hostage-taking at the Dubrovka theatre, Moscow, on October 23 2003, and the Beslan school siege in September 2004.

9 As many as 278,000 Bosnian Muslims, Serbs, and Croatians were killed, and 2 million displaced, in the Bosnian conflict of 1992–95, of which the highest proportion were Bosnian

We remind you of this call in the noble Qur'an: "Believers, respond to God and His Messenger when he calls you to that which gives you life."[10] And life, to which the Qur'an, God, and His Messenger are calling you, should be a life of self-respect in this world and victory in the next—a life of *jihad* for the sake of God Almighty.

And we remind you of the words of God Almighty: "If you do not go out and fight, God will punish you severely and put others in your place, but you cannot harm Him in any way."[11] The painful torment of which God warns those who refrain from *jihad* is that He will give authority to their enemies over them in this world.

And is there any torment—in the world, in the spirit, or the senses—worse for any believer than the humiliation and weakness that his *umma* is experiencing, not to mention the defilement of her holy places, occupation of her land, and violation and plundering of her sanctuaries?

Honorable and righteous scholars, the divine punishment afflicting the *umma* is due to the neglect of its religion and the abandonment of *jihad* for the sake of God Almighty. As the noble Prophetic saying goes: "If you have made a solemn pledge, but then follow cows' tails and are happy with your lot and abandon the *jihad*, God decrees humiliation for you and will not remove it until you return to your religion."[12]

Honorable and righteous scholars, come and lead your *umma*, and call her to God, and return her to her religion in order to correct beliefs, spread knowledge, enjoin good, and forbid evil. Call her to *jihad* for the sake of God Almighty and call her to motivate people for it. "Prophet, urge the believers to fight."[13] "Fight them: God will punish them at your hands, He will disgrace them, He will help you conquer them, He will heal the believers' feelings and remove the rage from their hearts."[14]

Muslims. The International Criminal Tribune for the Former Yugoslavia ruled as genocide the Srebrenica massacre of July 1995, in which members of the Serbian Army and special forces led by Ratko Mladic killed up to 8,000 Muslims.

10 Qur'an, 8:24.
11 Qur'an, 9:39.
12 From the collection of *hadith* of Abu Dawud, book 23, no. 3,455.
13 Qur'an, 8:65.
14 Qur'an, 9:14–15.

And if you cannot to do so in your own country, then emigrate for the sake of God Almighty.[15] "And if anyone leaves home as a migrant towards God and His Messenger and is then overtaken by death, his reward from God is sure. God is most forgiving and most merciful."[16]

Emigration is related to *jihad*, and *jihad* will go on until the Day of Judgment. For according to Jinada bin Abi Umayya, as related on Ahmad's authority, the Messenger of God said: "Emigration will never cease, so long as there is *jihad*."[17]

So, scholars of our *umma*, rise up for the sake of God Almighty and do not be one of those of whom God rightly said: "Why, when it is said to you, 'Go and fight in God's way,' do you dig your heels in the earth? Do you prefer this world to the life to come? How small the enjoyment of this world is, compared with the life to come! If you do not go out and fight, God will punish you severely and put others in your place, but you cannot harm Him in any way: God has power over all things."[18]

In conclusion, we ask God Almighty to give our *umma* true guidance, and to establish an order of guidance for our *umma* in which those who obey him will be proud and those who disobey him will be humbled, and in which good is enjoined and evil rejected.

God speaks the truth and leads us on the path of guidance.

Peace be with you and all God's mercy and blessings.

Your brother,
Osama bin Muhammad bin Laden

---

15 Emigration, or *hijra* (the exodus of Muhammad from Mecca to Medina in 622), has profound spiritual importance for bin Laden. Muhammad and his followers left Mecca under intense pressure from their fellow Meccans, pagans (*jahili*) who did not follow Islam. From Medina, Muhammad waged war for eight years until he retook Mecca from the unbelievers. This serves as a paradigm for bin Laden's own emigration under pressure from the Saudi government, first to the Sudan, and then to Afghanistan, and for his *jihad* against the "apostate" Saudi regime and the West. Afghanistan was to become for bin Laden the Medina of the 21st century. See below, Statement 3, p.27.

16 Qur'an, 4:100.

17 Quoted in ibn Manzur, *Makhtasar Tarikh Damashq*, p. 801.

18 Qur'an, 9:38–39.

II

IN KHURASAN 1996–1998

3

DECLARATION OF *JIHAD*

August 23 1996

The longest of bin Laden's early statements, reproduced here in an abbreviated version, this text has subsequently been dubbed the "Ladenese Epistle". It comes in the form of a juridical edict authorizing defensive war (jihad) against the Americans for their continued presence in the Kingdom of Saudi Arabia. The full document sums up the long and very detailed findings of the May 1991 letter of protest and July 1992 "Memorandum of Advice" sent by the sahwa to King Fahd. It was issued after the Sudanese government, under intense American and Egyptian pressure, had requested bin Laden—following various Saudi attempts to assassinate him—to leave Khartoum, and he had arrived in Afghanistan in May 1996, before the Taliban came to power in the autumn of that year. Its composition and transmission have been dated by various commentators to between August and October 1996.[1] In form, the Epistle is an adaptation of "Communiqué 17," an indictment of the Saudi regime and a call for the abdication of King Fahd, issued on March 8 1995 by the London office of the Advice and Reform Committee (ARC). The Epistle broadens the framework of bin Laden's appeals, addressed now not only to Muslims in the Arabian peninsula, but across the world, whose sufferings he invokes in the Middle East, Central Asia, the Horn of Africa, the Caucasus, the Balkans and Southeast Asia, under "the blatant imperial arrogance of the United States" and its cover in the United Nations. But in this panorama of desolation, "the greatest disaster to befall Muslims since the death of the Prophet" is "the occupation of Saudi Arabia, the cornerstone of the Islamic world", and most of

1 The full title of this statement is "A Declaration of *Jihad* against the Americans Occupying the Land of the Two Holy Sanctuaries." Rosalind Gwynne notes that the full text was published in three parts, on October 12, 13 and 14 1996, by the Muslim Student Association (Ohio State University). An English translation of the complete version of the Statement can be found at http://www.washingtonpost.com/ac2/wp-dyn/A4342-2001Sep21; Gwynne's exhaustive analysis of bin Laden's use of Qur'an and *hadith* references in the Ladenese epistle, "Al-Qa'ida and al-Qur'an: The 'Tafsir' of Usamah bin Ladin", September 18 2001, is published at http://web.utk.edu/~warda/bin_ladin_ and_quran.htm.

the Epistle concentrates on the fate that has overtaken it, as American troops camp in the land and the regime collaborates with Israel. Amid the stench of corruption, mass unemployment, inflation and poverty are spreading. Petitions are ignored and jails are filled. The country has become a volcano, in which resistance has already started, with attacks on American forces in Riyadh and Khobar. Calling for a boycott of American goods, and jihad against the 'Judeo-Crusader alliance', bin Laden exhorts the warriors who fought in Afghanistan and Bosnia not to lay down their swords. "Cavalry of Islam, be mounted!".

"Expel the Polytheists from the Arabian peninsula."[2]

A Letter from Sheikh Osama bin Muhammad bin Laden to his Muslim Brothers across the world, and particularly those in the Arabian peninsula.

Praise be to God. We beseech Him for help and forgiveness. We seek refuge in God from the evil of our souls and our bad deeds. He whom God guides will not go astray, and he whom He leads astray can have no guide. I testify that there is no god but God alone, who has no partners. And I testify that Muhammad is His Servant and Prophet.

"You who believe, be mindful of God, as is His due, and make sure you devote yourselves to Him, to your dying moment."[3]

"People, be mindful of your Lord, who created you from a single soul, and from it created its mate, and from the pair of them spread countless men and women far and wide; be mindful of God, in whose name you make requests of one another. Beware of the severing ties of kinship: God is always watching over you."[4]

"Believers, be mindful of God, speak in a direct fashion and to good purpose, and He will put your deeds right for you and forgive you your sins. Whoever obeys God and His Messenger will truly achieve a great triumph."[5]

Shu'ayb said: "I cannot succeed without God's help: I trust in Him, and always turn to Him."[6]

Thanks be to God, who said: "[Believers], you are the best community singled

---

2 From the *hadith* collection of al-Bukhari, no. 2,932; also found in the collection of Murdin, no. 3,089.

3 Qur'an, 3:102.

4 Qur'an, 4:1.

5 Qur'an, 33:70–71.

6 Qur'an, 11:88.

out for people: you order what is right, forbid what is wrong, and you believe in God."[7]

And blessings and peace upon His Servant and Prophet, who said: "The people are close to an all-encompassing punishment from God if they see the oppressor and fail to restrain him."[8]

It is no secret to you, my brothers, that the people of Islam have been afflicted with oppression, hostility, and injustice by the Judeo-Christian alliance and its supporters. This shows our enemies' belief that Muslims' blood is the cheapest and that their property and wealth is merely loot. Your blood has been spilt in Palestine and Iraq, and the horrific image of the massacre in Qana[9] in Lebanon are still fresh in people's minds. The massacres that have taken place in Tajikistan, Burma, Kashmir, Assam, the Philippines, Fatani, Ogaden, Somalia, Eritrea, Chechnya, and Bosnia-Herzegovina send shivers down our spines and stir up our passions. All this has happened before the eyes and ears of the world, but the blatant imperial arrogance of America, under the cover of the immoral United Nations, has prevented the dispossessed from arming themselves.

So the people of Islam realized that they were the fundamental target of the hostility of the Judeo-Crusader alliance. All the false propaganda about the supposed rights of Islam was abandoned in the face of the attacks and massacres committed against Muslims everywhere, the latest and most serious of which—the greatest disaster to befall the Muslims since the death of the Prophet Muhammad—is the occupation of Saudi Arabia, which is the cornerstone of the Islamic world, place of revelation,[10] source of the Prophetic mission, and home of the Noble Ka'ba where Muslims direct their prayers. Despite this, it was occupied by the armies of the Christians, the Americans, and their allies.

I meet you today in the midst of this gloomy scenario, but also in light of the tremendous, blessed awakening that has swept across the world, and particularly the Islamic world. After the scholars of Islam underwent an enforced absence—enforced due to the oppressive Crusader campaign led by America in the fear

---

7 Qur'an, 3:110.

8 From the *hadith* collection of Abu Dawud, book 37, no. 4,325.

9 On April 18 1996, Israeli forces launched a rocket and mortar attack on a UN compound near the village of Qana, Lebanon. 102 civilian refugees died and over 300 were wounded.

10 The place of revelation is the cave of Hira, where the Qur'an was revealed to Muhammad in 610. Hira is located on Jabal al-Nour ("Mountain of Light") in the Hijaz region of Saudi Arabia.

that these scholars will incite our Islamic *umma* against its enemies, in the same way as did the pious scholars of old (God bless their souls) such as ibn Taymiyya and al-Izz ibn Abd al-Salam[11]—this Judeo-Crusader alliance undertook to kill and arrest the righteous scholars and hardworking preachers. May God sanctify who He wishes. They killed the *mujahid* Sheikh Abdallah Azzam,[12] they arrested Sheikh Ahmed Yassin in Jerusalem,[13] and they killed the *mujahid* Sheikh Omar Abd al-Rahman[14] in America, as well as arresting—on the advice of America—a large number of scholars, preachers and youth in Saudi Arabia. The most prominent of these were Sheikh Salman al-Auda and Sheikh Safar al-Hawali[15] and their brothers.

This injustice was inflicted on us, too, as we were prevented from talking to Muslims and were hounded out of Saudi Arabia to Pakistan, Sudan, and then Afghanistan. That is what led to this long absence of mine, but by the grace of God there became available a safe base in Khurasan, high in the peaks of the Hindu Kush, the very same peaks upon which were smashed, by the grace of

11 For ibn Taymiyya, see above, p. 5, n. 7.

12 Abdallah Azzam (1941–89) was a radical Islamic scholar and preacher of Palestinian origin. He taught that *jihad* was a moral obligation of Muslims and the 'sixth pillar' of faith (conventionally, there are five such pillars of faith in Islam). Azzam taught in Saudi Arabia from 1978 to 1984, when he moved to Peshawar, where he worked in conjunction with bin Laden, setting up a recruitment centre, the Maktab al-Khidamat (MAK), to organize resistance against the Russians in Afghanistan; branches of which were subsequently opened throughout the Middle East, and in locations as far-flung as Brooklyn, New York. Azzam became revered as a father of the *jihad* against the USSR in Afghanistan. He was killed by a car bomb in Peshawar in November 1989.

13 Sheikh Ahmed Yassin (c.1937–2004) was founder of the Palestinian organization Hamas ("Harakat al-Muqawamah al-Islamiyyah" or "Islamic Resistance Movement") in 1987. In 1989 he was convicted of ordering the kidnapping and killing of two Israeli Defense Force (IDF) soldiers, and sentenced to life imprisonment. Released in 1997, the quadriplegic Yassin resumed his leadership of Hamas; he was assassinated by an Israeli helicopter gunship on March 22 2004.

14 Contrary to bin Laden's assertion, the blind Sheikh Omar Abdel Rahman (1938–) is still alive. An Egyptian cleric, after graduating with Qur'anic studies from al-Azhar university, Cairo, he became the leader of al-Gama'a al-Islamiyya ("the Islamic group"), which was responsible for the attacks at Deir el-Bahri, Luxor, on November 17 1997, that left 62 dead. During the 1970s, he developed links with another militant organization, Egyptian Islamic Jihad, led by Ayman al-Zawahiri, and spent three years in Egyptian jails, where he was tortured. In the mid-1980s, he rejoined his former university professor, Abdallah Azzam, in Afghanistan. In 1990, he was issued a US tourist visa by the CIA in acknowledgment of his role in opposing the Soviet invasion in Afghanistan. Arrested in 1993, he was convicted in October 1995, of conspiring to bomb locations in New York. He is currently serving a life sentence in Colorado.

15 See above, p. 8, n. 19.

God, the largest infidel military force in the world,[16] and on which the myth of the great powers perished before the cries of the holy warriors: God is greatest!

And today, in the same peaks of Afghanistan, we work to do away with the injustice that has befallen our *umma* at the hands of the Judeo-Crusader alliance, especially after its occupation of Jerusalem and its appropriation of Saudi Arabia. We pray to God that He might bless us with victory—He is our protector and is well capable of doing so.

And so here we are today, working and discussing with each other to find ways of rectifying what has happened to the Islamic world generally and Saudi Arabia in particular. We need to study the appropriate paths to take in order to restore things to good order, and to restore to the people their rights after the considerable damage and harm inflicted on their life and religion. This has afflicted every section of society, whether civilian or military or security personnel, whether employees or merchants, young or old, university students, graduates or the unemployed, who now represent a broad section of society numbering hundreds of thousands. The situation in Saudi Arabia has begun to resemble a huge volcano that is about to explode and destroy unbelief and corruption, wherever it comes from. The two explosions in Riyadh and Khobar[17] are merely warning signs pointing to this destructive torrent which is produced by bitter repression, terrible injustice, and the humiliating poverty that we see today.

People are struggling even with the basics of everyday life, and everyone talks frankly about economic recession, price inflation, mounting debts, and

16 Khurasan ("where the sun appears") was a Persian province commensurate with parts of modern-day Iran, Afghanistan, Tajikistan, Turkmenistan and Uzbekistan. Bin Laden is referring to the defeat of the Soviet army in Afghanistan by the *mujahidin*. Backed by Pakistan and the USA, the *mujahidin* succeeded in forcing the Soviet forces to withdraw, after ten years of occupation, with the loss of around 15,000 soldiers.

17 On November 13 1995, a car bomb was detonated outside the National Guard building in Riyadh. The first such attack of its kind in Saudi Arabia, it killed five Americans and two Indians. Subsequently, one of the four accused said that he had been influenced by the writings of bin Laden and by Egyptian Islamist groups. Three of the four had fought in Afghanistan, one of them, Maslah al-Shamrani, was appointed to the Egyptian-run "al-Farooq" training camp, near Khost, with which bin Laden had connections. Bin Laden denied direct responsibility for the attack, but drew a connection between the bombing and his role as an inciter to *jihad*. The four bombers were subsequently sentenced to death by a Saudi court and beheaded. On June 25 1996, an attack on the Khobar Towers military complex killed nineteen US servicemen and injured hundreds of others. Five years later, thirteen members of Saudi Hezbollah, a Shia group with Iranian links, were indicted in the USA for the bombing.

prison overcrowding. Low-income government employees talk to you about their debts in the tens or hundreds of thousands of riyals,[18] whilst complaining that the riyal's value is declining dramatically. Domestic debts owed by the government to its citizens have reached 340 billion riyals, and are rising daily due to usurious interest, let alone all the foreign debt. People are wondering: are we really the biggest source of oil in the world? They feel that God is bringing this torture upon them because they have not spoken out against the regime's injustice and illegitimate behaviour, the most prominent aspects of which are its failure to rule in accordance with God's law, its depriving of legal rights to its servants, its permitting the American occupiers into Saudi Arabia, and its arresting of righteous scholars—inheritors of the Prophets' legacy—and unjustly throwing them in prison. The regime has desecrated its legitimacy through many of its own actions, the most important being:

1. Its suspension of the rulings of the Islamic law[19] and replacement thereof with man-made laws, and its entering into a bloody confrontation with the righteous scholars and pious youth. May God sanctify whom He pleases.

2. Its inability to protect the land and its allowing the enemies of God to occupy it for years in the form of the American Crusaders, who have become the principal reason for all aspects of our land's disastrous predicament.

The voices of the shadows have spoken up, their eyes uncovering the veil of injustice and their noses smelling the stench of corruption. The voices of reform have spoken up, calling for the situation to be put right: they have sent petitions, testimonies, and requests for reform. In the year 1411 AH, at the time of the Gulf War, a petition was sent to the king with around 400 signatures calling for reform in the country, but he made a mockery of them by completely ignoring their advice, and the situation went from bad to worse.[20]

---

18 The currency of Saudi Arabia.

19 "Islamic law" throughout this volume represents the Arabic word *sharia*. Islam has no distinction between religious and secular life; *sharia* therefore covers not only religious rituals but many aspects of everyday life, including politics, economics, and banking.

20 It should be noted that the 1990–91 Gulf War is generally termed the Second Gulf War; the first was the Iran–Iraq War (1980–88). The petition bin Laden is referring to here is probably not the Memorandum of Advice sent after the Gulf War in July 1992, but a first petition sent in May 1991, which similarly called for the imposition of Islamic law, and for the Saudi regime to be accountable. See Headnote to Statement 1, p. 3.

Brother Muslims in Saudi Arabia, does it make any sense at all that our country is the biggest purchaser of weapons from America in the world and America's biggest trading partner in the region, while at the very same time the Americans are occupying Saudi Arabia and supporting—with money, arms, and manpower—their Jewish brothers in the occupation of Palestine and their murder and expulsion of Muslims there? Depriving these occupiers of the huge returns they receive from their trade with us is a very important way of supporting the *jihad* against them, and we expect you to boycott all American goods.

Men of the radiant future of our *umma* of Muhammad, raise the banner of *jihad* up high against the Judeo-American alliance that has occupied the holy places of Islam. God told his Prophet: "He will not let the deeds of those who are killed for His cause come to nothing; He will guide them and put them in a good state; He will admit them into the Garden He has already made known to them."[21] And the Prophet said: "There are one hundred levels in Heaven that God has prepared for the holy warriors who have died for Him, between two levels as between the earth and the sky."[22] And the *al-Jami al-Sahih* notes that the Prophet said: "The best martyrs are those who stay in the battle line and do not turn their faces away until they are killed. They will achieve the highest level of Heaven, and their Lord will look kindly upon them. When your Lord looks kindly upon a slave in the world, He will not hold him to account."[23] And he said: "The martyr has a guarantee from God: He forgives him at the first drop of his blood and shows him his seat in Heaven. He decorates him with the jewels of faith, protects him from the torment of the grave, keeps him safe on the day of judgment, places a crown of dignity on his head with the finest rubies in the world, marries him to seventy-two of the pure virgins of paradise and intercedes on behalf of seventy of his relatives," as related by Ahmad al-Tirmidhi in an authoritative *hadith*.[24]

I say to the youth of Islam who have waged *jihad* in Afghanistan and Bosnia-Herzegovina, with their financial, spiritual, linguistic, and scholarly resources,

---

21 Qur'an, 47: 4–6.
22 From the *hadith* collection of Muslim, book 20, no. 4,645.
23 The *al-Jami al-Sahih* is the title of al-Bukhari's collection of *hadith*. See above, p. 13, n. 34. Quoted in ibn Hajar al-Haitimi, *Majma al-Zawa'id wa Manba al-Fawa'id*, p. 909.
24 From the *hadith* collection of al-Tirmidhi, vol. 4, book 23, ch. 1, no. 1,620. Abu al-Tirmidhi (824–92), from Termez in modern-day Uzbekistan, was a collector of *hadith*. He wrote the *Jami al-Tirmidhi*, one of the six canonical collections of Prophetic traditions used in Sunni Islam.

that the battle is not yet over. I remind them of what Gabriel said to the Prophet, after the battle of Ahzab: "When the Messenger of God, prayers and peace be upon him, departed to Medina and laid down his sword, Gabriel came to him and said: 'You have laid down your sword? By God, the angels have not yet laid down their swords. Get up and go with whoever is with you to the Bani Qurayza, and I will go ahead of you to shake their fortresses and strike fear into them.' So Gabriel went off, accompanied by his pageant of angels, the Prophet, and his holy warriors and helpers."[25] This is as it was told by al-Bukhari.

I say to our Muslim brothers across the world: your brothers in Saudi Arabia and Palestine are calling for your help and asking you to share with them in the *jihad* against the enemies of God, your enemies the Israelis and Americans. They are asking you to defy them in whatever way you possibly can, so as to expel them in defeat and humiliation from the holy places of Islam. God Almighty has said: "If they seek help from you against persecution, it is your duty to assist them."[26]

Cavalry of Islam, be mounted! This is a difficult time, so you yourselves must be tough. You should know that your coming-together and cooperation in order to liberate the holy places of Islam is the right step towards unification of the word of our *umma* under the banner of God's unity. At this point we can only raise our palms humbly to ask God Almighty to provide good fortune and success in this matter.

Lord, bless your slave and messenger Muhammad, and his family and companions. Our final prayer is praise to God, Lord of the worlds.

Your brother in Islam,
Osama bin Muhammad bin Laden

---

25 From the *hadith* of al-Bukhari, vol. 5, book 59, no. 448. The Battle of the Trench (627) was fought between the forces of Muhammad and the coalition ("joint forces," or *al-Ahzab*) army of Mecca. Muhammad was victorious; in the aftermath of the battle, the Jewish tribe the Bani Qurayza, who had broken a peace treaty with Muhammad to side with the "joint forces" against him, were found guilty, the judge ruling that all the adult males in the tribe should be killed.

26 Qur'an 8:72. Bin Laden leaves out both the first part of the verse, which establishes the antecedent (the emigrants), and is also the conditional to the quoted clause, which reads, "except against people with whom you have a treaty: God sees all that you do."

4

THE SAUDI REGIME

November 1996

Apearing about the same time as the Ladenese Epistle, this interview appeared in Nida'ul Islam, *a journal edited by Muslim activists in Australia,[1] and can be regarded as an indication of bin Laden's efforts to expand media coverage of his appeal for a global* jihad. *In the brief biography he supplied to preface the interview, he dates his radicalization from 1973, the year of the Yom Kippur War, and dwells on his relationship with the Palestinian thinker Abdallah Azzam, who seems to have introduced the ideas of the Muslim Brotherhood to bin Laden—brought up in the conservative atmosphere of wahhabism—when he was a student at Jeddah. Of his services in the cause of militant Islam, bin Laden singles out battlefield actions against Communism in Yemen and Afghanistan. Denying any hand in the bombs exploded against American targets in Riyadh and Khobar, he expresses his satisfaction at these attacks, which he hopes may be causing elements within the Saudi ruling family and Gulf sheikhdoms to reconsider their policies. At this stage, he still holds out the possibility of a reconciliation between the regimes of the peninsula and their peoples. Rejecting charges of terrorism, he points to the recent Israeli bombing of a refugee camp in the Lebanon, and the hundreds of thousands of deaths, most of them children, caused by UN sanctions against Iraq, as the major slaughter of innocents of the time.*

BIOGRAPHY:

Name: Osama bin Muhammad bin Laden
Born in the city of Riyadh 1377 AH (1957).
Raised in Medina and Hijaz, and received his education in the schools of

---

1 First published under the title "The New Powder Keg in the Middle East," this English text was taken from the October/November 1996 issue (no. 15) of *Nida'ul Islam.* Spelling and syntax have been altered for consistency and clarity.

Jeddah, then studied management and economics in King Abdul Aziz University in Jeddah.
Married with children.

His outlook: The way of the people of the traditions of the Prophet and of the religious community in accordance with the understanding of the righteous predecessors, in total and in detail. From this emerges the necessity for armed struggle, preceded by the invitation to Islam[2] and military preparation in order to repel the greater unbelief,[3] and to cooperate with Muslims in order to unite their word under the banner of monotheism, and to set aside divisions and differences.

He began his interaction with the Islamic groups in 1393 AH (1973) and continued with this until the commencement of *jihad* in Afghanistan; he also participated, in the beginning of the 1980s, with the *mujahidin* against the Communist party in South Yemen, participating once again in the 1990s until the downfall of the Communist party.[4]

He established alongside Sheikh Dr Abdallah Azzam—May God bless his soul—the office for *mujahidin* services in Peshawar; he also established along with Sheikh Azzam the Sidda camp for the training of Arab *mujahidin* who came for *jihad* in Afghanistan. His first visit to assist the Afghan *mujahidin* came a few days after the entry of the Russians in 1399 AH (1979); he established "Ma'asadat Al-Ansar", which was a base for Arab *mujahidin* in Afghanistan.[5] In 1406 AH (1986) he participated in the battles of Jalalabad with the Arab

2 Throughout this volume, the "invitation to Islam" denotes the Arabic term *dawa*. *Dawa* is particularly significant in the context of bin Laden's later statements to America and its allies after 9/11, in which he offers them a chance to convert before further assaults, thereby "clearing the decks in Islamic terms: he has warned and invited before attacking." (Michael Scheuer, *Imperial Hubris: Why the West is Losing the War on Terror* [Potomac, 2005], p. 153).

3 "Unbelief" throughout this volume represents the Arabic word *kufr*, meaning unbelief or blasphemy. In Islamic law, the term is equivalent to the Christian "excommunication".

4 In July 1969, a radical branch of the Marxist National Liberation Front gained power in the People's Republic of South Yemen, which became the People's Democratic Republic of Yemen on December 1 1970, with Aden as its capital. In the early 1990s, Afghan Arabs returning from Afghanistan participated in a *jihad* to rid South Yemen of its socialist government; the Arab Afghans' leader, the *mujahid* Tariq al-Fadhli, was financed by bin Laden. In 1994, North Yemen went to war against the South, mobilizing the Afghan Arabs in the process. Aden was taken in July 1994, and a general amnesty declared. 10,000 civilians were killed during the course of the war.

5 "Ma'asadat al-Ansar" refers to "al Ma'asada", the training camp bin Laden established at Jaji in Paktia province near the Afghan border with Pakistan, built sometime from late 1996 onwards for the exclusive use of Arabs fighting in Afghanistan.

mujahidin, as he also did in 1409 AH (1989), which was one of the biggest battles which the Arabs fought in Afghanistan.[6]

He migrated from the Arabian peninsula on 16 Shawwal 1411 AH (May 1 1991), and was then asked by the Saudi government to return; however he refused, so they withdrew his citizenship, cancelled his passport, froze his assets, and then attacked him through the media by defaming his character both inside and outside Saudi Arabia.

He currently resides in Afghanistan, and has directed a call to the Muslims throughout the world to declare a *jihad* against the Judeo-Christian alliance which is occupying Islamic sacred land in Palestine and the Arabian peninsula.

INTERVIEWER: What is the policy that should be adopted by the Islamic movement towards the scholars who defend—intentionally or unintentionally—the likes of the Saudi regime?

OBL: It is not a concealed fact that the police states in the Arab world rely on some organizations in order to protect themselves. Amongst these organizations is the security organization, on which they spend generously, whose foremost mission is to spy on its own people in order to protect the person of the ruler, even if this is at the expense of the rights of the people and their security, as well as the military sector, which is prepared to strike the people if they wish to reject and remove this oppression and establish truth.

The media sector is in the same category, as it strives to beatify the persons of the leaders, to sedate the community, and to fulfil the plans of the enemies through keeping the people occupied with minor matters, and to stir their emotions and desires until corruption becomes widespread amongst the believers.

There is also another organization which takes priority with the leaders in the Arab world, and is used to leading the people astray, and to opening the door wide for the security factions to fulfil their aforementioned objectives. This is the organization of the scholars of the authorities, as the role of this

---

6 In March 1989, the *mujahidin* launched an assault on the government-held city of Jalalabad in eastern Afghanistan. The offensive was a failure: more than 1,000 Afghan fighters were killed and several thousand injured. Bin Laden was involved in fighting around the town of Chaprihar, southeast of Jalalabad; those who fought with him remember his lack of concern for his own safety. See Burke, *Al-Qaeda: The True Story of Radical Islam* (Penguin, 2004), p. 81.

organization is the most dangerous of roles throughout the Arabic countries. History is the best witness to this.

Every time a leader engages in the major unbelief, which takes them out of the fold of Islam in broad daylight and in front of all the people, you will find a juridical decree issued from their religious organization [justifying their actions]. The religious organization in Saudi Arabia, in particular, plays the most ominous of roles. Overlooking the question of whether or not it fulfils this role intentionally, the harm which has resulted from its efforts is no different from [that which resulted] from the efforts of the most ardent enemies of our *umma*.

The regime in Saudi Arabia has given a very high priority to this organization, which has been able to increase its stature in the estimation of the people, until some of the common people started worshipping it as an idol, separately from God, and without the will of the members of this organization.[7]

However, there remain in Saudi Arabia a good number of honest scholars and students who work according to their teachings, and who have taken visible and daring stances against the activities of unbelief which the regime is perpetrating.

The regime has striven to keep these scholars in the shadows and then to remove them, one way or another, from being effective elements in the lives of the people in the community. At the forefront of these scholars was the Sheikh Abdallah bin Hamid[8]—May God bless his soul—who was the jurist in the Arabian peninsula, and who headed the Supreme Council of Judges. However, the regime constrained him and tightened its grip on him until he offered his resignation. He has [authored] many famous writings in response to the unacceptable laws which the government introduced in place of the Law of God; one of these is a treatise dealing with the law of work and workers, which tackles many of the man-made laws which contradict the Law of God.

---

7 In return for endorsing official Saudi government policies, the council of *ulema*, headed by Sheikh bin Baz, obtained heightened influence within the country. When the *ulema* approved King Fahd's decision to call in US troops in 1990, the clerics demanded that the regime grant them new measures of social control in the name of Islam. Bin Laden argues that the prestige of the *ulema* among the Saudi population led to their laws being obeyed rather than true Islamic law; in his eyes, this constituted shirk, idolatry, which is forbidden in Islam.

8 See above, p. 12, n. 30.

At the same time, they promoted some of the scholars who were far below Sheikh bin Hamid, may God bless his soul; in a cunning plan which began more than twenty years ago, they foregrounded those known to be weak and soft. During this time, the regime enlarged the role of bin Baz because of what it knows of his weakness and flexibility, and because he was easily influenced by that usual practice of the interior ministry: providing him with false information. So, a generation of youth was raised believing that the most pious and knowledgeable of people is bin Baz, as a result of his promotion in the media through a concerted policy, a promotion which had progressed over twenty years.

After this, the government began to strike with the cane of bin Baz every corrective programme which the honest scholars put forward; further, it extracted a juridical decree to hand over Palestine to the Jews, and before this, to permit entry into Saudi Arabia to the modern-day crusaders under the rule of necessity; it then relied on a letter from bin Baz to the minister for internal affairs and placed the honest scholars in jail.[9]

However, a high price was paid for these actions, because the confidence of the people and the youth in bin Baz was shaken, whilst their confidence in the working scholars, particularly those in the prisons, increased.

The policy of the Advice and Reform Committee[10] towards these scholars is to continue providing advice to them openly and secretly (as there is no person above the law, and we are not immune) and particularly as regards the matters on which they have given public rulings, and to make public the rulings of the scholars who respond to them, in order to bring awareness to the people as to the correct ruling with respect to these issues, and not to forestall the rectification programme in order that the scholars are made aware [of their errors], as the pressure which is put on them [to issue rulings in support of government policy] is very great.

Also [the Committee aims] to promote the honest scholars as they deserve in front of the people, so that the support of the people swings behind them.

9 See above, Headnote to Statement 1, p. 3.
10 See above, p. 4, n. 2.

INTERVIEWER: How do you evaluate the Saudi regime's foreign policy towards the Muslim world in the past years?

OBL: The external policy of the Saudi regime towards Islamic issues is a policy which was tied to the British outlook from the establishment of Saudi Arabia until 1364 AH (1945); it then became attached to the American outlook after America gained prominence as a major power in the world after World War Two.[11]

It is well known that the policies of these two countries bear the greatest enmity towards the Islamic world.

To be taken out of this category is the final phase of the rule of King Faisal,[12] [during which] there was a clear engagement with Muslim issues, in particular Jerusalem and Palestine.

However, the regime does not cease to cry in the open over matters affecting Muslims, without making any serious effort to serve the interests of the Muslim community, apart from small gestures in order to confuse people and throw some dust into their eyes.

INTERVIEWER: The confrontation between the Islamic movement and the apostate Saudi regime reached a historical turning point following the latest attacks against the American occupiers. How did these attacks reflect [domestic attitudes], and how did they affect Saudi-American relations?

OBL: The two explosions in Riyadh had a significant impact on both the domestic and foreign fronts.[13] Most important amongst these is the people's awareness of the significance of the American occupation of Saudi Arabia, and that the original decrees of the regime are a reflection of the wishes of the American occupiers. So the people became aware that their main problems

11 At a meeting with the first king of Saudi Arabia, Abd al-Aziz ibn Saud, on February 14 1945, US President Roosevelt gave his political seal of approval to concessions granted to American firms to develop Saudi Arabia's oilfields. In so doing, he established US hegemony over the Kingdom, which had previously been a client state of the UK, and pledged US military support to counter any threat to the Saudi dynasty.

12 Faisal bin Abd al-Aziz al-Saud (1906–75) was the fourth son of King ibn Saud. After the United Nations partition of Palestine in 1947–48, Faisal petitioned his father to break off relations with the USA, to no avail. On becoming king in November 1964, Faisal introduced reforms, including making secondary education available to girls, opposed by many Saudis as against Islamic law. On October 17 1973, he removed Saudi oil from world markets, thereby quadrupling the price at the stroke and precipitating the 1973 energy crisis.

13 See above, p. 27, n. 17.

were caused by the American occupiers and their puppets in the Saudi regime, whether this was from the religious perspective or from other aspects of their daily lives. The sympathies of the people towards the working scholars who had been imprisoned also increased, as did their understanding of the [working scholars'] advice and guidance, which prompted the people to support the general reform movement led by the scholars and the callers to Islam. This movement—with the bounty of God—is increasing in power and in supporters day by day at the regime's expense. The sympathy with these missions at the civil and military levels was great, as were the sympathies of the Muslim world with the struggle against the Americans.

As for the relationship between the regime and the American occupiers, these operations have embarrassed both sides and have led to an exchange of accusations between them. So we have the Americans stating that the causes of the explosions are a result of the bad policies of the regime and the corruption of members of the ruling family, and the regime is accusing the Americans of exceeding their authority by taking advantage of it, forcing it to enter into military and civil contracts which are beyond its means, which has led to a major economic recession that has hit people hard. In addition to this are the Americans' crude and arrogant behaviour towards the Saudi army and their general behaviour with citizens, as well as the privileges which the Americans enjoy, distinct from the Saudi forces.

These missions [the Riyadh bombings] also paved the way for the raising of voices of opposition against the American occupation from within the ruling family and the armed forces; in fact, we can say that the remaining Gulf countries have been affected to the same degree, and that the voices of opposition to the American occupation have begun to be heard at the level of the ruling families and the governments of the Cooperative Council of Gulf countries. A difference in outlook between the Americans and the Gulf states has appeared for the first time since the Second Gulf War.[14] This was during the conference attended by the ministers of external affairs of the countries comprising the cooperative council of Gulf states which was held in Riyadh to look into the American missile aggression against Iraq.[15] These differences are

14 In Arab eyes, the first Gulf War was the 1980–88 Iran-Iraq conflict.
15 Bin Laden is here referring to the post-Gulf War conference held in Riyadh by the Cooperation Council for Arab States in the Gulf.

a sign of the strain which has appeared in the relationship between America and the countries of the region following the *jihad* missions against the Americans in Riyadh, and as a result of the fear of these regimes that similar *jihad* missions might take place in their own lands.

INTERVIEWER: *It was observed that the American and Saudi officials tried to link the latest operations to some foreign countries. What is behind this?*

OBL: A result of the increasing reaction of the people against the American occupation, and the great sympathy with the *jihad* missions against the Americans, is the eagerness of the Americans and the Saudis to propagate false information to disperse this sympathy. This can be witnessed in their statements that some of the countries in the region were behind the *jihad* missions inside Saudi Arabia; however, the people are aware that this is an internal Islamic movement against the American occupation which is revealing itself in the most clear picture after the killing of the four champions[16] who performed the Riyadh operation, whom we ask God to accept amongst the martyrs.

In the face of an internal calamity, it has become routine policy for countries to lay the responsibility on an external country. Before the puppetry of the Arabic countries to America became plainly obvious, the security sections never hesitated to accuse any rectifying Islamic movement of being a puppet of America and Israel.

INTERVIEWER: *What are the regime's options with regards to the Muslim uprising, and what are your expectations for the future?*

OBL: There are several choices for the regime. The first of these is reconciliation with all the different sections of the public, by releasing the honest scholars [who they have imprisoned], and offering essential changes, the most important of which is to bring back Islamic law, and to practise real consultative government. The regime may resort to this option after finding itself in the position of being a morsel of food for the Americans to consume, after it has sown discord among its people. These people today feel that the Americans have exceeded their limits both politically and economically, and the regime now knows that the public are aware that its sovereignty is shared

16 See above, p. 27, n. 7.

[with the Americans]. This was particularly evident in the recent period through the US press statements which give justification to the American occupation, which only exists to rob the wealth of the people to the benefit of the Americans. This option is dependent on the agreement of the people who hold the solution and have the ability to effect change; at the forefront of these would be the honest scholars.

As for the second option, this is a very difficult and dangerous one for the regime. It involves an escalation in the confrontation between the Muslim people and the American occupiers and confrontation of the economic hemorrhage [of the Kingdom]. Its most important goal would be to change the current regime, with the permission of God.

INTERVIEWER: As a part of the furious international campaign against the jihad *movement, you personally were the target of a prejudiced attack, which accused you of financing terrorism and being part of an international terrorist organization. What do you have to say about that?*

OBL: After the end of the Cold War, America escalated its campaign against the Muslim world in its entirety, aiming to get rid of Islam itself. Its main focus in this was to target the scholars and the reformers who were enlightening the people to the dangers of the Judeo-American alliance; it also targeted the *mujahidin*. We too have been hit with some of the traces of this campaign as we were accused of funding terrorism and being a member of an international terrorist organization.[17] America's aim in making these allegations was to place psychological pressure on the *mujahidin* and their supporters, so that they would forsake the obligation of *jihad* and the resistance of oppression and Israeli-American occupation of Islamic sacred lands. However, thanks be to God, America's campaign was not successful, because terrorizing the American occupiers is a religious and logical obligation. We are grateful to God Most Exalted in that He has facilitated *jihad* in His cause for us, against the Israeli-American attacks on the Holy Sanctuaries of Islam.

17 A US state department report in August 1996 noted that bin Laden was "one of the most significant financial sponsors of Islamic extremist activities in the world"; the previous April, the new Anti-Terrorism Act allowed the US to block assets of terrorist organizations, including bin Laden's access to his estimated US$250–300 million fortune. (Carol Giacomo, "US lists Saudi businessman as extremist sponsor", *Washington Post*, August 14 1996; cited in Ahmed Rashid, *Taliban: The Story of the Afghan Warlords* [Pan, 2001], p. 134.)

As for their accusations [that we] terrorize the innocent, the children, and the women, these fall into the category of "accusing others of their own affliction in order to fool the masses." The evidence overwhelmingly shows America and Israel killing the weaker men, women, and children in the Muslim world and elsewhere. A few examples of this are the recent Qana massacre in Lebanon,[18] and the death of more than 600,000 Iraqi children because of the shortage of food and medicine which resulted from the boycotts and sanctions,[19] also, their withholding of arms from the Muslims of Bosnia-Herzegovina, leaving them prey to the Christian Serbians who massacred and raped in a manner not seen in contemporary history. Nor should one forget the deliberate, premeditated dropping of the H bombs on cities with their entire populations of children, elderly, and women, as was the case with Hiroshima and Nagasaki. Then, killing hundreds of thousands of children in Iraq, whose numbers [of dead] continue to increase as a result of the sanctions. Despite the ongoing American occupation of Saudi Arabia, America continues to claim that it is upholding the banner of freedom and humanity, yet it perpetrated deeds which you would not find the most ravenous of animals debasing themselves to do.

As for what America accuses us of, the killing of innocent people, it has not been able to offer any evidence, despite the magnitude of its expenditure on intelligence services. Witness our history in the Afghan phase of the *jihad*. This was unstained with any blood of innocent people, despite the inhuman Russian campaign against our women, our children, and our brothers in Afghanistan.[20] Our history is similar with respect to our differences with the Saudi regime; all that has been proved is our joy at the killing of the American soldiers in Riyadh and Khobar. These are the sentiments of every Muslim.

18 See above, p. 25, n. 9.

19 Resolution 661, imposing sanctions on Iraq, was adopted by the United Nations Security Council on August 6 1990. A UNICEF report of 1998 found that sanctions had resulted in the deaths of an extra 90,000 Iraqi children a year since 1991. On May 10 1996, appearing on the US TV show *60 Minutes*, the US Ambassador to the UN, Madeleine Albright was presented with a figure of half a million children under five having died from the sanctions imposed on Iraq. Without challenging the statistic, Albright replied: "We think the price is worth it."

20 More than a million Afghans died in the Soviet-Afghan war (1979–89); 5 million became refugees in neighbouring countries. Economic production was drastically curtailed and much of the land laid waste. By the end of the war 5 million land mines had been laid in over 2 per cent of the country.

Our encouragement and call to Muslims to enter *jihad* against the American and the Israeli occupiers are actions which we undertake as religious obligations. God Most High has commanded us in many verses of the Qur'an to fight in His path and to urge the believers to do so. These are His words: "So [Prophet] fight in God's way. You are accountable only for yourself. Urge the believers on. God may well curb the power of the disbelievers, for He is stronger in might and more terrible in punishment."[21] and His words: "Why should you not fight in God's cause and for those oppressed men, women, and children who cry out, 'Lord, rescue us from this town whose people are oppressors! By Your grace, give us a protector and helper!'?"[22], and His words: "When you meet the disbelievers, strike them in the neck ..."[23] We have given an oath to God to continue in the struggle as long as we have blood coursing through our veins or a seeing eye, and we beg of God to accept and to grant a good outcome for us and for all the Muslims.

INTERVIEWER: Some media sources mentioned that the Afghan government demanded that you leave the country. How true is this?

OBL: The Afghan government[24] has not asked us to leave the country ... Thanks be to God, our relationship in with our brother *mujahidin* in Afghanistan is a deep and broad relationship where blood and sweat have mixed as have the links over long years of struggle against the Soviets; it is not a passing relationship, nor one based on personal interests.

They are committed to support the religion approved by God, and that country remains as the Muslims have known it, a stronghold of Islam, and its

21 Qur'an, 4:84.
22 Qur'an, 4:75.
23 Qur'an, 47:4. In its entirety, the verse reads "When you meet the disbelievers in battle, strike them in the neck, and once they are defeated, bind any captives firmly—later you can release them by grace or by ransom—until the toils of war have ended. That [is the way]. God could have defeated them Himself if He had willed, but His purpose is to test some of you by means of others. He will not let the deeds of those who are killed for his cause come to nothing."
24 Bin Laden arrived in Jalalabad, Afghanistan in May 1996 as a guest of the Taliban government. But his relations with it were not always easy. In a November 1996 interview with Abdel Bari Atwan, editor of the Arabic-language London newspaper, *Al-Quds Al-Arabi*, bin Laden contemplated leaving Afghanistan for his ancestral home of Yemen, with its armed tribesmen, mountainous terrain, and "clean air you can breathe without humiliation."

people are amongst the most protective of the religion approved by God, and the keenest to fulfil His laws and to establish an Islamic state.[25]

That passing phase of infighting has saddened us as it has saddened all the Muslims. However, we wish to indicate that the picture of events as painted by the international press is grossly distorted, and that this infighting is much smaller and less fierce than Muslims on the outside might imagine, and that most of the country is living a normal peaceful life, despite some petty crimes here and there as some elements attempt to create corruption under cover of the disputes amongst some of the groups. We are hoping that Afghanistan will regain very soon—God willing—its Islamic position which would befit its history of *jihad*.

INTERVIEWER: What is the responsibility of the Muslim peoples towards the international campaign against Islam?

OBL: What can be of no doubt in this fierce Judeo-Christian campaign against the Muslim world, the likes of which has never been seen before, is that Muslims must prepare with all their might to repel the enemy in military, economic, missionary, and all other areas. It is crucial for us to be patient and to cooperate in righteousness and piety, and to raise awareness of the fact that the highest priority, after faith, is to repel the invading enemy, which corrupts religion and the world, as the scholars have declared; and for this cause, it is crucial to overlook many of the issues of infighting in order to unite our ranks so that we can repel the greater unbelief.

All must act in order to give life to the words of the Most High: "[Messengers], this community of yours is one single community and I am your Lord, so serve Me."[26] And the Muslim should not be like those whom God has described with His words: "As for those who have divided their religion and broken up into factions, have nothing to do with them."[27] It is essential to volunteer and not to bicker, and the Muslim should not belittle righteousness in any way; the Messenger said: "Whoever believes in God and the last day must speak good or

25 Since the abolition of the Ottoman Caliphate, no country has replaced Turkey as the Muslim world's center. According to Sayyid Qutb, in order to bring about a new Caliphate governed by God's law there must be a revival in one Muslim country, enabling it to attain that status. When the Taliban captured Kabul in 1996, Afghanistan became an official Islamic state, or emirate, ruled by *sharia*, and in the view of bin Laden and others, the strongest candidate for a new Caliphate.
26 Qur'an, 21:92.
27 Qur'an, 6:159.

not speak at all."[28] And they must heed the words of the Messenger when they act: "Inform and do not repel, and make it easy and do not make it difficult."[29] And we ask God to give this community the guidance to exalt the people who obey Him and humiliate those who disobey Him, and to give us a law whereby decency is commanded and evil is forbidden. O God bless Muhammad, Your servant and messenger, and his family, and companions, and give them peace. All gratitude to God the Lord of the worlds.

28 From the *hadith* collection of Muslim, book 1, no. 78. Bin Laden quotes only the last third of the saying, the two omitted tasks being to do good to one's neighbor and to show hospitality to guests.

29 From the *hadith* collection of Muslim, book 23, no. 4,961.

5

FROM SOMALIA TO AFGHANISTAN

March 1997

This text is bin Laden's most comprehensive interview with a Western journalist, the CNN reporter Peter Arnett, whom he met near Jalalabad in March 1997. The occasion was set up by Arnett's colleague Peter Bergen, through the London-based Advice and Reform Committee (ARC).[1] The questions were submitted in advance, and all queries about bin Laden's personal life and finances were excised. The interview lasted an hour.

Though describing the Saudi regime as a branch of the United States, doing its will even in keeping oil prices down, bin Laden explains that the target of the jihad *is the American occupiers, not its local agents, and declines to outline any alternative to the House of Saud: "the young are concentrating their efforts on the sponsor and not on the sponsored". Today, after the fall of the Soviet Union, the United States displays greater arrogance than ever before, as now it is the sole superpower. It must be forced to withdraw not just from the Arabian peninsula but the whole Muslim world. American troops are the primary target of the* jihad, *but American civilians are at risk too, since the US itself spares no civilians in its aggressions against Palestine, Lebanon, and Iraq—just as it exterminated without a qualm the inhabitants of Hiroshima. American citizens, states bin Laden, are responsible for the actions of governments for which they voted, and cannot escape their consequences. Continually practising a double standard, the US sows terror and then calls whoever resists its injustices a terrorist. But it is weaker than it thinks: Arab* mujahidin, *fresh from victory in Afghanistan, routed US troops in Somalia and will do so again elsewhere; the Russians were tougher soldiers than the Americans, and Muslim fighters defeated them.*

---

1 The English transcript of this interview is reproduced by kind permission of CNN. For a full account of this encounter, see Bergen, *Holy War Inc*, pp. 1–23.

PA: *Could you give us your main criticisms of the Saudi royal family that is ruling Saudi Arabia today?*

OBL: Regarding the criticisms of the ruling regime in Saudi Arabia and the Arabian peninsula, the first one is their subordination to the US. So, our main problem is the US government, while the Saudi regime is but a branch or an agent of the US. By being loyal to the US regime, the Saudi regime has committed an act against Islam. And this, based on the ruling of *sharia*, casts the regime outside the religious community. Subsequently, the regime has stopped ruling people according to what God revealed, not to mention many other contradictory acts. When this main foundation was violated, other corrupt acts followed in every aspect of the country, the economic, the social, public services, and so on.

PA: *If the Islamic movement takes over Arabia, what kind of society will be created and will Saudi Arabia, for example, return to the laws of the Qur'an at the time of the Prophet?*

OBL: We are confident, with the permission of God, praise and glory be to Him, that Muslims will be victorious in the Arabian peninsula and that God's religion, praise and glory be to Him, will prevail in this peninsula. It is a great pride and a big hope that the revelation unto Muhammad will be resorted to for ruling. When we used to follow Muhammad's revelation, peace be upon him, we were in great happiness and in great dignity. To God belong credit and praise.

PA: *If the Islamic movement takes over Saudi Arabia, what would your attitude to the West be and will the price of oil be higher?*

OBL: We are an *umma* and have a long history, with the grace of God. We are now in the 15th century of this great religion,[2] whose complete and comprehensive methodology has clarified the dealing between one individual and another, the duties of the believer towards God, and the relationship between the Muslim country and other countries in times of peace and war. If we look

2 The Islamic calendar dates from Muhammad's emigration from Mecca to Medina. Year 1, AH (Anno Hegirae) therefore corresponds to 622 AD.

back at our history, we will find there were many types of dealings between the Muslim nation and the other nations in peacetime and wartime, including treaties and matters to do with commerce. So it is not a new thing that we need to create. Rather, it already exists. As for oil, it is a commodity that will be subject to the price of the market according to supply and demand. We believe that the current prices are not realistic due to the Saudi regime playing the role of a US agent and the pressures exercised by the US on the Saudi regime to increase production and flooding the market that caused a sharp decrease in oil prices.

PA: *You've declared a* jihad *against the United States. Can you tell us why? And is the* jihad *directed against the US government or the United States' troops in Arabia? What about US civilians in Arabia or the people of the United States?*

OBL: We declared *jihad* against the US government, because the US government is unjust, criminal, and tyrannical.[3] It has committed acts that are extremely unjust, hideous, and criminal, whether directly or through its support of the Israeli occupation of the Land of the Prophet's Night Journey.[4] And we believe the US is directly responsible for those who were killed in Palestine, Lebanon, and Iraq. The mention of the US reminds us before everything else of those innocent children who were dismembered, their heads and

---

3 The doctrine of *jihad* is traditionally split into two categories: "offensive" and "defensive". An offensive *jihad*, to conquer new lands for Islam and convert new peoples to the faith, is a collective responsibility of all Muslims; however, it must be called by a Caliph, the recognized leader of the world Islamic community. Bin Laden always describes his *jihad* as "defensive", something for which no formal declaration of war is required. In Michael Scheuer words, a defensive *jihad* is "an Islamic military reaction triggered by an attack by non-Muslims on the Islamic faith, on Muslims, on Muslim territory, or on all three. In this scenario, it is doctrinally incumbent on each Muslim to contribute to the fight against the attacker to the best of his ability. In such a *jihad*, there is no Qur'anic requirement for a central Muslim leader or leadership to authorize warlike actions. Once Islam is attacked, each Muslim knows his personal duty is to fight. He needs no one else's authority. Doctrine and historical practice therefore "void any claim that bin Laden cannot lead a *jihad* because he was not educated as an Islamic scholar and has no religious credentials ... Bin Laden's genius lies not in his call for a defensive *jihad*, but in constructing and articulating a consistent, convincing case that an attack on Islam is under way and is being led and directed by America." (Scheuer, *Imperial Hubris*, pp. 7–8; also ibid., pp. 17–18, 131–8.)

4 According to Islamic tradition, Muhammad was brought by night from Mecca to the Dome of the Rock (or *miraj*), Jerusalem, from where he ascended to heaven. Accompanied by the angel Gabriel, he was consulted by numerous other prophets and given the obligatory Islamic prayers before returning to earth. The "Land of the Prophet's Night Journey" is Palestine.

arms cut off in the recent explosion that took place in Qana [in Lebanon]. This US government abandoned even humanitarian feelings by these hideous crimes. It transgressed all bounds and behaved in a way not witnessed before by any power or any imperialist power in the world. They should have been sensitive to the fact that the *qibla*[5] of the Muslims raises the emotion of the entire Muslim world. Due to its subordination to the Jews, the arrogance and haughtiness of the US regime has reached such an extent that it occupied the *qibla* of the Muslims, who are more than a billion in the world today. For this and other acts of aggression and injustice, we have declared *jihad* against the US, because in our religion it is our duty to make *jihad* so that God's word is the one exalted to the heights and so that we drive the Americans away from all Muslim countries. As for what you asked, whether *jihad* is directed against US soldiers, the civilians in Saudi Arabia, or against the civilians in America, we have focused our declaration on striking at the soldiers in Saudi Arabia. This country has in our religion a significance of its own over the other Muslim countries. In our religion, it is not permissible for any non-Muslim to stay in our country. Therefore, even though American civilians are not targeted in our plan, they must leave. We do not guarantee their safety, because we are in a society of more than a billion Muslims. A reaction might take place as a result of the US government's targeting of Muslim civilians and executing more than 600,000 Muslim children in Iraq by preventing food and medicine from reaching them. So, the US is responsible for any reaction, because it extended its war against troops to civilians. This is what we say. As for what you asked regarding the American people, they are not exonerated from responsibility, because they chose this government and voted for it despite their knowledge of its crimes in Palestine, Lebanon, Iraq, and in other places, and its support of its client regimes who filled their prisons with our best children and scholars. We ask that God may release them.

PA: *Will the end of the United States' presence in Saudi Arabia, their withdrawal, will that end your call for* jihad *against the United States and against the US?*

OBL: The cause of the reaction must be sought and the act that triggered this reaction must be eliminated. The reaction came as a result of the aggressive US

5   See above, p. 16, n. 1.

policy towards the entire Muslim world and not just towards the Arabian peninsula. So if the cause that has called for this act comes to an end, this act, in turn, will come to an end. So, the defensive *jihad* against the US does not stop with its withdrawal from the Arabian peninsula; rather, it must desist from aggressive intervention against Muslims throughout the whole world.

PA: *Tell us about your experience during the Afghan war and what you did during that jihad?*

OBL: Praise be to God, Lord of the Worlds, that He made it possible for us to aid the *mujahidin* in Afghanistan without any declaration of *jihad*, [but instead through] the news that was broadcast by radio stations that the Soviet Union invaded a Muslim country. This was a sufficient motivation for me to start to aid our brothers in Afghanistan. I have benefited so greatly from the *jihad* in Afghanistan that it would have been impossible for me to gain such a benefit from any other opportunity, and this cannot be measured by tens of years but rather more than that. In spite of the Soviet power, we used to move with confidence and God conferred favors on us so that we transported heavy equipment from Saudi Arabia estimated at hundreds of tons altogether that included bulldozers, loaders, dump trucks, and equipment for digging trenches. When we saw the brutality of the Russians bombing *mujahidin* positions, we dug a good number of huge tunnels and built in them some storage places and in some others we built a hospital. We also dug some roads, one of which you came by to us tonight. So our experience in this *jihad* was great, by the grace of God, praise and glory be to Him, and what we benefited from most was that the myth of the superpower was destroyed not only in my mind but also in the minds of all Muslims. Slumber and fatigue vanished and so did the terror which the US would use in its media by attributing to itself superpower status or which the Soviet Union used by labelling itself as a superpower. Today, the entire Muslim world has imbibed the faithful spirit of strength and started to interact in a good manner in order to bring an end to occupation and the Western and American influence on our countries.

PA: *What was the significance of the Afghan war for the Islamic movement? Veterans of that war are fighting for Islamic movements and conflicts from the former Soviet republics such as Chechnya to Bosnia to Algeria. Can you explain that phenomenon to us?*

OBL: As I mentioned in my answer to the previous question, the effect of *jihad* has been great not only at the level of the Islamic movement but also at the level of the Muslim nation in the whole world. The spirit of power, dignity, and confidence has grown in our sons and brothers for this religion and the power of God. And it has become apparent even to the Islamic movement that there is no choice but to return to the original source, to this religion, to God's Book, and to the *sunna* of His Prophet, as understood by our predecessors, may God be pleased with them. Of this, the peak of this religion is *jihad*. The nation has had a strong conviction that there is no way to obtain faithful strength but by returning to this *jihad*. The influence of the Afghan *jihad* on the Islamic world was so great; it necessitated that people should rise above many of their differences and unite their efforts against their enemy. Today, the nation is interacting well by uniting its efforts through *jihad* against the US, which has, in collaboration with the Israeli government, led the ferocious campaign against the Islamic world in occupying the holy sites of the Muslims. As for the young men who participated in *jihad* here, their number was quite big, praise and gratitude be to Him, and they spread in every place in which non-believers' injustice is perpetuated against Muslims. Their going to Bosnia, Chechnya, Tajikistan and other countries is but a fulfilment of a duty, because we believe that these states are part of the Islamic world. Therefore, any act of aggression against even a hand's span of this land makes it a duty for Muslims to send a sufficient number of their sons to fight off that aggression.

PA: *Can you tell us now about your expulsion from Saudi Arabia and your time you spent in Sudan and your arrival here in Afghanistan?*

OBL: I was, by the grace of God, in the great spot that is dear to Him, al-Hijaz, especially Venerable Mecca, where is God's Ancient House.[6] However, the Saudi regime imposed on the people a life that does not appeal to the free believer. They wanted the people to eat and drink and sing the praise of God, but if the people wanted to encourage what is right and forbid what is wrong, they could not. Rather, the regime dismisses them from their jobs and in the event the people continue to do so [encourage what is right], they are detained in prisons. I have refused to live this submissive life, which is not befitting of

6 The Ka'ba.

man let alone a believer. So, I waited for the chance when God made it possible for me to leave Saudi Arabia. I hope He would confer upon me His favor to return one day, when God's law rules in that country. I went to the Sudan and stayed there for about five years, during which I visited Afghanistan and Pakistan to work against the Communist government in Kabul. When the Saudi government transgressed in oppressing all voices of the scholars and the voices of those who call for Islam, I found myself forced—especially after the government prevented Sheikh Salman al-Auda and Sheikh Safar al-Hawali and some other scholars from doing so—to carry out a small part of my duty of enjoining what is right and forbidding what is wrong. So, I collaborated with some brothers and established a committee for offering advice (the Advice and Reformation Committee), and we started to publish some declarations. However, the Saudi regime did not like this and started to exercise pressure on the Sudanese regime. The US government, the Egyptian government, and the Yemeni government also helped in doing so. They asked the Sudanese regime to extradite me, and the pressure continued. Saudi Arabia dropped all conditions agreed with the Sudanese regime in return that I be driven out of the Sudan. The US government had already taken the same stance and pulled out from its diplomatic mission from Khartoum, saying that it would only return after I had left. Unfortunately, the Sudanese government was in some difficult circumstances and there was a tendency inside the government that inclined to reconciliation or surrender. Then, when they insisted initially that I should keep my mouth shut, I decided to look for a land in which I could breathe a pure, free air to perform my duty in enjoining what is right and forbidding what is wrong. I ask God to increase the prosperity of this great land of Khurasan in order to carry on this duty. So, we implore God to accept [our deeds and most of all] Muslims.

PA: *Now, the United States government says that you are still funding military training camps here in Afghanistan for militant, Islamic fighters and that you are a sponsor of international terrorism; but others describe you as the new hero of the Arab-Islamic world. Are these accusations true? How do you describe yourself?*

OBL: After the collapse of the Soviet Union—in which the US has no mentionable role, but rather the credit goes to God and the *mujahidin* in Afghanistan—this collapse made the US more haughty and arrogant, and it has started to see itself as a Master of this world and established what it calls the new world order. It wanted to delude people [into thinking] that it can do whatever it wants, but it can't do this. It levelled against me and others as many accusations as it desired and wished. It is these [accusations] that you mentioned. The US today, as a result of this arrogance, has set a double standard, calling whoever goes against its injustice a terrorist. It wants to occupy our countries, steal our resources, install collaborators to rule us with man-made laws, and wants us to agree on all these issues. If we refuse to do so, it will say we are terrorists. With a fleeting glance at US behavior, we find that it judges the behavior of the poor Palestinian children whose country was occupied: if they throw stones against the Israeli occupation it says they are terrorists, whereas when the Israeli pilots bombed the United Nations building in Qana, Lebanon, while it was full of children and women, the US stopped any plan to condemn Israel. At the same time that they condemn any Muslim who calls for his rights, they receive the highest official of the Irish Republican Army [Gerry Adams] at the White House as a political leader, while woe, all woe if the Muslims cry out for their rights. Wherever we look, we see the US as the leader of terrorism and crime in the world. The US does not consider it a terrorist act to launch atomic bombs at nations thousands of miles away, when it would not be possible for those bombs to hit only military troops. Rather, those bombs were dropped on entire nations, including women, children, and elderly people and up to this day the traces of those bombs remain in Japan. The US does not consider it terrorism when hundreds of thousands of our sons and brothers in Iraq died for lack of food or medicine. So, there is no basis for what the US says, and these words do not affect us, because we, by the grace of God, are dependent on Him, getting help from Him against the US. As for the last part of your question, we are fulfilling a duty which God decreed for us. We look upon those heroes, those men who undertook to kill the American occupiers in Riyadh and Khobar. We describe them as heroes and as men. They have wiped disgrace and submissiveness off the forehead of their nation. We ask God, praise and glory be to Him, to accept them as martyrs.

PA: *Let's go to the bombings of United States troops in Riyadh and Dhahran. Why did they happen and were you and your supporters involved in these attacks?*

OBL: We ask about the main reason behind this explosion. This explosion was a reaction to US provocation of the Muslim peoples, in which the US transgressed in its aggression until it reached the *qibla* of the Muslims in the whole world. So, the purpose of the two explosions is to end the American occupation [of Saudi Arabia]. So if the US does not want to kill its own sons who are in the army, it has to get out.

PA: *On the same issue of the American troops in Saudi Arabia, do you think there will be more bombing attacks on them? Or attacks on US civilians in Arabia? Or assassination attempts, for example on the Saudi royal family?*

OBL: As for the previous question, the explosion of Riyadh and the one in Khobar, it is no secret that during the two explosions, I was not in Saudi Arabia, but I have great respect for the people who did this action. I say, as I said before, they are heroes. We look upon them as men who wanted to raise the flag of "There is no god but God", and to put an end to the nonbelievers and the state of injustice that the US brought. I also say that they did a great job; theirs was a big honor that I missed participating in.

PA: *Do you think there will be more bombing attacks on American troops in Saudi Arabia? Or attacks on American civilians in Saudi Arabia? Or will there be assassination attempts on the Saudi Arabian ruling family?*

OBL: It is known that every action has its reaction. If the American presence continues, and that is an action, then it is natural for reactions to continue against this presence. In other words, explosions, and killings of American soldiers, will continue. These are the troops who left their country and their families and came here with all arrogance to steal our oil and disgrace us, and attack our religion. As for what was mentioned about the ruling [Saudi] family, those in charge bear the full responsibility for everything that may happen. They are the shadow of the American presence. The people and the young men are concentrating their efforts on the sponsor and not on the sponsored. The concentration at this point of *jihad* is against the American occupiers.

PA: *What are your views about Sheik Omar Abdul Rahman and have you ever met him? Do you know him?*

OBL: Sheikh Omar Abdul Rahman is a Muslim scholar well known all over the Muslim world. He represents the kind of injustice that is adopted by the US. A baseless case was fabricated against him, even though he is a blind old man. We ask God, the Almighty, to relieve him. The US sentenced him to hundreds of years just to please its caprice and the whims of the Egyptian regime. He is now very badly treated and in a way unfit for an old man like him or any Muslim scholar.

PA: *The US State Department quoting a Pakistani official says that Ramzi Yousef, a convicted bomber in the World Trade Center in New York City stayed in the house you funded in Peshawar, Pakistan for those receiving training during the Afghan conflict after the Trade Center bombing: is that true? Did Ramzi Yousef stay in your house in Peshawar?*

OBL: I do not know Ramzi Yousef.[7] What the American government and Pakistani intelligence has been reporting is not true at all. But I say if the American government is serious about avoiding the explosions inside the US, then let it stop provoking the feelings of 1.25 billion Muslims. Those hundreds of thousands who have been killed or displaced in Iraq, Palestine, and Lebanon, do have brothers and relatives, [who] will make of Ramzi Yousef a symbol and a teacher. The US will drive them to transfer the battle into the United States. Everything is made possible to protect the blood of the American citizen while the bloodshed of Muslims is permitted everywhere. With this kind of behavior, the US government is hurting itself, hurting Muslims and hurting the American people.

PA: *Were you involved in financing the bombing of the World Trade Center in New York City?*

OBL: I have no connection or relation with this explosion.

---

7 On February 26 1993, a bomb was detonated under the World Trade Center in New York, killing six people and injuring more than 1,000; it also caused over $300 million damage. The attacks were supervised by the Pakistani/Kuwaiti Ramzi Yousef (1968–), who was arrested two years later in Islamabad, found guilty of masterminding the 1993 bombing and sentenced to life imprisonment; he is currently held in a high-security prison in Florence, Colorado. His uncle, Khalid Sheikh Mohammed, who reportedly helped fund the bombing, is described by the *9/11 Commission Report* as "the principal architect of the 9/11 attacks".

PA: *In a recent interview with an Arabic newspaper, you said that Arabs who fought in the Afghan war killed US troops in Mogadishu, Somalia. Can you tell us about that?*

OBL: The US government went [to Somalia] with great pride and stayed there for some time with a strong media presence, wanting to frighten people [and show] that it is the greatest power on earth. It went there with pride and with over 28,000 soldiers, to fight a poor unarmed people.[8] The goal of this was to scare the Muslim world and the whole world, saying that it is able to do whatever it desires. As soon as the troops reached the Mogadishu beaches, they found no one but children. The CNN and other media cameras started photographing them [the soldiers] with their camouflage and heavy arms, entering with a parade crawling [on the ground] and showing themselves to the world as the "greatest power on earth". Resistance started against the American invasion, because Muslims do not believe the US allegations that they came to save the Somalis. A man with human feelings in his heart does not distinguish between a child killed in Palestine or in Lebanon, in Iraq or in Bosnia. So how can we believe your claims that you came to save our children in Somalia while you kill our children in all of those places?

With God's grace, Muslims over there cooperated with some Arab *mujahidin* who were in Afghanistan. They participated with their brothers in Somalia against the American occupation troops and killed large numbers of them. The American administration was aware of that. After a little resistance, the American troops left after achieving nothing. They left after claiming that they were the largest power on earth. They left after some resistance from powerless, poor, unarmed people whose only weapon is the belief in God Almighty, and who do not fear the fabricated American media lies. We learned from those who fought there, that they were surprised to see the low spiritual morale of the American fighters in comparison with the experience they had with the Russian fighters. The Americans ran away from those fighters who fought and killed them, while the latter stayed. If the US still thinks and brags that it still has this kind of power, even after all these successive defeats in

---

8 Operation Restore Hope was an American military operation, conducted under the auspices of the UN, which in March 1993 officially took over administration of the country. In the battle of Mogadishu, in August 1993, between 500–1000 Somilian militia and civilians were killed; eighteen US troops and one Malaysian soldier died.

Vietnam, Beirut, Aden, and Somalia, then let its troops go back to those who are awaiting its return.

PA: *Your family is a rich powerful family in Saudi Arabia. Have they, or the Saudi Arabian government, asked you to stop your activities?*

OBL: They have done that a lot. They have pressured us greatly, especially since a lot of our money is still in the hands of the Saudi ruling family due to the activities of our family and company.[9] They sent my mother, my uncle, and my brothers on almost nine visits to me in Khartoum, asking me to stop and return to Arabia to apologize to King Fahd. I apologized to my family kindly because I know that they were driven by force to come to talk to me. This regime wants to create a problem between me and my family in order to take some measures against them. But, with God's grace, this regime did not get its wish fulfilled. I refused to go back. They [my family] conveyed the Saudi government's message that if I did not go back, they'll freeze all my assets, deprive me of my citizenship, my passport, and my Saudi ID, and distort my picture in the Saudi and foreign media. They think that a Muslim may bargain on his religion. I said to them: do whatever you may wish. It is with God's bounty that we refused to go back. We are living in dignity and honor for which we thank God. It is much better for us to live under a tree here on these mountains than to live in palaces in the land most sacred to God, subjected to the disgrace of not worshipping God even in the most sacred land on earth, where injustice is so widespread. There is no strength except with God.

PA: *Have Saudi agents attempted to assassinate you? Are you targeted by the US government? Are you in fact in fear of your life?*

---

9 The Saudi BinLaden group (SBG) is run by one of bin Laden's brothers, Bakr, who is the chairman; other top jobs in the company are also held by brothers. By the mid-1990s, the estimated worth of the bin Laden group of companies was $5 billion; SBG employed 37,000 people in 1999. Construction projects undertaken by SBG include: the construction of a new suburb of Cairo; a Hyatt hotel in Amman, Jordan; a mosque in Kuala Lumpur, and a $150 million base for more than 4,000 US servicemen in Saudi Arabia. Its other ventures include distribution of products including Snapple drinks; it is licensed by Disney to produce Arabic books based on its animated features; and it continues to maintain and renovate the holy mosques of Mecca and Medina, expanding their capacity to a million worshippers each: Bergen, *Holy War Inc*, pp. 48–50.

OBL: The US pressures are no secret to you. The Saudi pressures are also in response to American pressures. There were several attempts to arrest me or to assassinate me. This has been going on for more than seven years. With God's grace, none of these attempts succeeded. This is in itself proof to Muslims and to the world that the US is incapable and weaker than the picture it wants to paint in people's minds. A believer must rest assured that life is only in the hands of God, and sustenance is also in the hands of God, the Almighty. As for fearing for one's life, it is difficult to explain to you how we think of ourselves, unless you have full belief. We believe that no one could take out one breath of our written life as ordained by God. We see that getting killed in the cause of God is a great honor wished for by our Prophet. He said in his *hadith*: "I swear to God, I wish to fight for God's cause and be killed, I'll do it again and be killed, and I'll do it again and be killed."[10] Being killed for God's cause is a great honor achieved by only those who are the elite of the nation. We love this kind of death for God's cause as much as you like to live. We have nothing to fear for. It is something we wish for.

PA: *What are your future plans?*

OBL: You'll see them and hear about them in the media, God willing.

PA: *If you had an opportunity to give a message to President Clinton, what would that message be?*

OBL: Mentioning the name of Clinton or that of the American government provokes disgust and revulsion. This is because the name of the American government and the name of Clinton and [George HW] Bush directly reflect in our minds the picture of children with their heads cut off before even reaching one year of age. It reflects the picture of children with their hands cut off, the picture of the children who died in Iraq, the picture of the hands of the Israelis with weapons destroying our children. The hearts of Muslims are filled with hatred towards the United States of America and the American president. The President has a heart that knows no words. A heart that kills hundreds of children definitely knows no words. Our people in the Arabian peninsula will send him messages with no words because he does not know any words. If

10 From the *hadith* collection of Muslim, book 20, no. 4,626.

there is a message that I may send through you, then it is a message I address to the mothers of the American troops who came here with their military uniform walking proudly up and down our land while the scholars of our country are thrown in prisons. I say that this represents a blatant provocation to 1.25 billion Muslims. To these mothers I say that if they are concerned for their sons, then let them object to the American government's policy and to the American president. Do not let themselves be cheated by his standing before the bodies of the killed soldiers describing the freedom fighters in Saudi Arabia as terrorists. It is he who is a terrorist who pushed their sons into this for the sake of the Israeli interest. We believe that the American army in Saudi Arabia came to separate the Muslims and the people for not ruling in accordance with God's wish. They came to support of the Israeli forces in occupied Palestine, the land of the night journey of our Prophet.

6

THE WORLD ISLAMIC FRONT
February 23 1998

This declaration, by the newly formed "World Islamic Front," announces a jihad *against Jews and Crusaders. It has four signatories, perhaps in answer to criticisms that bin Laden lacked the necessary religious qualifications to interpret the Qur'an and issue authoritative legal opinions* (fatwa). *They include the Egyptian Ayman al-Zawahiri, who has been bin Laden's closest associate since the assassination of Abdallah Azzam in 1989, and is often thought to be the principal strategist of global* jihad; *Abu Yasir Rifa'i Ahmad Taha, a representative of al-Gamaa al-Islamiyya (Egyptian Islamic Group); Sheikh Mir Hamzah, secretary-general of the Jamiat e Ulema of Pakistan, and Maulana Fazlur Rahman, currently a leader of the opposition in Pakistan's National Assembly, who would convene the April 2001 conference at which bin Laden issued Statement 8, below. The declaration condemns US policies in the Middle East as "a clear proclamation of war against God, his messenger and Muslims", and argues that religious scholars throughout history have agreed that* jihad *becomes an individual duty when an enemy attacks Muslim countries. Iraq, in particular, has become a target of intensifying aggression. The declaration already warns of American "eagerness to destroy Iraq, the strongest neighbouring state", and of US efforts to weaken all the other countries of the region. A fatwa follows, citing seven passages of the Qur'an in support of the obligation to wage* jihad *against Americans, military and civilian, until they quit the lands of the* umma.

Sheikh Osamah bin Muhammad bin Laden
Ayman al-Zawahiri, amir of the Jihad Group in Egypt[1]

---

1 The Cairo-born Ayman al-Zawahiri (1951–) is leader of the Egyptian organization Islamic Jihad. At the age of 14 he joined the Muslim Brotherhood, becoming a student and follower of Sayyid Qutb, and by 1979 had joined Islamic Jihad. He was one of hundreds arrested after the

Abu-Yasir Rif'ai Ahmad Taha, Egyptian Islamic Group[2]

Sheikh Mir Hamzah, secretary of the Jamiat-ul-Ulema-e-Pakistan[3]

Fazlur Rahman, amir of the Jihad Movement in Bangladesh[4]

Praise be to God, revealer of the Book, controller of the clouds, defeater of factionalism, who says in His Book: "When the forbidden months are over, wherever you find the polytheists, kill them, seize them, besiege them, ambush them."[5] Prayers and peace be upon our Prophet Muhammad bin Abdallah, who said: "I have been sent with a sword in my hands so that only God may be worshipped, God who placed my livelihood under the shadow of my spear and who condemns those who disobey my orders to servility and humiliation."[6]

Ever since God made the Arabian peninsula flat, created desert in it and surrounded it with seas, it has never suffered such a calamity as these Crusader hordes that have spread through it like locusts, consuming its wealth and destroying its fertility. All this at a time when nations have joined forces against the Muslims as if fighting over a bowl of food. When the matter is this grave and support is scarce, we must discuss current events and agree collectively on how best to settle the issue.

There is now no longer any debate about three well acknowledged and commonly agreed facts that require no further proof, but we will repeat them so that people remember them. They are as follows:

Firstly, for over seven years America has occupied the holiest parts of the Islamic lands, the Arabian peninsula, plundering its wealth, dictating to its

assassination Anwar Sadat on October 6 1981 by members of Islamic Jihad. In the 1980s he travelled to Afghanistan to participate in the resistance against the Soviet invasion. Long associated with bin Laden, on August 4 2005 he issued a televised statement blaming British Prime Minister Blair's foreign policy for the July 7 2005 London bombings.

2 Abu Yasir Rif'ai Ahmad Taha is a representative of al-Gamaa al-Islamiyya, whose leader, Sheikh Omar Abdel Rahman was sentenced to life imprisonment by a US Court in 1995.

3 Sheikh Mir Hamza is secretary-general of the Jamiat Ulema-e-Pakistan (JUP), the largest Barelvi religio-political party in Pakistan.

4 Maulana Fazlur Rahman is now leader of the opposition in Pakistan's national assembly, head of the Jamiat Ulema–i-Islam (Islamic Party of Religious Leaders, or JUI), and secretary-general of the Muttahida Majlis-e-Amal (MMA), a six-party religious alliance.

5 Qur'an, 9:5. The second half of the verse reads, "but if they turn [to God], maintain the prayer, and pay the prescribed alms, let them go on their way, for God is most forgiving and merciful."

6 From the *hadith* collection of Musnad of Ahmad ibn Hanbal, vol. 5, book 3, no. 5,409.

leaders, humiliating its people, terrorizing its neighbours and turning its bases there into a spearhead with which to fight the neighbouring Muslim peoples.

Some might have disputed the reality of this occupation before, but all the people of the Arabian peninsula have now acknowledged it. There is no clearer proof than America's excessive aggression against the people of Iraq, using the Peninsula as a base. It is true that all its leaders have rejected such use of their lands, but they are powerless.

Secondly, despite the great devastation inflicted upon the Iraqi people at the hands of the Judeo-Crusader alliance, and despite the terrible number of deaths—over one million—despite all this, the Americans are trying to repeat these horrific massacres again, as if they are not satisfied with the long period of sanctions after the vicious war, or with all the fragmentation and destruction.[7]

Today they come to annihilate what is left of this people and humiliate their Muslim neighbours.

Thirdly, while these wars are being waged by the Americans for religious and economic purposes, they also serve the interests of the petty Jewish state, diverting attention from its occupation of Jerusalem and its murder of Muslims there.

There is no better proof of this than their eagerness to destroy Iraq, the strongest neighbouring Arab state, and their efforts to fragment all the states in the region, like Iraq, Saudi Arabia, Egypt, and Sudan, into paper mini-states whose weakness and disunity will guarantee Israel's survival and the continuation of the brutal Crusader occupation of the Peninsula.

All these American crimes and sins are a clear proclamation of war against God, his Messenger, and the Muslims. Religious scholars throughout Islamic history have agreed that *jihad* is an individual duty when an enemy attacks Muslim countries. This was related by the Imam ibn Qudama in "The Resource," by Imam al-Kisa'i in "The Marvels," by al-Qurtubi[8] in his exegesis, and by the Sheikh of Islam when he states in his chronicles that "As for fighting

7 This may be a reference to the internationally televised "town hall" meeting in Ohio to discuss a possible war with Iraq, attended by US Secretary of Defense William Cohen and US National Security Adviser Sandy Berger, which took place on February 18 1998, five days before this declaration was issued.

8 Born in Jerusalem, Muwaffaq al-Din ibn Qudama (1147–1223) was a celebrated scholar of the Hanbali *madhhab* and author of, among other books, *Al-Mughni*, the main Hanbali jurisprudence manual. He is often cited by modern radicals for enumerating the situations in which *jihad* becomes compulsory. Al-Kisa'i wrote his book in the 11th century, but very little is known about him outside of this work, which tells numerous stories from the time of the Prophet. Al-Qurtubi,

to repel an enemy, which is the strongest way to defend freedom and religion, it is agreed that this is a duty. After faith, there is no greater duty than fighting an enemy who is corrupting religion and the world."[9]

On this basis, and in accordance with God's will, we pronounce to all Muslims the following judgment:[10]

To kill the American and their allies—civilians and military—is an individual duty incumbent upon every Muslim in all countries, in order to liberate the al-Aqsa Mosque and the Holy Mosque[11] from their grip, so that their armies leave all the territory of Islam, defeated, broken, and unable to threaten any Muslim. This is in accordance with the words of God Almighty: "Fight the idolators at any time, if they first fight you;" "Fight them until there is no more persecution and until worship is devoted to God;"[12] "Why should you not fight in God's cause and for those oppressed men, women, and children who cry out: 'Lord, rescue us from this town whose people are oppressors! By Your grace, give us a protector and a helper!'?"[13]

With God's permission we call on everyone who believes in God and wants reward to comply with His will to kill the Americans and seize their money wherever and whenever they find them. We also call on the religious scholars, their leaders, their youth, and their soldiers, to launch the raid on the soldiers of Satan, the Americans, and whichever devil's supporters are allied with them, to rout those behind them so that they will not forget it.

---

whose name identifies him as a Cordoban, was an Islamic scholar specializing in the sayings of the Prophet and jurisprudence in the 13th century. Bin Laden refers to his masterwork, an exegesis of the Qur'an.

9 The "Sheikh of Islam" is ibn Taymiyya.

10 The word that bin Laden uses here means "considered judgment" (*hukm*) which carries a less binding authority than a "juridical decree" (*fatwa*).

11 The al-Aqsa ("farthest") mosque is located in Jerusalem, on the al-Haram al-Sharif ("Noble Sanctuary") to Muslims and the Temple Mount to Jews and Christians. It is the third holiest shrine in Islam. By referring to al-Aqsa's liberation, bin Laden is also denoting all of Palestine. In this instance, the Holy, or "Haram" Mosque in Mecca, which holds the Ka'ba, is also synecdoche for all of Arabia.

12 Qur'an, 2:193 and 8:39. This clause is listed at the beginning of both Qur'anic verses. The conclusion to the first reads: "If they cease hostilities, there can be no [further] hostility, except towards aggressors"; and to the second: "if they desist, then God sees all that they do."

13 Qur'an, 4:75.

God Almighty said: "Believers, respond to God and His Messenger when he calls you to that which gives you life. Know that God comes between a man and his heart, and that you will be gathered to Him."[14]

God Almighty said: "Believers, why, when it is said to you, 'Go and fight in God's way,' do you dig your heels into the earth? Do you prefer this world to the life to come? How small the enjoyment of this world is, compared with the life to come! If you do not go out and fight, God will punish you severely and put others in your place, but you cannot harm Him in any way: God has power over all things."[15]

God Almighty also said: "Do not lose heart or despair—if you are true believers you will have the upper hand."[16]

14 Qur'an, 8:24.
15 Qur'an, 9:38–39.
16 Qur'an, 3:139.

III

TOWARDS 9/11 1998–2002

7

A MUSLIM BOMB

December 1998

On August 7 1998, simultaneous bomb attacks in the US embassies in Kenya and Tanzania killed over two hundred people, and injured many more. These were the first terrorist actions that could unequivocally be connected to bin Laden. In retaliation, the US launched Cruise missiles on August 17 against a training camp in Khost, eastern Afghanistan, where he was thought to be found. Operation Infinite Reach killed 34 militants on the ground, but failed to strike bin Laden. In November 1998, the US announced a $5 million reward for information leading to his arrest. In mid-December, Clinton—within hours of indictment for perjury and obstruction of justice in the House of Representatives—unleashed 70 hours of round-the-clock bombing of Iraq with high explosives, in "Operation Desert Fox," named after General Rommel of the German Army in World War Two. In the wake of this attack, Osama bin Laden gave his first interview to the Qatari satellite television network, al-Jazeera, running for ninety minutes. Al-Jazeera's commitment to report stories that were newsworthy, regardless of ideological orientation—in sharp contrast with official Arab media—would henceforward make it the natural conduit for bin Laden's efforts to reach a global audience. Three years later, the interview was rerun in full by al-Jazeera nine days after the attacks of September 11, when footage and stills from it were shown throughout the world.

The interview covered a broad range of issues, many of them new in bin Laden's public statements. Highlighting Israeli possession of a large stockpile of nuclear bombs, he remarks that it is not only a right but a duty for Muslim countries to acquire corresponding weapons, and congratulates Pakistan on being the first to do so. He further states that US support for Israel is a function of the power of the Jewish community in American political life, but three-quarters of the American people in any case support Clinton's attack on Iraq. Disclaiming any responsibility for the bombings in East Africa, other than by general incitement to such actions, he at the same time praises them as legitimate self-defense against Crusader aggression, even if the loss of innocent lives is to be regretted. Bin Laden also denies having received any help from the CIA in the struggle against communism in Afghanistan. After the victory of the mujahidin *over the Russians, however, internecine fighting among the faithful was deplorable; fortunately, the Taliban have put an end to this, and their state—which can be compared to the tiny city of Medina where Muhammad was driven after his expulsion from Mecca—merits all the help Muslims can give it. While Mullah Omar has decided that no actions against other states should be launched from Afghanistan, bin Laden emphasizes that the defense of the* umma *cannot be confined to its soil, if the Islamic world as a whole is not to undergo the historic fate of Andalusia, and fall prey to the Crusaders.*

AL-JAZEERA: *Recently there has been a joint American-British attack on Iraq. Firstly, what is your view on these attacks? And secondly, have the popular and official Arab and Islamic reactions up to this point not been—as it were—at the required level to resist such attacks, or they have not been what the Iraqi people would expect in response to this attack. What is your position on this?*

OBL: Praise be to God. The recent American and British attack on Iraq a few days ago told us many serious and important things. We are not talking about the material and human losses of our Muslim brothers who have been killed in Iraq. We are talking about what this attack has revealed. America accuses Iraq of using poison gas against the Kurds, against its own people. It also accuses Iraq of using lethal weapons against Iran; however, what people should realise is that America was not accusing Iraq at that time, but rather was supporting it through various means and agents in the region.[1] But from the point when Iraq became a notable regional power, and even became the biggest Arab power in the region, threatening the security of Jews and Israelis who are occupying Jerusalem, America started to dig all these issues up again and to claim that it would have to hold Iraq to account, saying that "it's true that there are weapons of mass destruction, as in Israel, but Israel is not using them—Iraq has." This kind of nonsense can be answered. America is the

---

1 On March 16–17 1988, the Iraqi Kurdish town of Halabja was attacked with chemical weapons; estimates of casualties range from several hundred to 5,000 people. Most accounts of the incident hold Iraqi government forces responsible for the attack, which occurred in the eighth year of the Iran-Iraq war. Halabja, a few miles from the Iranian border, was held by Iranian soldiers and Iraqi Kurdish militias allied with Tehran. At the time, there was little international protest; two years later, when the Western powers had stopped supporting Saddam Hussein, the attacks were attributed to Iraq. In the aftermath of the incident the US state department instructed its diplomats to say that Iran was partly to blame.

country that owns this weapon, and it is the one that has bombed people in the Far East, in Nagasaki and Hiroshima, after Japan had surrendered and World War Two had begun to end.

Despite this, America insisted on attacking entire peoples, including their children, their women, and their elderly. It is now clear that it is Israel that is behind all the attacks on states in the Islamic world. However, for fear that great popular movements will rise up and topple them, these collaborator regimes have conspired to save their own skin, regardless of their duties to Islam and Muslims. The feelings of these people were desensitized as much as America wanted, so the Jews were able to employ American and British Christians to do the job of attacking Iraq. America claims that it is bringing Iraq to account and to justice, but the fact is that the Israeli authority and the Jewish authority, which has become powerful inside the White House, as everyone can see—the Defence Minister is Jewish, the Secretary of State is Jewish, the CIA and National Security officials are Jewish, all the biggest officials are Jews—led the Christians to clip the wings of the Islamic world. Their real target is not Saddam Hussein but the growing power of the Arab and Islamic world, even if they struck the Iraqi people or—as they previously alleged in the sanctions against Libya—because they had a chemical weapons factory, or when they bombed the al-Shifa factory in Sudan, which was a pharmaceutical factory.[2] So that we should be very aware of this issue, which again goes to show that no sane Muslim should take his grievances to the United Nations. As for Muslims, according to God's law, they are not allowed to seek the help of these infidel, man-made organizations. And we should also point out that wise non-Muslims also do not go to the UN. North Korea, for example—would any sane man, even if he is an infidel, take his case to a court in which the judge decided to give a painful, decisive blow under the deceitful pretext of so-called "international legitimacy"? In any case, America can also use its right of veto at the United Nations. So no Muslim goes there at all, because this contradicts faith, and no sensible person goes there, even if he is an infidel. Those who talk so much about the UN and its resolutions either do not understand their religion,

---

2 In Operation Infinite Reach, on August 20 1998, the USA launched cruise missile strikes against targets in Afghanistan and Sudan, as reprisal for the attacks on US embassies in Kenya and Tanzania, which killed 224 people and injured 5,000. Several cruise missiles destroyed the al-Shifa chemical factory in Khartoum, which US officials claimed was helping bin Laden develop chemical weapons. Subsequent investigation revealed that the factory was in fact a pharmaceutical plant that produced half of Sudan's medicines.

or want to abandon our *umma* by placing their hopes in a mirage and an illusion. There is no strength or power save in God.

AL-JAZEERA: *Do you think that the American-British attack on Iraq will increase support for the organizations that are opposed to America, or will it terrify and subdue them and make them afraid to undertake any act—military or non-military—against the United States and its interests?*

OBL: Just as I answered the previous question, the time has come for Muslim peoples to realize after these attacks that the states of the region do not have their own sovereignty. For our enemies are disporting themselves in our seas and on our lands and in our airspace, striking without anyone's permission. In this particular case, this barefaced, shameful plot to attack Iraq, America and Britain could not get anyone else on board. But these other regimes no longer have any real power. They are either colluding with America and Britain or have lost the power to do anything against this barefaced occupation. What Muslims should do, especially the resourceful ones and the righteous scholars and faithful businessmen and tribal leaders who have opinions, is to emigrate for the sake of God and find for themselves a place to raise the banner of *jihad* and to enlist our *umma* to maintain their religion and their world, otherwise they will lose everything. If they do not consider what happened to our brothers in Palestine, even though the Palestinian people were famous for their activity and agriculture, which they exported together with their citrus fruits, their textiles, and soap, this people—and they are our brothers—became homeless, chased all over the world. In the end they became low-wage workers for this colonialist Jew, who lets them enter when it wants, and then prevents them from entering when it does not want them. The matter is serious, and if we don't move and the Noble Sanctuary is attacked, and the direction of prayer of 1200 million Muslims is attacked, when will people begin to stir? This is a momentous matter which requires much effort. As for those who think that this airstrike will terrify the Islamic movements, they are fooling themselves. For we Muslims believe that death is predestined and decided; it will come before or after its appointed time, from the time we were in our mothers' wombs. Provision is in the hands of God Almighty and these souls are His creation. Money is His provision, and it is He who "purchases" their souls for Heaven. So why do Muslims hold back from helping their religion?

AL-JAZEERA: *After the first American attack on Afghanistan last summer, your statements or delegates said in the media that you will respond to this attack. But up to this point there has been no response from you, nor have we heard of any response. In the event of a new American attack on Afghanistan, do you expect there to be a real reaction against them, and what might it be?*

OBL: Our duty—which we have undertaken—is to motivate our *umma* to *jihad* for the sake of God against America and Israel and their allies. And we are still doing this, motivating people; the popular mobilization that happened in these last months is moving in the right direction to remove the Americans from Muslim countries. In light of all the circumstances around us, and not being able to move out of Afghanistan to devote ourselves to the work more closely whenever we can, we have formed with a large number of our brothers, the "Global Islamic Front for Jihad against Jews and Crusaders." So I believe that the work of many of those brothers is going well and that they have a broad campaign. We pray to God that He will open the way for them to help the religion, and to wreak revenge on the Jews and the Americans.

AL-JAZEERA: *Seven or eight months have gone by since the formation of this "Global Islamic Front", or at least since the announcement of its formation, and until now no one has heard anything other than the statement that you referred to, or the press conference that you convened in the city of Khost last summer.³ Should this "Front" now be considered to be in abeyance, in practical terms?*

OBL: No, it is not in abeyance. Its members are from very many nationalities and they have a wide range of movement, and they do not necessarily advertise everything they do. Moreover, these months cannot be considered a long time in the renaissance of our *umma* and resistance against the biggest enemy in the world.

---

3 Bin Laden convened a press conference on May 28 1998 at a camp near the eastern Afghan town of Khost, the heart of Islamic militancy in Afghanistan. This was the culmination of a series of press statements and interviews given by bin Laden to British and US journalists over the previous eighteen months, including Peter Arnett of CNN (see above, Statement 5), Robert Fisk of the London *Independent*, and John Miller of the American news network ABC. For an eyewitness account of the conference by Rahimullah Yusufzai, one of the journalists attending the event, see http://www. newsline.com.pk/NewsOct2001/cover4.htm). Yusufzai interviewed bin Laden for *Time Asia* magazine in December 1998.

AL-JAZEERA: *The United States of America has warned its subjects in the Gulf and the region in general about operations that you and your helpers will undertake, especially in the current month of Ramadan. Firstly, to what extent should these warnings to America's subjects be taken seriously, and secondly, will you target American subjects in general or just the American troops located in the Gulf and some other Islamic areas?*

OBL: I heard this news a few days ago on the radio, and happiness entered my heart. For it tells of the resurgence of our *umma*, by the grace of God Almighty. But as for the extent to which this threat can be taken seriously, if I knew who was behind it then I would say so. Unfortunately I still do not know who did this blessed deed. But we pray to God Almighty to make them successful, and to open the way for them to defeat the infidels and Americans and others. As for the previous juridical decree,[4] it discussed the fact that we make a different distinction in our faith than the infidels call for in theirs. They preach one thing and do another; we differentiate between men and women, and between children and old people. Men are fighters; whether they carry arms or merely help our struggle by paying taxes, they are fighters. The infidels tell Muslims that bin Laden is threatening to kill civilians—yet what are they doing in Palestine? They're not only killing innocents, but children as well! And America has taken over the media sphere, manipulating in different measures these enormous powers as it sees fit. Every American is our enemy, whether he fights directly or whether he pays taxes. Perhaps you have heard the recent news that three-quarters of the American people support Clinton in attacking Iraq. This is a people whose votes are won when innocents die, whose leader commits adultery and great sins and then sees his popularity rise—a vile people who have never understood the meaning of values.

AL-JAZEERA: *The Pentagon has published reports about your health and mentioned in these reports attributed to Pakistani intelligence saying that you are suffering from an incurable disease and that you are not expected to live much longer. According to these reports, you will not live more than five to six months at the most. Firstly, to what extent are these reports authentic, and secondly, what is the goal of publishing*

---

4 Bin Laden is referring to the *fatwa* issued in Statement 6; see above, pp. 58–62.

such reports in these circumstances, after publishing the warning to the subjects of America about the possibility that you and your helpers will undertake operations?

OBL: As for my health, all thanks and praise be to God, we thank Him always, for I enjoy very good health. As you can see, we are in the mountains, which means that we have to endure this biting cold, and we also have to endure the heat of this region during the summer. I still practise my favourite hobby, horseriding—even now I can ride for 70 kilometres without stopping. These are biased and tendentious rumours, the purpose of which might be an attempt to sow caution among the feelings of the Muslims that sympathize with us, or to calm the fears of the Americans that bin Laden might do something. But the fact is that these deeds have nothing to do with bin Laden. This is an *umma* of 1200 million Muslims, and there is no way that it will allow these dirty pestering Jews and Christians into the Noble Ka'ba of God. For our *umma* is continuing on its path, and we are sure that it will continue the *jihad* and give America and its allies a painful beating.

AL-JAZEERA: *On the 20th of last month, the 20th of August, when the American bombardment on Afghanistan was perpetrated, it was said that you were preparing for a meeting in the Khost region, that was subjected to American aerial bombardment, and that the bombardment was timed to coincide with your meeting. Firstly, were you at that meeting, or was there even a meeting at all? And secondly, it was said that a letter arrived for you from a neighbouring country—meaning Pakistan—asking you to leave this place immediately because of the possibility that it might be bombed. What is the extent of your relationship with Pakistan and how do you evaluate its position towards you? Do you think that Pakistan might cooperate with the United States in making a strike at you?*

OBL: The information that the Americans had was clearly incorrect. I was not in Khost, nor in the state of Paktia at all; I was hundreds of kilometers away from there. As for the information that was supposed to have reached us, we found a sympathetic and generous people in Pakistan who exceeded all our expectations, and we receive information from our beloved ones and helpers of *jihad* for the sake of God against the Americans. The people in Pakistan gave a clear measure of the extent of their hatred at American arrogance towards the Islamic world. As for what we said with regard to Pakistan, there are groups that are sympathetic to Islam and to the *jihad* against the

Americans. There are also a few groups that are unfortunately still cooperating with the enemies of our *umma*, the Americans.

AL-JAZEERA: *You mean at an official level?*

OBL: I mean the government, there are elements within the government.

AL-JAZEERA: *There were also published in some Arabic and foreign newspapers some details about your attempts to acquire nuclear, chemical, or biological weapons, especially by means of some businessmen from Central Asian or ex-Soviet countries.[5] What is the truth of these reports, especially that the American administration—which has made 235 accusations against you—has made the accusation that you are really attempting to acquire this kind of weapon?*

OBL: As I said, at a time when Israel is stocking up on hundreds of nuclear warheads and atomic bombs, and when the Christian controls a vast proportion of these weapons, this is not an accusation but a fact. We cannot accept that anyone should accuse us of this. How can it be claimed that a man is a brave warrior when the claimant is backward and stupid? We supported and congratulated the Pakistani people when God blessed them with possession of a nuclear weapon,[6] because we consider it the Muslims' right to have it, and we will not pay any attention to these shabby American accusations.

AL-JAZEERA: *Can this be taken as confirmation that you are seeking to acquire this weapon?*

OBL: We say this is not an accusation. There is a duty on Muslims to acquire them, and America knows today that Muslims are in possession of such a weapon, by the grace of God Almighty.

AL-JAZEERA: *Regarding the accusations directed at you by the American administration, or those concerning issues—in their words—related to terrorism and supporting terrorist*

---

5 See for example "Report Links bin-Laden, Nuclear Weapons," *Al-Watan Al-Arabi*, November 13 1998.

6 On May 28 1998, the government of Pakistan first announced that it had successfully conducted five nuclear tests.

groups, and so forth; are you prepared to face such accusations and go on trial in another country and in a neutral court?

OBL: I say that there are two sides in the struggle: one side is the global Crusader alliance with the Zionist Jews, led by America, Britain, and Israel, and the other side is the Islamic world. It is not acceptable in such a struggle as this that he [the Crusader] should attack and enter my land and holy sanctuaries, and plunder Muslims' oil, and then when he encounters any resistance from Muslims, to label them terrorists. This is stupidity, or considering others stupid. We believe that it is our legal duty to resist this occupation with all our might, and punish it in the same way as it punishes us.

AL-JAZEERA: *But the Taliban government announced that it is seeking to put you on trial in the event that there is any real evidence from any state or any party regarding the allegations that have been directed against you by these countries.*[7] *Would you accept a trial according to the laws applied by the Taliban and Islamic law?*

OBL: We came out of our country to wage *jihad* for the sake of God Almighty. He blessed us with this gift of emigration, wishing us to strive to implement His law and be judged by it. This is our demand and this is what we set out to do. What legitimate court is applying Islamic law away from the pressures imposed by dissenters? This is our goal and our demand. We are prepared at any time for any legitimate court that has an accuser and an accused. But if the accuser is the United States of America, we too accuse it of many things, all the terrible things it has committed in the lands of Muslims. But America— may God fight it—when it asked for me from the Taliban,[8] refused to abide by

7 According to some sources, by mid-1998, relations between bin Laden and Mullah Omar had grown strained (Burke, *Al-Qaeda*, pp. 186–87). A different picture of the relationship is painted by Peter Bergen (*Holy War Inc*, pp. 146–47) and Michael Scheuer (*Imperial Hubris*, pp. 140–41), who suggest that it was never under any serious threat.

8 In April 1998, the Taliban received a high-level US delegation in Kabul and two months later, Mullah Omar met the head of Saudi intelligence, Prince Turki al-Faisal, in Kandahar to discuss a deal to hand bin Laden over for trial in Saudi Arabia for treason (a crime carrying the death penalty). An arrangement was agreed in principle, but it came unstuck when the US launched Operation Infinite Reach. Three weeks after the strikes, Prince Turki arrived in Kandahar to detain bin Laden, but after a stormy meeting Omar reneged on the deal and sent Turki away empty-handed. For detailed analysis of Mullah Omar's contact with the USA and Saudi Arabia regarding a possible handover of bin Laden, see Chapter 4 of The Final Report of the National Commission on Terrorist Attacks upon the United States, Official Government Edition, http://www.gpoaccess.gov/911.

Islamic law, and said: "We are only asking for one thing, that you give us Osama bin Laden." In its arrogance, it treats people as if they were slaves. We pray to God that He will humble it.

AL-JAZEERA: *There are allegations against you regarding the explosions that occurred in the American embassies in East Africa, in Nairobi, and Dar es-Salaam, through the confessions, published by the Pakistani and international newspapers, attributed to Muhammad Sadiq Howayda, who was arrested in Pakistan and handed over to the United States and the Kenyan authorities. He alleged that you gave him orders and asked him to carry out these explosions. What is your real position on these explosions? What is your relation to Muhammad Sadiq Howayda?*[9]

OBL: By the grace of God Almighty, I have brought happiness to Muslims in the Islamic world, and anyone who follows the global media will see the extent of the sympathy in the Islamic world for strikes against Americans, even if people are sorry to see the killing of innocents in these countries. But what is clear is the enormous wave of joy and happiness that is spreading across the Islamic world [in response to these attacks], because they believe that the Jews and America have gone too far in their tyranny and their contempt for Muslims. And people were unable to move the Islamic states to defend them or to avenge them, so these acts are nothing but a popular response from young men who have put themselves forward and are striving to please God Almighty. I look at these men with much admiration and respect, for they have removed the shame from the forehead of our *umma*, whether they carried out the explosions in Riyadh or Khobar or East Africa or the like. I also admire our brothers the lions in Palestine, who are teaching the Jews great lessons about faith and about the pride of the believer. But unfortunately, after these courageous attacks in Palestine, global unbelief has crystallized in the land of Canaan, in Egypt, with their collaborators from among the rulers of the region, the rulers of the Arabs, who have laughed at our *umma* for more than half a century. Every time a king meets a president they say they have "discussed the Palestinian issue", but over half a century a clear picture has

---

9 "Mohammed Sadiq Howayda" may be the Saudi Mohammed Rashid Daoud Owhali, arrested in Nairobi on August 12 and convicted of the attacks in 2001; he remains in prison in America. For al-Owhali's responses to his FBI interrogators, including a description of his relationship with bin Laden, see Burke, *Al-Qaeda*, pp. 169–74.

emerged: they have abandoned the *mujahidin* in Palestine. In fact they have given a guilty verdict on those lions whose fathers and brothers have been killed, imprisoned, tortured, and persecuted in the defense of their religion and their attempts to drive the infidels away. "From mysteries come the clearest things," as they say. I don't know what people are waiting for after this clearest of betrayals, and after the shameful way in which the Arab rulers have acted in the interests of the Jews or America.

AL-JAZEERA: *Yes, but the United States says that it is convinced, and has evidence, of your involvement in these operations, and even now it has not revealed this evidence except to say that it is under further investigation. It is said that someone from your group, or one of your helpers, has confessed to the American intelligence services many things about your organization and your link to the operations, even the explosion of the International Trade Centre.*[10]

OBL: America makes many allegations, but—even supposing they're true—they don't mean a thing. These people are resisting global unbelief that has occupied our lands. How angry America gets when it attacks people and those people resist! But in any case, the allegations are false, except for the fact that I have a link to motivating these people. That is clearly true, and I admit to it every time, when I was one of the ones who signed the juridical decree inciting our *umma* to *jihad*; I have been doing just that for some years. And this decree was responded to by many people, by the grace of God, among whom were those brothers we consider martyrs, brother Abd al-Aziz al-Mu'zim, who was killed in Riyadh—there is no strength or power save in God—and brother Maslah al-Shamrani, brother Riyadh al-Hajiri, and we ask God Almighty to accept them all as martyrs, and brother Khaled al-Sa'id.[11] These men confessed during the investigation that they were influenced by

10 The "helper" may have been Abdul Hakim Murad (1968–), an alleged conspirator in the abortive terrorist scheme named Operation Boyinka. This was a series of plots, developed by Ramzi Yousef and his uncle, Khalid Sheikh Mohammed, to destroy 11 airliners on January 21 and 22 1995, to kill John Paul II on January 15 1995, and to crash a plane into CIA headquarters in Langley, Virginia. The plots were discovered when Filipino police found their plans on Yousef's laptop computer in his Manila apartment in 1994; Murad subsequently confessed to Filipino interrogators under torture, and was extradited to the USA on April 12 1995; his testimony would help convict Yousef.

11 The four men who carried out the Riyadh car bomb attack on November 13 1995; see above, p. 27, n. 16).

some of our statements that we have made to the people in which we discussed the juridical decrees of the men of knowledge concerning the duty of *jihad* against these occupying Americans. As I said earlier, what is wrong with resisting those who attack you? All religious communities have such a principle, for example these Buddhists, both the North Koreans and Vietnamese who fought America. This is a legal right, so by any right the Arab or Islamic media should be able to follow the *mujahidin* who have followed the example of the master of mankind, Muhammad, and have been guided by him." This is reassurance for us that we are fighting for the sake of God. I previously told some Western media outlets that a great honor passed us by that it was not us who participated in the killing of Americans in Riyadh. These accusations are utterly false, except that it is true that I am linked to inciting: I have incited our *umma* to *jihad* with all my brothers and Muslim scholars.

AL-JAZEERA: *Muhammad Sadiq Howayda claimed that he had been trained in one of your camps, and that he had a personal relationship to you. To what extent are these claims— or at least the claims that have been attributed to him in some of the media—true?*

OBL: What I do know is that in the *jihad* camps in Afghanistan, which we helped to open in the days of the *jihad* against the Soviet Union, more than 15,000 young men were trained in those camps, by the grace of God Almighty. Most of them were from Arab countries, and some were brothers from Islamic countries. As for this idea that I commissioned this explosion to be carried out, I really think that this is an illusion and a fallacy put about by the American government, for which it has no evidence. Even if brother Howayda did confess to these things, he would have done so under torture— the types of torture in Pakistan and East Africa are no secret.

AL-JAZEERA: *But Muhammad Sadiq Howayda also claimed that you had given orders for Sheikh Abdallah Azzam to be killed in Peshawar in 1989, and that there was a struggle for the leadership of the Arabs—the Afghan Arabs, as the Arab* mujahidin *in Afghanistan were called—between you and Sheikh Azzam, who was head of the* mujahidin *Services Office.[12] To what extent are these claims true, and what is your*

12 The MAK (Maktab al-Khidamat, or Afghan Services Bureau) played a major role during the Soviet-Afghanistan war, training an estimated 10,000 *mujahidin* and dispersing around $2 billion in donations sourced through a network of offices around the world, including the USA. With the

position on them? How would you describe your relations with the Sheikh at the time of his murder?

OBL: Sheikh Abdallah Azzam, may God rest his soul, is a man of our *umma*. He is someone who has demonstrated very clearly after his murder the extent of the barrenness that has afflicted Muslim women in failing to conceive another man like himself.

Mujahidin who were in the theatre of war and lived through that era know that no one benefited the Islamic *jihad* in Afghanistan more than Sheikh Abdallah Azzam, God bless his soul, who motivated our *umma* throughout the world. Since that time, Sheikh Azzam increased his activity with the *mujahidin* in Palestine, and specifically with Hamas. His books, especially *Signs of the Merciful*, circulated around Palestine, motivating the population to *jihad* against the Jews. When the Sheikh started out, the atmosphere among the Islamists and sheikhs was limited, location-specific, and regional, each dealing with their own particular locale, but he inspired the Islamic movement and motivated Muslims to the broader *jihad*. At that point we were both in the same boat, and you are all aware of the numerous conspiracies there were to murder us all. I used to ask Sheikh Azzam to keep a safe distance from Peshawar because of the increasing number of plots against us, particularly when a week or two before his death we found a bomb in the middle of the night at the same mosque where he was eventually killed. The Jews were the ones who were complaining most about the Sheikh's movement, and who were constantly targeting him. It is therefore believed that Israel, in collusion with some of its Arab agents, killed the Sheikh. As for this accusation against me, it was fabricated by the Americans, the Jews, and some of their agents. It doesn't even merit a response. Those who witnessed events know of the close relationship between Sheikh Azzam and myself. Alleged disagreements that some people have mentioned have no basis in truth, and there was no competition

---

war's end, there seems to have been a difference in opinion between Azzam and bin Laden over the future direction of MAK. Azzam wanted to use the network and its resources to help install an Islamic state in postwar Afghanistan; bin Laden—influenced by the Egyptian members of the Muslim Brotherhood, including Ayman al-Zawahiri and Omar Abdel Rahman—wanted to use it to fund a global *jihad*. When Azzam and his sons was killed by a land mine in Peshawar on November 24 1989, bin Laden assumed control of MAK.

between us whatsoever.[13] Sheikh Abdallah Azzam's mission was motivation and calling people to their duty. When we were inside the Paktia mountains, he sent young men to us to fight, and we took instructions and directions from him. We ask God to accept him and his sons, Muhammad and Ibrahim, as martyrs, and for our *umma* to be compensated for his loss by another who can take up his duty like he did.

AL-JAZEERA: *After the American aerial bombardment of Afghanistan, the US President demanded economic sanctions against you, and against the commercial and financial institutions managed by you, or with whom you deal. It was said that a period of "drying the swamps" had started, of draining your financial resources.[14] Could it be that this is straining your financial resources to the limit, that it has caused you financial difficulties, and that it will cause your helpers to be scattered away from you in the coming period?*

OBL: War has its ups and downs—sometimes it goes our way, sometimes not. America applied severe pressures against our activities since early on, and this has had an effect on us. Some countries who are on our side and have possessions and funds have responded and ordered us to stop attacking America, but we believe that these attacks are a duty incumbent upon us, as is motivating our *umma*. So we have continued to motivate our *umma*, and by the grace of God Almighty, we have carried on. There has been American pressure on us for some years now—it did not start with the recent bombing. But some Arab states also applied economic pressure on us, depriving us of our rights, and making life difficult for us. Our own people were even prevented from paying our money to us, and in this they were guided by Abdallah bin Ubay bin Sulul, leader of the hypocrites, and by the hypocrites themselves, of whom God said: "They are the ones who say, 'Give nothing to those who follow God's Messenger, until they abandon him,' but to God belong the treasures of heaven and earth, though the hypocrites do not understand this."[15] God Almighty will be their punisher. And now, because they made us live in dire

13 Jason Burke concludes that "there is little evidence to implicate bin Laden in the assassination [of Azzam] and a host of more likely suspects": *Al-Qaeda*, p. 82.

14 Clinton ordered a freeze of bin Laden's assets following the August 7 1998 bombings of US embassies in Nairobi and Dar-es-Salaam.

15 Qur'an, 63:7. Abdallah bin Ubay bin Sulul is the reputed leader of the hypocrites from the Prophet Muhammad's time to whom a verse like this could be directed.

straits, they are also doing so. As for us, our Prophet said: "Whoever remains a true believer in his heart, remains healthy of body and has enough food for the day, will inherit the entire world."[16] For by the one God, we feel that the world is giving us plenty, and money is merely transitory. But we say to Muslims to give their money to the *jihad* and *jihadi* movements who apply themselves specifically to fighting Jews and Crusaders.

AL-JAZEERA: *Last February, in the juridical decree that you issued, you made a call for* jihad *against Crusaders and Jews, and especially against Americans. This announcement came at a time when many Islamic movements that had previously undertaken armed action began to return to this armed action (as we're now hearing in Egypt or in Algeria);*[17] *however, in many Arabic countries, as we have seen, many Islamic movements are beginning to shift towards sympathy with parliaments, or with what is called the democratic game. Don't you think that, with your call to* jihad *at that time, you are going against the current of the other Islamic movements?*

OBL: We believe that *jihad* is now an individual duty on our *umma*, but we have to distinguish between the judgment itself and the ability to carry it out. In any country containing the necessary conditions for *jihad* to be successfully implemented, Muslims are obliged to perform their legal duty of *jihad* against what is clearly the biggest unbelief. However, in some countries it might have been shown to some people that the necessary conditions [for *jihad*] are in place, but after a while they gain experience and know-how and realise that this is in fact not the case; in this instance they are charged with pardon and forgiveness.

But the question remains: who defines what the right conditions are? Should it be those who have relied on the world, or those who have taken no share in legal knowledge? If circumstances prevent them from taking any share in military knowledge, then in this case it is true that *jihad*, as long as it is an individual duty, is sometimes impossible, but real preparation requires good numbers and equipment.[18] As for this widespread idea among Muslims

16 From the *hadith* collection of al-Tirmidhi; vol. 16, book 30, no. 2,268.
17 Al-Gama'a al-Islamiyya, whose representative had signed bin Laden's February 23 1998 *fatwa*, was responsible for a series of attacks in the mid-1990s, including the massacre at Luxor in 1997. The civil war in Algeria, which erupted in 1992 when the military prevented an Islamist political party from taking power after the country's first multi-party elections, held in December 1991, left 100,000 people dead.
18 Cf. Qur'an, 9:46.

today that now is not time for *jihad*, then this idea—if it is not an obligation—is wrong. Many scholars say that now is not the time for *jihad*, and unless they can justify this they are quite wrong. And if *jihad* is decreed to be an individual duty today, then we are obliged to strive with all our might to complete the preparation and the necessary conditions for it. For these words are true. The Sheikh of Islam ibn Taymiyya makes it clear in this regard that he who issues a juridical decree regarding *jihad* is he who has knowledge of the legal aspects of religion, who has knowledge of *jihad* and when it should be waged. In other words, he should wage *jihad* himself. But after *jihad* had been absent from our *umma* for a long period there rose up a new generation of students of knowledge who had not embarked on the battles of *jihad*. They were infuriated by America's media imperialism, by which it conquered Saudi Arabia without a fight. This psychological blow made them say: "It is true that *jihad* is obligatory, but we cannot fight". Know, on the contrary, that it is right that whoever those whom God Almighty has blessed with *jihad* [should fight], as happened in Afghanistan, Bosnia and Chechnya—and God blessed us with that, for we are certain that our *umma* today is able to wage *jihad* against the enemies of Islam, and especially against the greatest external enemy, the Crusader-Jewish alliance.

I'm referring here to the issue whereby some of the youth—God bless them —have noticed the unwillingness of some important people, and concluded that these important and famous people have only been unwilling because they knew what was in their interest. On further investigation it wasn't that at all, it wasn't necessarily the hesitation of famous people as a result of his knowing what was in his interest. When we contemplate God's book, we find that the best men were reprimanded by God for holding back, for these pious, righteous men were afflicted by this disease, the disease of holding back from *jihad*. How can we claim that our best men today are holding back in order to safeguard their own interests? In the chapter of the Battle Gains[19] in the Qur'an God addresses His Prophet and the men of Badr, who are the best of men: "For it was your Lord who made you venture from your home for a true

19 The chapter of the Battle Gains (al-Anfal), the 8th *sura* of the Qur'an, is a comment on the Battle of Badr, the first battle fought between the Muslims and their Meccan opponents after the migration (622). The Muslims won despite being vastly outnumbered, and began to question the distribution of the spoils of war. The *sura* reminds them that it was God who brought about the victory (summary taken from *The Qur'an*, ed. MAS Abdel Haleem (OUP, 2005), p. 110.

purpose—though a group of believers disliked it and argued with you about the truth, after it had been made clear, as if they were being driven towards a death they could see with their own eyes."[20] This is how even the best men were described, so it's only natural that it applies to us too. There is a long Prophetic saying in the books of both al-Bukhari and Muslim which goes that on the day of Tabuk, Ka'b bin Malik said: "I did not remain behind God's Prophet in any battle that he fought except the battle of Tabuk ... I never had two she-camels before, but I did have at the time of this battle ... I said, 'I will prepare myself [for departure] one or two days after him [the Prophet], and then join them.' In the morning after their departure, I went out to get myself ready but returned having done nothing. And he said, "God's Prophet fought that battle at the time when the fruits had ripened and their shade looked pleasant."[21]

For man is pulled back and forth by the burdens of the earth. He was one of the ones who took the blessed greater oath of allegiance at al-Aqaba,[22] from which resulted the state of Islam in Medina, the City of Light. He held back without apology, and in his long discussion of this it becomes clear that there were three of them, just as when it says in God's book: "And to the three men who stayed behind ...".[23] The stories in the Prophetic biography that those who went out to Tabuk were thirty thousand. What is three compared to thirty thousand? An utterly inconsequential number, if we asked any military commander: if three out of thirty thousand of your men stayed behind, a tiny number? But to show what a great misdeed this is, God Almighty sent down from the seven heavens a Qu'ran which will be recited until the Day of Judgment calling these men to account. Of it Ka'b bin Malik says: "When the earth closed in around me I climbed a wall to my cousin Abu

20 Qur'an, 8:5.
21 From the *hadith* collection of al-Bukhari, vol. 5, book 59, no. 702. The battle of Tabuk (in northwestern Saudi Arabia), between the Muslims and the Byzantines, took place in 630, during the month of Ramadan. In it, the soldiers of Islam, under Muhammad's leadership, established a training and fighting camp during the sacred month of fasting, so as to demonstrate their strength and endurance.
22 Aqaba: not the modern-day port of Aqaba in Jordan, but a town near Medina (then Yathrib). There were two pledges of Aqaba, both undertaken just before Muhammad's flight from Mecca to Medina in 622. The first pledge was a commitment to fight, the second to fight to the death. The one referred to here is the second pledge.
23 Qur'an, 9:118. Bin Laden quotes only the first clause of this verse, assuming the listeners know the remainder.

Qatada, the dearest person to me, and said to him: 'Abu Qatada, I appeal to you by God, do you know that I love God and His Messenger?' This was a very serious matter—he wanted to be assured of the greatest thing in existence, the love of God and His Messenger, for there was no meaning to our existence other than loving them. But he did not answer me. So I appealed to him a second time. But again he did not answer me. So I appealed to him a third time. But Abu Qatada could not testify that he loved God and His Messenger – how could he when he was sitting with those who stayed behind? This is the religion of God. News had come that the Byzantines wanted to attack him in Tabuk, and so the Messenger of God got up in the midst of the tumult and hot wind, wanting to help his religion, and you are sitting and doing the opposite—how can he testify that you love God and His Messenger? So he did not testify for him, but he did not deny it either. Instead he said: 'God and His Messenger know best.' So I was overcome and my eyes flooded over."[24] And so you see, the dearest of his friends could not testify on his behalf over this great matter. It is clear then that this *jihad* today is an obligation on the *umma*. It could fall short, but we believe that those who fought in Afghanistan did more than their share of duty. They knew that they were fighting with sparse supplies—very few RPGs, very few anti-tank mines, and very few Kalashnikovs—yet they managed to destroy the myth of the largest military machine ever known to mankind and utterly annihilated the idea of the so-called superpowers. We believe that America is much weaker than Russia, and we have learned from our brothers who fought in the *jihad* in Somalia of the incredible weakness and cowardice of the American soldier. Not even eighty of them had been killed and they fled in total darkness in the middle of the night, unable to see a thing. After this, great commotion filled the globe about the new world order. People can, if they fear God—who knows that it is in His power—wage *jihad*, and who knows that the situation now still needs the right conditions. God knows best.

AL-JAZEERA: *The amount that the American administration has set aside for your capture or for provision of information leading to your capture and arrest is five million dollars. Some people think that this amount might be tempting to some of your helpers,*

---

24   From the *hadith* collection of al-Bukhari, vol. 5, book 59, no. 702.

and it might induce them to provide information about you, or betray you. Aren't you afraid that someone might betray you?

OBL: Well, you have come here and you see the situation. These young men— I pray that God will accept them and those of them who have died throughout this blessed *jihad* as martyrs—have left the material world and come to these mountains and this land; they have left their families, they have left their fathers and mothers, they have left their universities, and they have come here to face bombardment by American cruise missiles. As you know, some of our brothers have been killed, six of our Arab brothers, and one Turk—we pray that God will accept them all as martyrs.[25] Among them was our brother Siddiq from Egypt, our brother Hamdi also from Egypt, and three of our brothers from Yemen, including Bashar, who is also known as Saraqa, and our brother Abu Jihad, as well as our brother from the Illumined Medina, Sa'd Salah Mutbiqani. These men left the material world and came for the *jihad*. But America, because it worships money, thinks that the people here are of the same persuasion. But by God we have not sent away a single man following this propaganda, because we do not doubt our brothers. We consider them the best, and they are. God is their only reckoner.

AL-JAZEERA: *With regard to the relationship between you and the Afghan government, or the Taliban movement, what is the nature of this movement? Are you a follower of it or a part of it, or are you working independently, but on Afghan soil?*

OBL: God Almighty blessed us with the Taliban movement fourteen years after the *jihad* that the former *mujahidin* undertook, in which the students also played a role.[26] God Almighty brought them the success of defeating the Soviet Union at that time, and He opened the way for those who raised the banner of *jihad* at that early time to defeat the biggest state in the world, the biggest military state. But unfortunately they did not continue along the path after that and there were some disagreements, into which America, and some of the Arab

25 They are the seven outsiders (three Yemenis, two Egyptians, a Saudi, and a Turk) killed by the US missile attacks on bin Laden's camps around Khost and Jalalabad on August 20 1998. Bin Laden omits to mention the seven Pakistanis and twenty Afghans also killed in the attacks.

26 The term Taliban means "students". From 1994 to 1999, tens of thousands of boys studying in the *madrassas* in Pakistan crossed the border into Afghanistan to fight for the movement; on occasion the religious schools would be shut to allow reinforcements to be drafted in for specific operations.

states who have a strong connection to America, intervened and set about sowing strife between the *mujahidin*. To everyone's regret, fighting took place, which only increased the suffering of the Muslim people of Afghanistan.[27] What is unfortunate here is that many good people discontinued their support for Afghanistan because of this internal fighting. And in truth this was conduct that it should not have condoned, for it only heaped more misery on the widows and orphans whose husbands and fathers had been killed. What good Muslims should have done is come here to look after these orphans and widows, but the devil led them to believe that they should stop helping the Muslims who had defended Islam here, just as they had defended all the Islamic world, especially the Gulf states. One look at a map would tell you that Afghanistan was not so much a target in itself, but was rather a passage for the Soviet forces, after they had achieved large gains in the world at that time. For the Russians thought that they could strike a decisive blow to the West by occupying the Straits of Hormuz and all the Gulf states, thereby taking possession of the biggest petroleum reserves in the world. So the real reason why some—indeed all—of the Gulf states suported the Afghan jihad, was that they saw it as self-defense. For they were themselves participants in the battle. After the Russians were defeated these states turned their backs completely and began—to my great regret—to publicly denounce the *jihad* and the *mujahidin*. Some of them also colluded in sowing discord within the *mujahidin* themselves, until God blessed the Muslims with the coming of the Taliban government, which is not a force influenced from the outside, as the Crusader Western media would have it, but a force that has come from within.

People had become weary of ambushes and of the stealing of taxes and dues, so any tribe that had in it scholars of Islamic studies and had a link with the Taliban went and asked them to go to this or that province. This explains why we saw Gulbuddin Hikmetyar[28] getting to the edge—even within a few metres—of Kabul with the public support of Pakistan, but he wasn't able to take it. It is well known that the Islamic party, under Hikmetyar's leadership,

---

27 For an overview of Afghanistan's descent into civil war following the Soviet withdrawal, and the coming of the Taliban, see Ahmed Rashid, *Taliban: The Story of the Afghan Warlords*, (Pan, 2001), pp. 21–3.
28 Gulbuddin Hikmetyar was a US-trained leader of the Afghan resistance against the USSR in the 1980s. He later became the leader of the radical movement Hizb-i Islami (of which the Taliban leader Mullah Omar was previously a member) which had the short-lived support of the Pakistani government, but later lost control of the Afghan capital to the Taliban after losing Pakistan's support.

was the was the best of the Afghan parties in terms of power, organization, and area covered within Afghanistan. Conversely, the Taliban were the youngest of all parties and most of them had not even participated in the fighting, but because of the great numbers of people in Afghanistan who had reached such a degree of despair with former events, God opened the way for the Taliban.

So we advise Muslims both within and outside Afghanistan to help these students,[29] and we advise Muslims outside [Afghanistan] that much of the effort that is being made is doing hardly anything to promote the existence of a state of Islam. For our Prophet Muhammad spent thirteen years preaching in Mecca, the result being a few hundred emigrants [to his cause], but when the state of Medina was founded, despite its tiny size, its location in the middle of the Persian and Byzantine states and in the middle of Abs, Thabyan and Ghatfan and neighbouring Arab tribes, all ready to tear this little state to pieces—despite all this, good prevailed. And we call on Muslims to help this state [Afghanistan] with all their might, their ideas, their charitable donations and funds, for with God's will it represents the banner of Islam today. And aggression by America today against Afghanistan is not just against Afghanistan itself, but against Afghanistan in its capacity as the raiser of the banner of Islam in the Islamic world, the true Islam of *jihad* for the sake of God. So our relationship with the Taliban is very strong and firm, and it is a doctrinal relationship based on us sharing the same belief, not a political or business relationship. Many states have participated and attempted to put pressure on the Taliban, trying to tempt it or scare it, but God Almighty has made them firm.

AL–JAZEERA: *But how authentic are these reports that have talked about the Taliban movement, or the Taliban government, possibly being prepared to give you over to any state in the event that official charges are made against you, or in the event of there being any evidence against you?*

OBL: From what I have heard, the Taliban have denied these reports, and as we know they are not true in any case. God knows best.

---

29 Bin Laden uses a word here that is from the same root as the word "Taliban," simultaneously indicating the Taliban as his explicit subject while emphasizing that they considered themselves students of Islamic learning.

AL-JAZEERA: *You spoke a little earlier about your participation in the Afghan jihad and about how some states, especially Gulf states, encouraged the mujahidin, even supporting and giving them assistance. Among the other states who provided assistance to support the mujahidin at that time against the Soviet Union was the United States. The Western and international media talk about there being a link between you and the US administration, or the CIA, during the jihad against the Soviet Union. What is the truth behind this alleged link, if there was one? What is your position on this? And is it true that they played any part in developing your activities against the Soviet Union at that time?*

OBL: Going back to the previous question, when you asked whether we are working here in an independent capacity, the truth of the matter is that we are not here independently, but are here in a state that includes the Commander of the Faithful.[30] We are committed under God's law to obey him, there is no dispute about that, and we are committed to this state. We call others to help it, and we warn—as I mentioned—of the confusion that America is making. It wants to strike the State of Islam in Afghanistan, but it does so under the slogan of striking Osama bin Laden. That will not help it. As for us, by the will of God we have come out here and we know our path from the outset; America's rockets do not scare us. But we warn it that any strike against this people is a strike against the State of Islam, and for various reasons pertaining to the circumstances in Afghanistan there is an opinion amongst the Taliban that we should not move from within Afghanistan against any other state. This was the decision of the Commander of the Faithful, as is known. But the success of our efforts to motivate the *umma*, by God's help, is not constrained by our limited abilities at this point. By the grace of God we are certain that our *umma* is on a rapid course towards the work of *jihad* against America, which is a duty for all Muslims, as I mentioned.

AL-JAZEERA: *There has been talk in the international media about America's support for the Afghan jihad against the Soviet Union, in which you took part both physically and financially, and it has also been mentioned that you were linked to the CIA, or that it was the CIA who were funding your activities and supporting you in this jihad*

30 "Commander of the Faithful" (*amir al-muminin*) is the title applied to the early leaders of Islam who ruled in both religious and civil spheres. This is a reference to Mullah Omar, head of the Taliban, who was voted *amir al-muminin* at a meeting of the Taliban in Kandahar in March 1996.

against the Soviet Union. What is the truth of these allegations and what is the truth of the link between you and America at that time?

OBL: It's an attempt to distort by the Americans, and praise be to God that He has thwarted their conspiracy.[31] Every Muslim, from the moment they realise the distinction in their hearts, hates Americans, hates Jews, and hates Christians. This is a part of our belief and our religion. For as long as I can remember, I have felt tormented and at war, and have felt hatred and animosity for Americans. What they say happened did not in fact take place. And as for their claim that they supported the *jihad* and the struggle against the Soviets, well, this support came from Arab countries, especially from the Gulf. They supported this war not for the sake of God Almighty, as they claim, but for fear of losing their positions of power and privilege from the Russian advance. Carter, the American president at the time, was unable to utter anything of any value whatsoever for over twenty days. On the 20th of January he made a statement that any Russian interference in the Gulf region would be considered as a direct act of aggression against America.[32] This is because they had already occupied this area and appropriated its oil. He also said that they would use military force if such an invasion took place. The Americans are lying when they claim they helped us at any point, and we challenge them to present a single shred of evidence to prove it. In fact, they were a burden on us and the *mujahidin* in Afghanistan, and there was no agreement between us. We were doing our duty, which is supporting Islam in Afghanistan, even if this did coincide with American interests. When the Muslims were fighting the Byzantines, during the fierce war between the Byzantines and the Persians, no one in their right mind could say that the Muslims were fighting as agents of the Persians against the Byzantines.[33] There was merely a common interest

---

31 According to Peter Bergen, a "source familiar with bin Laden's organization" has explained that bin Laden "never had any relations with America or American officials ... He was saying very early in the eighties that the next battle is going to be with America ... No aid or training or other support have ever been given to bin Laden from Americans." Bergen adds that "A senior US official unequivocally says that 'bin Laden never met with the CIA'." *Holy War Inc*, p. 67.

32 This seems to be in reference to an interview given by President Carter on NBC's "Meet the Press" on January 20 1980, in which he criticized the Russian invasion of Afghanistan and called for a boycott of the Moscow Olympic Games.

33 This refers to the early period in the expansion of Islam, when the Byzantines were a common enemy of the Persians and the Muslims.

between the Muslims and the Persians. Fighting the Byzantines was a duty, but after their victories over the Byzantines, by the grace of God, they set about fighting the Persians. Unintended confluence of interests does not mean there is any kind of link or tacit agreement. We have been advancing since those days and, with the grace of God, have been spreading our message in Hijaz and Najd[34] for more than twelve years on the duty of boycotting American goods, attacking its military forces and its economy.

AL-JAZEERA: *Reports have been published in the Arab and international media about the presence of the activities of your followers or helpers in some Arab states, including Yemen, for example. Is there any truth in these reports?*

OBL: You know, we are linked to all of the Islamic world, whether that be Yemen, Pakistan, or wherever. We are part of one unified *umma*, and by the grace of God the numbers of those who have conviction and have set out to wage *jihad* are increasing every day. Their numbers are good news for us, both in Yemen and elsewhere. In Yemen we have strong and old links, by the grace of God Almighty, besides the fact that my roots and my father's roots go back there.[35]

AL-JAZEERA: *As for your relations with the other Islamic organizations in the Arab world, how would you describe them and what would you say about them at the present time? What is the true position of the Egyptian Islamic Group vis-à-vis the World Islamic Front? Have they withdrawn from it?*

OBL: By the grace of God, our relationship with Islamic organizations in the Islamic world, overall, are very good. We collaborate with them piously and devoutly to help this religion, all in the sphere that God opened up for us. We call Muslims, and especially those working for Islam, to transcend all the less important problems—although unfortunately the devils and demons among mankind, and especially the Crusaders, have been able to divert the states,

---

34 These are both regions of Saudi Arabia; the Hijaz is the region along the Red Sea which is the location of Mecca and Medina; the Najd is further inland and includes the capital city Riyadh.

35 The bin Laden ancestral home is the village of al-Rubat, in the Hadramaut region of Yemen. Burke notes that, as well as family ties, bin Laden "has long had connections with Yemeni militants ... Phone records from bin Laden's personal satellite phone show hundreds of calls made to the Yemen made between 1996 and 1998." Burke, *Al-Qaeda*, p. 214.

apart from the smaller organizations in them, towards regional issues. So you find Egypt has problems with Libya, and Yemen with Saudi Arabia, and likewise the organizations—except those on whom God has taken mercy— generally experience severe problems, while the greatest unbelief, the Crusader-American alliance, remains unchallenged, tearing the Islamic world apart and plundering the wealth of Muslims in an unprecedented manner. And the second part of the question?

AL-JAZEERA: *The Egyptian Islamic Group?*

OBL: They have links to us.

AL-JAZEERA: *Was it part of the World Islamic Front, and has it withdrawn?*

OBL: Yes, we have very strong links with them, by the grace of God Almighty, since the days of the *jihad*, when we were fighting in the same trenches against the Soviet Union. They played a supportive, supervisory role in the signing of the juridical ruling calling for American and Jewish blood to be shed. They signed the juridical ruling, but there was some confusion with an administrative issue when it came to the issuing of the juridical ruling. Since the issuing of the juridical ruling coincided with the founding of the Front, people became uncertain as to whether the Islamic Group was part of the Front, so it was forced to clarify its position. It did sign the juridical ruling, but it is not part of the World Islamic Front.

AL-JAZEERA: *What exactly are the goals that you see for yourself? What is the general message that you want to bring to the Arab or Islamic world?*

OBL: As I've said, we believe very firmly—and I say this in light of the severity with which the regimes and the media deal with us, in their desire to strip us of our virility—we believe that we are men, Muslim men who have a duty to defend the greatest house in the world, the Noble Ka'ba, and to be honored in doing so, not so that Christian and Jewish American recruits can come to defend the descendants of Sa'd, Muthanna, Abu Bakr and Umar[36]—and if

---

36 The first two men are unknown. Abu Bakr and Umar are the first two of the four Rightly Guided Caliphs, the first four Caliphs who in the Sunni tradition are seen as model leaders. They wre close companions of Muhammad. Abu Bakr (c.573–684) ruled from 632–34, succeeding

God had not blessed us with Islam then our ancestors in the pagan age would not have let these people come either—not so that these infidel asses can come using as their excuse this invitation that wouldn't even fool a child. As far as this region is concerned, the ruling said: "... the coming of the Americans for a few months ..." but they lied from beginning to end. "And three of them God will not look at on the Day of Judgment," as our Prophet said, "For they were said to be liars."[37] The months passed, the first year passed, then the second, and we are now in the ninth year, and the Americans are all lying, saying "We have interests in the region, and we will not move before we can guarantee them." So basically an enemy comes in and steals what is yours, and you ask him why he is stealing? He tells you: "No, these are my interests, my interests." They are tricking us with their sophistry. So perhaps the virility of the rulers in this region has been stolen, and they think people are women. By God, the noble women of the Muslims would not let these American and Jewish whores defend them. Our goal is to work under the law of God Almighty and to defend the Noble Ka'ba, this great Ka'ba and this ancient house. God Almighty, in his Unity, put men into servitude on this earth, the greatest servitude, greater than those after faith and prayers, as the Prophet said: "Islam is the camel's head, prayer is his body, and *jihad* is the tip of his hump."[38] God Almighty does not accept any written prayer from us unless it is directed towards the Noble Ka'ba. He has chosen the best of men for himself: Abraham, father of the Prophets after our Prophet, to build it, and Ismail.[39] This is our goal, to liberate the lands of Islam from unbelief and to

---

Muhammad. Bakr nominated Umar as his successor. Umar ibn al-Khattab (c.581–644) was the second caliph of Islam (634–644), and was part of the emigration (*hijra*) to Medina in 622 (1 AH), and a companion of Muhammad. When war broke out between Mecca and Medina, Umar fought bravely, according to Sunni Muslims. Conversely, the Shia regard Umar as a coward and usurper, since in the disputed succession to Muhammad, he persecuted Ali ibn Ali Talib (598–661), Muhammad's cousin and son-in-law, and (according to the Shia), the first imam and the first rightful caliph. Sunnis, however, believe that Umar was a strong and wise ruler. During his Caliphate, the Islamic empire grew rapidly, absorbing Mesopotamia and parts of Persia from the Sassanids, and Egypt, Palestine, Syria, North Africa, and Armenia from the Byzantines.

37 From the *hadith* collection of al-Bukhari, vol. 5, book 59, no. 702.

38 From the *hadith* collection of ibn Hanbal, vol. 12, book 54, no. 21,054.

39 Ismail is the firstborn son of Abraham from his second wife Hagar, and an appointed Prophet of God. According to the Qur'an, the Ka'ba was built by Abraham and Ismail (Qur'an, 2:125–127).

apply the law of God Almighty in it until we meet Him and He is pleased with us.

To all those brothers who are still waiting for their situation to improve, without actually getting up and doing something about it, I tell you that the Americans are bargaining with us in silence. America and some of its agents in the region have bargained with us discreetly more than ten times, I tell you: [they say] shut up and we'll give you back your passport and possessions, we'll give you back your ID card, but shut up. These people think that people live in this world for its own sake, but they have forgotten that our existence has no meaning if we do not strive for the pleasure of God Almighty. So I tell you: this graph[40] shows the proportions of the population [of Saudi Arabia] according to their ages. For these last ten years people have been living in this thin section, from the moment they are born, they are the biggest sector of any normal society, then those who follow them, then the ones after that, and our *umma* for sixty to seventy years has been restricted to this section that is devoted to the service of religion and to *jihad* in particular. As is known, from birth to fifteen years of age people do not look after themselves, nor are they really aware of great events, and from the age of 25 and above people enter into family commitments, they go out and have working commitments. A man will have a wife and children, so his mind becomes more mature, but the ability to give becomes weaker. He tells you: "Who can I leave the children to? If I leave, who will look after them?," and so on. And if we're really honest we find that this section, between the ages of 15 to 25, is when people are able to wage *jihad*. In Afghanistan most of the *mujahidin* are of this age. So when the Americans came in during Muharram at the beginning of 1411 AH [c. July 1990], these young men were not really aware of the event, and juridical decrees were unfortunately issued. One country, and the Gulf states, took part in pressuring these scholars to issue such juridical decrees, which they claimed were temporary, and we spoke to those who issued the juridical decrees, such as Sheikh Muhammad bin Salih al-Uthaimain in his council and his house.[41] He said: "We did not issue a juridical decree, but when the Americans entered the country they got us together and said: 'You have to issue a juridi-

40 At this point on the videotape, bin Laden is referring to a graph that he is holding in his hand.
41 Muhammad bin Salih al-Uthaimain is a Saudi jurist from the highest council of scholars of Islamic studies in Saudi Arabia.

cal decree, or otherwise the youth will fight the American soldiers.'" I spoke to the Sheikh for a long time about the duty of issuing a juridical decree expelling them from the Higher Council of Scholars, but he told me in no uncertain terms, as God is my witness, he said: "Bin Laden, we in the Higher Council do not have the right to issue juridical decrees ourselves, but if those in power give us the permission to issue a *fatwa*, then we will do so. I'm sorry to say that this is our predicament." So when people are silent, this section of the demographic from 15 to 25 do not know the truth of the matter. We are now nine years after the invasion, and all of this section, except those who are 16, and all of the people in this section [of the graph], who have now reached the age of 34, have become intellectully mature, and can no longer give anything. As for the small section that can now give, people are now stopping from showing them what the situation is. If we are silent then what happened to al-Andalus will happen to us.[42] You go forward ten years and gradually the original zeal dissipates. It's a serious matter— people have to do whatever they can, with their voices, their pens, and their souls, to motivate our *umma*, and we, by the grace of God, have taken up this duty in our belief that we are obliged to do so. We are continuing on this path until we meet God Almighty.

In conclusion I direct some advice to all Muslims to contemplate God's Book. He is the Creator and He is the one who rescued us from the stinking depths of paganism in those dark ages. Our remedy is in the Qur'an and the traditions of the Prophet, and when people read the Qur'an they will be amazed at the slackness of so many people. Are they not reading the Qur'an, or are they reading it and not thinking about it? God Almighty says: "You who believe, do not take the Jews and Christians as allies: they are allies only to each other. Anyone who takes them as an ally becomes one of them—God does not guide such wrongdoers."[43] The men of knowledge said: "Whichever of them is in unbelief, becomes like them an infidel." And then the verse of the Qur'an that follows it says: "yet you [Prophet] will see the perverse at heart rushing to them for protection, saying, 'We are afraid fortune may turn against us.' But God may well bring about a triumph or some other event of

---

42 The reconquest of Moorish Spain by Christian rulers proceeded from 718 to 1492. It culmi-nated on January 2 1492, when the Catholic monarchs Ferdinand and Isabella expelled the last Moorish ruler, Boabdil of Granada, from the Iberian Peninsula.

43 Qur'an, 5:51.

His own making: then they will rue the secrets they harbored in their hearts."[44]

So I urge my Muslim brothers to read the Qur'an and to read the exegesis of these verses. God's book contains many warnings about befriending the infidels. They should read the exegesis of ibn Kathir, and the short exegesis of ibn Kathir for Sheikh Muhammad Nasim al-Rif'ai.[45] I say that the world has agreed to devour the Islamic world. The Crusader world has agreed to devour us, and nations have rallied together against us. And all we have left to cope with them, besides God Almighty, is the young men who have not been weighed down by the filth of the world. God Almighty has taught us how to respond to those who argue falsely that *jihad* should be postponed. He said: "When fighting was ordained for them, some of them feared men as much as, or even more than, they feared God, saying, 'Lord, why have you ordained fighting for us? If only you would give us just a little more time.'"[46] So whoever has realised that the rewards of this world are few and that the next world is better and more permanent, he is the one who responds to the command of God Almighty. Among the verses that we have been sent are: "You who believe, do not take the Jews and Christians as friends."[47] Ibn Kathir shows that Muslims discovered the hypocrites on the day when they defended and befriended the Jewish Bani Qainuqa.[48] And today Arab rulers are all befriending the Jews and Christians too, and people are still praising the enemies of Islam and Muslims. There is no strength or power save in God.

We need to make a serious and honest stand by which we can seek the pleasure of God Almighty, showing that this life, this world, is an illusory pleasure. Every Muslim can make haste, so he must do so, and he must look for the right places for *jihad* and for preparation to meet God Almighty—who

44 Qur'an, 5:52.

45 The Syrian ibn Kathir (1301–72) studied with ibn Taymiyya in Damascus, and went on to become a celebrated Islamic scholar. His commentary on the Qur'an remains one of the most widely used analyses of the Qur'an today, in particular by wahhabi/salafi muslims. The reference is to his commentary on Qur'an 63, the chapter on the hypocrites, at whose head was Abdullah ibn Ubayy ibn Salul. 46 Qur'an, 4:77.

47 Qur'an, 5:51.

48 The Bani Qainuqa was one of three Jewish tribes (the other two being the Bani Nadhir and the Bani Qurayza) who lived in Medina. In 627, the army of Mecca enlisted the tribe as allies in its attack on Medina, where Muhammad had emigrated in 622 following persecution and assassination attempts against him.

will be pleased with him. He must motivate himself and the believers with the words of the one who, after these great disasters, said:

> He prepared himself for battle
> For the matter was very grave.
> I will don my armor and defend her
> With teeth and stones
> Would you leave us beseiged by
> The infidel wolves, eating my wing?
> They have not ceased harrying us
> These sons of evil, from all sides
> So where is the nobleman among the sons of my religion
> Who will defend his noble brothers with the sword?
> Death is better than a life of humiliation
> And some shame none can erase.

I ask great God on high to bless the Muslims with a return to His noble religion, and to help the young men who have come out to wage *jihad* for His sake, to seek His pleasure.

Lord, give us patience and make us stand firm and help us against the infidels.

God is the one who reveals the book and directs the clouds. It is He who defeats factionalism and helps us against the different parties. Lord, bring us surely into this world and into the next world. Spare us the torment of the fire, and help us against the Americans and Israel and their supporters. You are capable of all things.

Our final prayer is praise be to God, lord of the worlds.

Pray to God and blessings upon Muhammad, his family, and his companions.

8

UNDER MULLAH OMAR

April 9 2001

This statement by bin Laden was recorded on an audiotape for the delegates to the International Conference of Deobandis, held at Taro Jaba near Peshawar, Pakistan, from April 9 to 11 2001.[1] This was an event attracting an estimated 500,000 delegates, most of them from madrassas *in Pakistan, with others attending from Afghanistan, India, and Iran, the UK, UAE, Libya, and Saudi Arabia. It was organized by the Jamiat-Ulema-I-Islam (JUI), headed by Maulana Fazlur Rehman, the high-ranking cleric and opposition leader in Pakistan's National Assembly, who had been a signatory to the* fatwa *issued by the World Islamic Front for Jihad (see above, Statement 6). Lauding the occasion as an example of the unity of the* umma *needed to fight the forces of global unbelief, bin Laden reminds them not only of their general duty to preach* jihad *for the sake of God, but presses them quite particularly to adopt a resolution calling for help to the Islamic Emirate of Afghanistan by all possible means. At this point, bin Laden was going out of his way to pledge allegiance to Mullah Omar, according him the supreme title of Commander of the Faithful, as if to dispel any notion of strain in his relationship with the Taliban.*

Praise be to God, who said: "You who believe, be mindful of God and make sure you devote yourselves to him, to your dying moment. Hold fast to God's rope all together; do not split into factions."[2]

---

1 The Deobandi are Muslims of South Asia and Afghanistan who follow *fiqh* (Islamic jurisprudence; see above, p. 12, n. 28). Their name comes from Deoband, India, where the *madrassa* Darul Uloom Deoband is located. The Deoband have reformist tendencies similar to those of the *wahhabi*. Many Deobandi *madrassas* were set up in Pakistan's remote and rural Northwest Frontier Province and Baluchistan, and run by semi-educated mullahs whose interpretation of *sharia* was influenced by Pashtunwali, the tribal code of the Pashtuns, and *wahhabi* doctrines. The *madrassas* were a key source of Taliban doctrine and volunteers.

2 Qur'an, 3:102–103.

Honorable scholars, peace be upon you, and all God's mercy and blessings.

You are gathered here from many different places and regions, representing a wide spectrum of the unity of Islam, which neither recognizes race nor colour; nor does it pay any heed to borders and walls.

By gathering here you are enraging all the global forces of unbelief who are taking every account of your meeting, and who are using every ploy to divide you and preoccupy you from the issues of your *umma*.

Honorable scholars, I write these lines to you, proud in the knowledge that there still remains in our *umma* a remnant of those who prevent corruption on this earth, after injustice and oppression have flooded the world.

Honorable scholars, it is no secret to you that a great duty has been thrown upon your shoulders, for you are the inheritors of the Prophets' legacy, you are the leaders among men, who publish your juridical decrees and work in the light of your guidance.

God has tested you by sending you at a time when tyranny prevails, when sanctity has been violated, and when holy sanctuaries have been occupied. He is asking you: what you have done about it?

Honorable scholars, I write these lines to you at a time when every single inch of our *umma*'s body is being stabbed by a spear, struck by a sword, or pierced by an arrow.

I write these lines to you at a time when even the blood of children and innocents has been deemed fair game, when the holy places of Islam have been violated in more than one place, under the supervision of the new world order and under the auspices of the United Nations, which has clearly become a tool with which the plans of global unbelief against Muslims are implemented. This is an organization that is overseeing with all its capabilities the annihilation and blockade of millions of Muslims under the sanctions, and yet still is not ashamed to talk about human rights!

According to al-Bukhari, God's Prophet said that "A woman entered the fire in Hira and didn't invite her to eat insects until she died."[3] That was in Hira, servants of God, so what about someone who has imprisoned a Muslim woman and imposed sanctions upon her until the death of ... how many people? Oh Lord, you should not be blamed for what these people have done,

3 From the *hadith* collection of al-Bukhari, vol. 3, book 40, no. 553.

and I apologize to you for the slackers among the Muslims who do not help their brothers that are suffering under sanctions.

Scholars of Islam, however deep this wound is, however terrible these crises, there is great trust in God, for He has promised the victory of his religion and has said that there still remains a group in the Prophet's Nation [the *mujahidin*] that knows the truth and fights for it.[4] The traitors and turn-coats cannot harm them until God's command comes at their hands.

For it is a duty, as you well know, to stand up for the truth and show the way to the waiting throngs who crane their necks to see you.

Teach them that there is no pride or victory except in *jihad* for the sake of God, by which the first generation [of Muslims] overcame this sense of estrangement and exile in the world [by becoming Muslims], and by which the latter generations are victorious and are able to overcome their own estrangement.

Teach them that *jihad* for the sake of God can only be done by a group that listens to and obeys a single commander, through which God unites them from their differences and disarray. As the Prophet said to al-Ash'ari, as related by al-Tirmidhi: "I command you to do five things that God has commanded me to do: to gather, to listen, to obey, to emigrate, and to perform *jihad* for His sake. For whoever splits the group even a little has removed the noose of Islam from his neck, unless he repents, and whoever calls for paganism is but one of the corpses of hell, even if he fasts and claims that he is a Muslim. So make the call for God, by which you have been raised up high as Muslim believers and servants of God."[5]

And when Hadhi asked him: for guidance, he said: "Commit to the com-munity of Muslims and their leader," as related by al-Bukhari and Muslim.[6]

And in the story of the group of companions, as related by al-Tirmidhi: "Three women cannot overcome the heart of a Muslim man who is sincere in

---

4 There is a saying of the Prophet about schisms which will divide the community of believers into 72 groups, but only one of the 72 will know the truth. The saying is apocryphal and not found in any of the eight trusted collections.

5 Quoted in ibn Qayiyim Juziyya, *A'lam Muwaqi'in an Kahb al-Alimin*, p. 108.

6 From the *hadith* collection of al-Bukhari, vol. 6, book 60, no. 108; and the *hadith* of Muslim, book 20, no. 4517. Both refer to a verse from the Qur'an (4:59) that is slightly misquoted by bin Laden; it does not speak of the "community of Muslims," just their leader.

his work for God and in his counsel to the leaders of the Muslims and the obligation of their community. For their prayer gives them good protection."

And he said: "Whoever dies without the pledge around his neck has died a pagan death", as related by Muslim.[7]

Teach them that there is no Islam without a spirit of kinship, no kinship without authority, and no authority without listening and obeying.

You yourselves know that God has ordained for this *umma* in these difficult times to establish an Islamic state that abides by God's law and raises the banner of His unity, and that is the Islamic Emirate of Afghanistan under the leadership of the Commander of the Faithful Mullah Muhammad Omar, may God keep him.

So it is your duty to call the people to commit to this Emirate and to help it in any way they possibly can, and to stand with it in the confrontation of this torrential current of global unbelief.

In order to achieve this we urge that you include in the final statements of the conference a call to help the Islamic Emirate of Afghanistan by all possible means:

Spiritually: that is, by motivating the youth to prepare themselves for *jihad* in Afghanistan. For with the current state of the *umma*, *jihad* has been affirmed as an individual duty.

Financially: that is, by calling on wealthy Muslims to donate money to the Emirate, to pay their alms to it, and to invest their businesses in it.

Verbally: that is, by issuing juridical decrees on the legitimacy of the Emirate and how it is a duty to help it.

On this occasion I assure you and Muslims across the world that I submit to God on the duty of allegiance to Mullah Muhammad Omar, and that I have taken my oath of allegiance to him. This act has great legitimacy in the texts, such as the Prophetic saying: "Commit to the community of Muslims and their leader" and "Whoever dies without the pledge around his neck has died a pagan death." For Mullah Omar is the ruler and rightful commander who rules by God's law in this age.

His great Islamic decisions, the most recent of which include the destruction of the idols,[8] the prohibition of growing opium, and the proud stance

7 From the *hadith* collection of Muslim, book 20, no. 4555.

8 In early March 2001, the Taliban started to destroy the millennia-old Buddha statues carved into the mountains in the Bamiyan valley of central Afghanistan.

against the campaign of global unbelief, are but some of his historic Islamic positions that affirm his honesty and steadfastness on the path, for which we admire him. God is his only reckoner.

Honorable scholars, the *umma* is expecting you to do what God has made your duty: to speak the truth and not to fear any blame. For God Almighty said: "[To] those who deliver God's messages and fear only Him and no other: God's reckoning is enough."[9] And He said: "God took a pledge from those who were given the Scripture—'Make it known to people; do not conceal it.'"[10]

In conclusion, please accept our sincere thanks and our prayers for steadfastness on this path.

We ask God to make both us and you aware of whom he said: "God will soon replace you with people He loves and who love Him, people who are humble towards the believers, hard on the disbelievers, and who strive in God's way without fearing anyone's reproach. Such is God's favor. He grants it to whoever He will. God has endless bounty and knowledge."[11]

Peace be with you and all God's mercy and blessings

Your brother,
Osama bin Muhammad bin Laden

9 Qur'an, 33:39.
10 Qur'an, 3:187.
11 Qur'an, 5:54. The first part of the verse reads "You who believe, if any of you go back on your faith ..."

9

TO OUR BROTHERS IN PAKISTAN

September 24 2001

On September 11 2001 coordinated aerial attacks were launched on the Pentagon and the World Trade Centre. On September 16, with the War on Terror announced by the American administration, the military ruler of Pakistan, General Pervez Musharraf, promised full cooperation with the United States in hunting down bin Laden as the author of the assaults, and with the War on Terror. Popular riots and demonstrations against this pledge of allegiance followed over the next days, violently repressed in Karachi. On September 24 a statement was faxed to al-Jazeera, consisting of a typewritten note hand-signed with bin Laden's full name, Osama bin Muhammad bin Laden. It was read out by an al-Jazeera announcer, while a still picture showing a copy of the statement occupied the entire screen. Voicing his grief for those who had died protesting the Pakistani military's alignment with the United States, bin Laden made no reference to September 11, simply expressing confidence that Pakistan would rise up to defend Islam against the 'neo-Crusader-Jewish campaign led by Bush, the biggest Crusader, under the banner of the cross'. The American President had used the word 'crusade' several times to describe the American response to 9/11, declaring on the White House lawn on September 16: 'This crusade, this war on terrorism is going to take a while. The American people must be patient. I'm going to be patient.'[1]

"Those who believe in God and His messengers are the truthful ones who will bear witness before their Lord: they will have their reward and their light."[2] To our Muslim brothers in Pakistan, peace be upon you and all God's mercy and blessings.

1 See Miles, *Al-Jazeera*, pp. 110–11.
2 Qur'an, 57:19.

It was with great sorrow that I learned the news of our Muslim brothers who were killed in Karachi while expressing their opposition to the hostility of the American Crusader forces and their allies against the Muslim lands of Pakistan and Afghanistan.[3] We ask God to accept them among the martyrs and place them among the prophets, martyrs, and the pious, true, and good men. We ask Him to provide their families with endurance and solace, to bless them, along with their sons and property, and to give them the greatest reward. The children they left behind are my children and with the permission of God Almighty I will provide for them.

It is no surprise that the Muslim nation in Pakistan will rise up to defend its Islam, for it is considered Islam's first line of defense in this region, just as Afghanistan was considered the first line of defense for itself and Pakistan against the Russian invasion more than twenty years ago.

We urge these brothers to be considered the first martyrs in the battle of Islam against the neo-Crusader-Jewish campaign led by Bush, the biggest Crusader, under the banner of the cross. This battle can be seen as merely one of the battles of eternal Islam.

We exhort our Muslim brothers in Pakistan to fight with all their might to prevent the American Crusader forces from conquering Pakistan and Afghanistan. The Prophet said: "Before the Day of Resurrection God will punish with calamity whoever did not fight, was not prepared to fight or was not successful in fighting," as related by Abu Dawud.[4]

Dear brothers, I bring you the good news that we are established on the path of *jihad* for God, following God's Prophet, with the Afghan people, who are heroes and believers, and under the command of our Emir the proud *mujahid* Commander of the Faithful Mullah Muhammad Omar.[5]

---

3 Pakistanis demonstrated for days following President Pervez Musharraf's announcement on September 16 2001 that he would cooperate with the American military in the "war on terror". The protests, which took place across Pakistan, degenerated into riots in Karachi, where at least three men were killed by police. See http://www.guardian.co.uk/september11/story/0,11209, 601645,00.html.

4 From the *hadith* collection of Abu Dawud, book 14, no. 2,497. Abu Dawud (817–88), from Sijistan in Khurasan, was a noted collector of *hadith*. He wrote the third of the six canonical *hadith* collections recognized by Sunni Muslims, the *Sunan Abu Dawud*, comprising 4,800 *hadith*.

5 See above, Headnote to Statement 8, p. 95.

We ask God to help us defeat the forces of unbelief and tyranny, and to smash the neo-Crusader-Jewish alliance in the lands of Pakistan and Afghanistan. "If God helps you, no one can overcome you; if He forsakes you, who else can help you?"[6]

Your brother in Islam,
Osama bin Muhammad bin Laden

6 Qur'an, 3:160.

10

THE WINDS OF FAITH

October 7 2001

By the end of September 2001, it was clear that a US attack on the Taliban regime in Afghanistan, held responsible for not delivering bin Laden to American justice, was imminent. On October 7, a massive bombing assault was launched by the United States, with British and French air support. A few days earlier, a video was delivered to al-Jazeera correspondent Taysir Alluni at the television network's offices in Kabul, containing a message from bin Laden. Pre-recorded, it was sent in order to be transmitted immediately after the commencement of hostilities, and was broadcast on the first night of the war, a few hours after Bush had addressed the nation in Washington, and some minutes after Blair had spoken in Britain.[1]

Once again, as with the bombings in Riyadh and Khobar, Nairobi and Dar-es-Salaam, bin Laden praises—but does not take responsibility for—9/11, which he describes as divine retribution for American-backed atrocities. These include the deaths of Iraqis as a result of UN-imposed economic sanctions, and the suffering of Palestinians under Israeli rule: he lists key towns in the West Bank and Gaza Strip that had been the targets of severe Israeli repression since the start of the second (or "al-Aqsa") intifada in September 2000. Drawing attention to the disparity between the world's silence in the face of such crimes—he includes the atomic destruction visited on non-Muslim Japan in 1945—and the international outcry whenever Americans are killed, he ends by saying that the world has now been split into two camps: one of faith, the other of unbelief.

Praise be to God. We beseech Him for help and forgiveness. We seek refuge in God from the evil of our souls and our bad deeds. He whom God guides will not go astray, and he whom He leads astray can have no guide. I testify

---

1 See Miles, *Al-Jazeera*, pp. 126–32.

that there is no god but God alone, Who has no partners, and that Muhammad is His slave and messenger.

God has struck America at its Achilles heel and destroyed its greatest buildings, praise and blessings to Him. America has been filled with terror from north to south and from east to west, praise and blessings to God. What America is tasting today is but a fraction of what we have tasted for decades. For over eighty years our *umma* has endured this humiliation and contempt. Its sons have been killed, its blood has been shed, its holy sanctuaries have been violated, all in a manner contrary to that revealed by God, without anyone listening or responding. So when God Almighty granted success to one of the vanguard groups of Islam, He opened the way for them to destroy America utterly. I pray to God Almighty to lift them up to the highest Paradise. When these men retaliated on behalf of their poor, oppressed sons, their brothers and sisters in Palestine and in many of the other lands of Islam, the whole world cried out. The infidels cried out [in protest at 9/11], and the hypocrites followed them.[2]

Until this point, a million innocent children have been killed in Iraq, although they had done nothing wrong. But we do not hear anyone condemning this, nor do we hear any juridical decree from the official scholars. As I speak, Israeli tanks and bulldozers are going in and wreaking havoc and sin in Palestine—in Jenin, in Ramallah, in Rafah, in Beit Jala[3]—and other parts of the domain of Islam, and we do not hear anyone protesting or even lifting a finger to stop it. But when after eighty years the sword comes down on America, the hypocrites rise up to lament these killers who have scorned the blood, honor, and holy places of Muslims.

The very least you can say about these people is that they are immoral, dissolute, apostates, who help the butcher slaughter his victim and help the oppressor against the innocent child. May God Almighty protect me against them, and may He give them what they deserve.

I tell you, the matter is very clear. After this event, now that senior officials in the United States of America—starting with the head of global unbelief,

2 Here, bin Laden is saying that the infidels—that is, the rest of the world—cried out in protest at 9/11. They were then followed by all those who bin Laden sees as Muslim hypocrites, who abandon the cause of jihad by also condemning 9/11.

3 Jenin, Ramallah, and Beit Jala in the West Bank, and Rafah in the Gaza Strip, were all towns administered by the Palestinian Authority.

Bush, and those with him—have spoken, every Muslim should rise up and defend his religion. They [the Americans] have come with their men and their horses, conspiring against us until even the countries that belong to Islam joined their side against this group [the 9/11 attackers] who came with their religion to God Almighty, refusing to abandon their religion. They came to fight Islam and its people on the pretext of fighting terrorism. Hundreds of thousands, young and old, were killed in Japan, the most distant land—but this is not a war crime, just an issue to be looked into. And today, in Iraq, the same applies. But when a few of them were killed in Nairobi and Dar es-Salaam, they bombed Afghanistan and Iraq and the hypocrites all stood behind the head of global unbelief, behind the Hubal[4] of the modern age, America and its supporters. I tell you that these events have split the entire world into two camps: one of faith, with no hypocrites, and one of unbelief—may God protect us from it. Every Muslim must give what he can to help his religion. The winds of faith and change have blown to remove falsehood from the peninsula of Muhammad.

I have only a few words for America and its people: I swear by God Almighty Who raised the heavens without effort that neither America nor anyone who lives there will enjoy safety until safety becomes a reality for us living in Palestine and before all the infidel armies leave the land of Muhammad. God is greatest and glory to Islam.

Peace be upon you and all God's mercy and blessings.

---

4 Before Islam, the moon god Hubal was worshipped as the pagan manifestation of the "One God", the chief among 360 idols worshipped at the Ka'ba in Mecca. Muhammad liberated his tribe from their pagan worship by smashing all the idols, including Hubal.

11

TERROR FOR TERROR

October 21 2001

In the second week of the American bombing of Afghanistan, when the Taliban were still in control of most of the country, one of al-Jazeera's most celebrated reporters, Taysir Alluni, head of the network's bureau in Kabul during the Afghanistan war, and recipient of bin Laden's communication on the outbreak of the war, interviewed bin Laden at an undisclosed location south of Kabul. The interview was conducted on October 20 2001, but aired for the first time some three months later, on January 31 2002. A Syrian-born Spanish national, Alluni caused great discomfort to the Pentagon by his televised reportage of civilian deaths under America's blitz of Afghan towns and villages. Al-Jazeera offices were bombed by US aircraft, and he was seized and beaten up by Northern Alliance forces when they entered Kabul. On returning to Spain, he was arrested by Spanish police in September 2003, on charges of supporting al-Qaeda, and imprisoned without trial, including a spell of 119 days in solitary confinement, until his release in March 2005.[1]

Alluni is the most penetrating and informed reporter to have interviewed with bin Laden, as at once a devout Muslim and a wary professional, and his questions and objections make this the most revealing exchange with bin Laden on record. Alluni pressed bin Laden hard on his justifications of terrorism, both in particular—the attacks of 9/11—and in general. In reply, bin Laden insists that historically the United States has been the intruder and aggressor in the Middle East, and that in striking back at it, Muslims are acting in self-defense: many civilians, in Palestine, Iraq, and elsewhere have died at its hands. The Qur'an forbids the killing of women and children, or innocent civilians, but enjoins retaliation if infidels commit such crimes, as they have done. Such terror, says bin Laden, must therefore be met by terror: "America and Israel practise ill-advised terrorism, and we practise terrorism that is a good act, because it deters those from killing our children in Palestine and other places". Nevertheless, he observes, the attacks of 9/11 had targeted military and financial institutions, not schools or residences. They inflicted great economic damage on the US—bin

<hr />

1 See Miles, *Al-Jazeera*, pp. 305–13.

Laden overestimates this—and have forced the West to talk suddenly of the need to do something about Palestine. Muslims everywhere, he continues, should rally to the cause of the defensive jihad, not just in the Middle East, but in Southeast Asia, the Subcontinent and as far afield as Mauritania. With the outcome of the war over Afghanistan still undecided, bin Laden's references to Arab regimes continue to be very prudent: though condemning unspecified governments for befriending Christians and Jews, he remarks that "it is no use to name names", and expresses no more than disappointment at the stance of Pakistan in the conflict. As for America's allies, why should countries like Japan, Australia, or Germany become involved in the war? The only possible reason is that they wish to be Crusaders too, as Richard of England, Louis of France, and Barbarossa of Germany were once in the Middle Ages.

OBL: May God greet you.

TA: *A question that is repeated on the tongues of a lot of people all around the world: The USA claims that it has convincing proof of your involvement in the events of New York and Washington. What is your answer to that?*

OBL: Praise be to God, the Lord of the Worlds. May God's Peace and Blessings be upon Muhammad, his pure family and his noble Companions. To proceed: As far as concerns [America's] description of these attacks as terrorist acts, that description is wrong. These young men, for whom God has created a path, have shifted the battle to the heart of the United States, and they have destroyed its most outstanding landmarks, its economic and military landmarks, by the grace of God. And they have done this because of our words—and we have previously incited and roused them to action—in self-defense, defense of our brothers and sons in Palestine, and in order to free our holy sanctuaries. And if inciting for these reasons is terrorism, and if killing those that kill our sons is terrorism, then let history witness that we are terrorists.

TA: *Alright, but Sheikh, those who monitor your speeches and documents have noted the oath you have given recently, in which you have said, word for word: "I swear to Almighty God who raised the heavens, that neither America nor anyone who lives there will be able to dream of security until we live it as a reality in Palestine." So, it is easy for any follower of these events to make a connection between the terrorist events that happened in New York and Washington, and your previous statement. So what is your opinion on these observations?*

OBL: Making connections is easy. If this implies that we have incited these attacks, then yes, we've been inciting for years, and we have released decrees and documents concerning this issue, and other incitements which were published and broadcast in the media. So if they mean, or if you mean, that there is a connection as a result of our incitement, then that is true. So we incite, and incitement is a duty—and God has asked it from the best of humans, the Prophet.

God said: "Then fight [O Muhammad] in the Cause of God, you are not held responsible except for yourself, and incite the believers [to fight along with you]—it may be that God will restrain the evil might of the disbelievers. And God is Stronger in Might and Stronger in punishing."[2]

And what He meant is fighting and combat against the disbelievers. So this connection is indeed right. We have incited and urged the killing of Americans and Jews. That is true.

TA: *Now, Sheikh Osama bin Laden, the al-Qaeda organization is today facing a state that dominates the world militarily, politically, and technologically. The material capabilities of the al-Qaeda organization don't come remotely close to the capabilities of the USA, so by what logic can an organization of this kind defeat the USA—militarily, for example?*

OBL: I say that the battle isn't between the al-Qaeda organization and the global Crusaders. Rather, the battle is between Muslims—the people of Islam—and the global Crusaders. And that organization, with the grace of God, used to work with our Afghan *mujahidin* brothers,[3] and people used to

2 Qur'an, 4:84.

3 Bin Laden uses the term "al-Qaeda" very rarely throughout his statements; indeed, this is the first instance of its use in this collection. In May 2001, he issued a communiqué to "members of al-Qaeda". The term itself (the "foundation" or "the base") is a common Arabic word used by Islamic radicals drawn from all over the Muslim world to fight alongside local resistance groups in the Soviet-Afghan War. It was also a term used by those who believed that their struggle would not end with the Soviet withdrawal from Afghanistan. Bin Laden's mentor Abdallah Azzam referred to a "vanguard" that "constitutes the strong foundation [*"al-qaeda al-sulbah"*] for the expected society." (See Rohan Gunaratna, *Inside Al-Qaeda* [Hurst, 2002], p. 3.) The first reference to "al-Qaeda" appeared in a CIA report in 1996; it was used by the State Department for the first time in 1998 (who described it not as an organized group, but rather as "an operational hub, predominantly for like-minded Sunni extremists". In Jason Burke's view, "it is important to avoid seeing 'al-Qaeda' as a coherent and structured terrorist organization with cells everywhere ... This would be profoundly to misconceive the nature of modern Islamic militancy"; *Al-Qaeda*, pp. 5–6.

ask us: "How will you defeat the Soviet Empire?" And at that time, the Soviet Empire was a mighty power that scared the whole world—NATO used to shake in fear in front of the Soviet Empire. So where now is that strong force that God sent to us and our *mujahidin* brothers?

The Soviet Empire has become—with God's grace—a figment of the imagination. Today, there is no more Soviet Empire; it split into smaller states and only Russia is left. So the One God, who sustained us with one of His helping Hands and stabilized us to defeat the Soviet Empire, is capable of sustaining us again and of allowing us to defeat America on the same land, and with the same sayings. So we believe that the defeat of America is something achievable—with the permission of God—and it is easier for us—with the permission of God—than the defeat of the Soviet Empire previously.

TA: *How do you think it's easy? Why do you think it's easier?*

OBL: We have already fought them—like our brothers who have engaged in battle with the Americans, as in Somalia. We have not yet found a significant force of note. There is a great aura about America, which it uses to scare people before it engages in battle. So our brothers that were here in Afghanistan tried to overcome this, and God has cleared the path for them through some of the *mujahidin* in Somalia. So America left, dragging behind it tails of humiliation, defeat, and loss, without looking back; it retreated unexpectedly, and it forgot all that great media enthusiasm about the New World Order, and how it was the master of that order, and could do whatever it pleased. It forgot all that and picked up its armies and retreated in defeat, with God's grace. So we fought against the Russians for ten years from 1979 until 1989; we then we continued against the Communists in Afghanistan. Today we are at the end of the second week [of the bombing], and what a difference there is, like night and day, between both battles. So we implore God to sustain us with one of His helping Hands and to break America, for He is capable of that.

TA: *In connection to Afghanistan, you have said that you will defeat America in this country. Don't you think that the existence of the al-Qaeda organization on the land of Afghanistan is making the Afghan people pay a high price?*

OBL: Well, this view is partial and incomplete, and only from one perspective. When we first arrived in Afghanistan, and when assistance came to aid the *mujahidin* victory, after the Russians entered, in 1399 AH [1979], the Saudi government officially asked us to not enter Afghanistan. Due to my arrival in Afghanistan, and due to my family's closeness to the Saudi governmental system, a letter arrived commanding Osama not to enter Afghanistan, and to stay with the immigrants in Peshawar, because if the Russians were to capture or imprison him, it would be construed as proof of Saudi backing for the *mujahidin* against the Soviet Empire. During that time, the whole world shook in fear from the Soviet Empire—and I am not exaggerating about this prohibition [to enter Afghanistan], as it was damaging to the Saudi government, from their point of view. They were forced to issue the prohibition as a result of their policies. So when we joined the Afghans for the first time, we endured what we had to endure, in our desire to awaken the Islamic self, and to safeguard the Muslim children and offspring here, and for victory for the religion. And this is a duty incumbent on all Muslims, not just the Afghans. So if I, or some of my brothers that came to perform *jihad*, have acted upon this duty, [which is] to bring victory to our brothers in Palestine, it does not mean that bin Laden alone has to endure this, but that it is a duty on all of our *umma* to do so, because it is in the Way of God, and *jihad* is today obligatory for all of us, Afghans and others, and it is true that they endure, but this is an Islamic duty for them and others to support this ... [*interjection by Taysir Alluni*]

TA: *Let's get back to the question ...*

OBL: ... and in addition to the matters related to the bombing of the Afghans [and those who] say that [the bombing] is only because of us [the *mujahidin*], the reason for it is not down to me. America didn't start by taking my money and didn't hurt me personally at all, but it made claims about me as a result of our incitement against the Jews and the Americans, in protection of our Islamic *umma*. And it is a known fact that America is against the establishment of any Islamic state; the Commander of the Faithful [Mullah Omar] has declared this on more than one occasion, as have a lot of the prominent students, which shows that they are being targeted because of their religion, not just because of the presence of Osama bin Laden. And as Omar has said, the British invaded and were defeated in Afghanistan before bin Laden was to be found here,[4] and the Russians came, before we did, and now the Americans have come, and we implore God to defeat them like He defeated their previous allies.

TA: *Let us go back to the transgressions that happened in New York and Washington. What is your analysis about what happened—its effect on America, and its effect on the Islamic world? Please note that this question is in two parts.*

OBL: I say that the events that happened on Tuesday September 11 in New York and Washington are truly great events by any measure, and their repercussions are not yet over. And if the fall of the twin towers was a huge event, then consider the events that followed it ... let us talk about the economic effects, which are still continuing. According to their own admission, the share of the losses on the Wall Street Market reached 16 per cent.[5] They said that this number is a record, which has never happened since the market opened more than 230 years ago. A collapse of this scale has never happened before. The gross amount that is traded in that market reaches $4 trillion. So if we multiply 16 per cent by $4 trillion to find out the loss that affected the stocks, it reaches $640 billion of losses from stocks, with God's grace, an amount that is equivalent to the budget of Sudan for 640 years. They have lost this through an attack that happened with the permission of God, lasting one hour only. The daily income of the American nation is $20 billion. The first week [after the attack] they didn't work at all as a result of the psychological shock of the attack, and even today some still don't work because of it. So if you multiply $20 billion by 1 week, it comes to $140 billion—and the actual amount is even bigger than this. If you add it to the $640 billion, we've reached how much? Approximately

---

4 British forces invaded Afghanistan three times, resulting in three "Anglo-Afghan Wars": on each occasion, they were unable to hold their positions in Afghanistan, having to settle for diplomatic concessions and making full retreats. The first war, in 1838, led to British retreat from Kabul four years later: of the 4,500 military and 12,000 camp followers, all but a few dozen were killed on the way back to India. The second war, from 1878–81, was almost as disastrous and again led to the British pulling out of Kabul; in 1919, the third war followed the assassination of the then ruler, Habibullah Khan.

5 When the stock markets reopened on September 17 2001 (the longest closure since the 1929 Great Depression), the Dow Jones Industrial Average (DJIA) stock market index fell 684 points (7.1 per cent) to 8920, its biggest-ever single-day decline. By the end of the week, it had fallen 1369.7 points, or 14.3 per cent, its largest one-week point decline in history. US stocks lost $1.2 trillion in value for the week.

$800 billion. The cost of building and construction losses? Let us say more than $30 billion. So far, they have fired or liquidated more than 170,000 employees from airline companies, including airfreight companies and commercial airlines.[6] American studies and analysis have mentioned that 70 per cent of the American people are still suffering from depression and psychological trauma as a result of the incident of the two towers, and the attack on the Defense Ministry, the Pentagon. One of the well-known American hotel companies, Intercontinental, has fired 20,000 employees, thanks to God's grace. These repercussions cannot be calculated by anyone, due to their very large—and increasing—scale, multitude, and complexity, so watch as the amount reaches no less than $1 trillion by the lowest estimate, due to these successful and blessed attacks. We implore God to accept those brothers within the ranks of the martyrs, and to admit them to the highest levels of Paradise.

But I mention that there are also other events that took place, bigger, greater, and more dangerous than the collapse of the towers. It is that this Western civilization, which is backed by America, has lost its values and appeal. The immense materialistic towers, which preach Freedom, Human Rights, and Equality, were destroyed. These values were revealed as a total mockery, as was made clear when the US government interfered and banned the media outlets from airing our words (which don't exceed a few minutes), because they felt that the truth started to appear to the American people,[7] and that we aren't really terrorists in the way they want to define the term, but rather because we

6 North American airspace was closed after the 9/11 attacks; when it reopened, air travel significantly decreased. The US airline industry has still not fully recovered.

7 On October 10 2001, the White House announced that it had asked the five major US television networks, ABC, CBS, CNN, Fox, and NBC, to censor al-Qaeda footage, "which meant in practical terms material from al-Jazeera, since it was the only network in a position to deliver it." In a 30-minute conference call, National Security Adviser Condoleezza Rice "urged all the American network chiefs not to screen videos of bin Laden." (Miles, *Al-Jazeera*, p. 116). All five networks agreed they would vet all their clips from the war in Afghanistan, and would not use al-Jazeera's footage live. On October 11, White House press secretary Ari Fleischer "asked America's newspaper editors not to publish full transcripts of bin Laden's or al-Qaeda's statements." Britain also tried to exert pressure on the press, Tony Blair summoning the BBC, ITN, and Sky News to Downing Street, where his media adviser, Alistair Campbell, "gave them a stern lesson on what would constitute acceptable reporting ... Any more bin Laden footage which materialized, the three networks were told, would have to be censored, for there was a 'real danger that they could be sending out messages to terrorist members of their network'." Hugh Miles notes that "These calls for censorship demonstrated a dim appreciation of al-Qaeda's proven ability to manipulate modern communications," something articulated by bin Laden himself later in this interview, when he ridicules American and British efforts to censor him.

are being violated in Palestine, in Iraq, in Lebanon, in Sudan, in Somalia, in Kashmir, in the Philippines, and throughout the world, and that this is a reaction from the young men of our *umma* against the violations of the British Government.[8] So, they declared what they declared, and they ordered what they ordered, and they forgot everything they mentioned about free speech, and unbiased opinion and all those matters. So I say that freedom and human rights in America have been sent to the guillotine with no prospect of return, unless these values are quickly reinstated. The government will take the American people and the West in general into a choking life, into an unsupportable hell, because of the fact that it has very strong ties with and are under the payroll of, the Zionist lobby, which serves the needs of Israel, which kills our sons and our children without right so that it can keep on ruling with total control.

TA: *There has been a clash of opinions regarding the effects of these actions [the 9/11 attacks] on the Islamic world. There are some who have made statements that have been accepted in the Islamic world: you hear all the official statements saying that those attacks are terrorist actions and that these people are innocent civilians, and that the attacks are unacceptable, and that they don't concord with the modern Islamic religion, and so on. So what is your opinion on what you have been able to follow of news concerning the Islamic world's reaction to the network that you own or run all around the world?*

OBL: I say that the events have proved very clearly the magnitude of the terrorism America inflicts in the world. Bush admitted that there can only be two kinds of people: one kind being Bush and his followers; and any nation that doesn't follow the Bush government, or the World Crusade, is guaranteed to be included with the terrorists.[9] What kind of terrorism is more terrifying and evident than this? A lot of countries that can't speak for them-

8 Here, bin Laden may be referring to the Sykes–Picot agreement of May 16 1916, in which the Middle East was secretly divided up into British and French areas of control; and to the Balfour dclaration of November 2 1917, which outlined the British government's support for Zionist plans for a Jewish "national home" in Palestine.

9 At a press conference in Washington on November 6 2001, President George W Bush stated that there is no room for neutrality in the "war against terrorism": "Over time it's going to be important for nations to know they will be held accountable for inactivity," he said. "You're either with us or against us in the fight against terror."

selves followed this powerful world terrorism, and were also forced to say at the beginning that they were with him [Bush], even though they all know without any doubt that we are fighting to protect our brothers and our holy sanctuaries. So the declarations of the leaders, both in the East and West, stated that the causes and roots of terrorism have to be removed. When they were asked to identify these causes, they mentioned the Palestine issue. We are part of a rightful cause, but in fear of America, these countries could not say that our cause is just—so they call us terrorists, and then ask us to fix the Palestine issue. In light of these recent attacks and what ensued from them, Bush and Blair quickly reacted and said that now is the time to create an independent nation for Palestine.[10] Amazing! And yet there was apparently no suitable time in the last 10 years to address this issue before the [9/11] attacks happened? They evidently won't wisen up without the language of beatings and killings. So, as they kill us, without a doubt we have to kill them, until we obtain a balance in terror. This is the first time, in recent years, that the balance of terror has evened out between the Muslims and the Americans; previously, the Americans did to us whatever they pleased, and the victim wasn't even allowed to complain. And then Clinton comes out and tells us that Israel has the right to defend itself, after the slaughter of Qana. They didn't even give the Israelis a warning! And when the new President Bush came [into office] with Minister Colin Powell, they said within the first months of their rule that they would move the US embassy from Tel Aviv to Jerusalem, and that Jerusalem would be the eternal capital of Israel, and the Congress and the Senate applauded them.[11] That is hypocrisy beyond any hypocrisy, and a clear violation. They will not come to their senses unless the attacks fall on their heads and, with the grace of God, until the battle has moved inside America. We will strive to maintain the fight until victory is attained or until we meet God [through martyrdom].

10 On October 11 2001, the Bush administration unveiled a new blueprint for the Middle East, with Jerusalem as a shared Israeli–Palestinian capital. Two days later, Blair said that military action in Afghanistan had to be balanced with progress in the Israeli–Palestinian peace process. In October, Israel launched its most far-reaching military operation since the start of the second *intifada*, entering several West Bank towns.

11 During his presidential campaign in 2000, George W Bush vowed to move the US embassy in Israel from Tel Aviv to Jerusalem. This decision has been deferred at six-monthly intervals since the US Congress passed a bill approving the move in 1995. The move continues to be postponed; as of 2005, the embassy remains in Tel Aviv.

TA: *But Sheikh, from what I see from your answers, you always concentrate on Palestine and the Palestinian issue. So let me ask you this question. In your latest statements, or more precisely in a statement that appeared a few years ago that preached the killing of Jews and Crusaders (and we remember that the title had between quotes a famous hadith, "Expel the polytheists from the Arabian peninsula"),[12] you concentrated on the expulsion of the Americans from the Arabian peninsula. But in your latest statements we see less mention of this. You have instead foregrounded the Palestinian issue—or as you like to call it the "Aqsa issue"[13]—and have relegated, so to speak, the issue of Saudi Arabia. So what is your opinion or argument on this matter?*

OBL: I say that *jihad* is without doubt mandatory for all Muslims, to free al-Aqsa, or to save the weak in Palestine, Lebanon, Iraq, and all Islamic lands; there is no doubt that freeing the Arabian peninsula from the polytheists is also compulsory. And concerning this talk about Osama pushing the Palestinian issue to the forefront: that is not true. The humble servant [bin Laden] made a speech in the year 1407 AH [1986] that urged Muslims to boycott American products, and I used to say that the Americans take our money and give it to the Jews, so they can kill our children with it in Palestine. Such boycotting is mandatory for all Muslims, as is freeing the Arabian peninsula from the polytheists, and there are a lot of mandatory things in *jihad*—such as Kashmir,[14] for example, and the battlefront that was created a few years ago, the title of which was called: "The World Islamic Front for *Jihad* Against the Jews and Crusaders." So our mention of these two issues [Palestine and Saudi Arabia] is of the utmost importance. Some of the events of recent times might foreground a certain issue, so we move in that direction, without ignoring the other.

12 The quotation is from the *hadith* collection of al-Bukhari, no. 2,932; also found in the *hadith* collection of Muslim, no. 3,089. Here, Alluni refers to Statement 3 (see above, pp. 23–30), in whose title this *hadith* is incorporated.

13 The "al-Aqsa issue" refers to the "al-Aqsa" mosque, which together with the Dome of the Rock, constitute the third holiest site in Islam; by extension, bin Laden uses "al-Aqsa" to denote all Palestine. The Israeli Prime Minister Ariel Sharon's controversial visit to the Temple Mount in September 2000 is generally held to have the beginning of the second Palestinian *intifada*, or "uprising", also known as the "al-Aqsa *intifada*".

14 From the late 1980s armed militancy in the majority-Muslim region of Jammu and Kashmir has grown significantly, transforming what began as an essentially indigenous popular challenge to Indian rule. Many militant groups fighting in Kashmir are based in Pakistan, and Pakistan-administered Kashmir, and have ties with radical Islamic organizations, including al-Qaeda, Hamas, and the Taliban. One of the most prominent groups, Lashkar-e-Taiba ("The Army of the Pure") has defined its agenda as the restoration of Islamic rule throughout India.

TA: *What are the events that have pushed you towards the Palestinian issue?*

OBL: In recent times, the new rise of the blessed *intifada*, the *intifada* of Rajab.[15] It helped focus us on this issue, and was the biggest reason for our foregrounding it; in this we only strive to do our duty so as not to feel religiously ashamed. All the above issues affect each other. The attack on the Americans concerning the Palestine issue helps in regards to the Saudi Arabia issue, and vice versa, as does attacking the Americans because they are considered to be a protective shield for the Jews in the areas of Tabuk[16] and the eastern regions of Saudi Arabia.

TA: *Alright Sheikh, now, to move on to the Jews and the Crusaders: you have as you say written legal rulings concerning the duty of* jihad *against the Jews and Crusaders. From what we have seen from other legal rulings written by scholars, there are some that support you, but there are also some who have argued and protested against your legal rulings. They ask what grounds we can have for killing a Jew, just because of his religion? Or the Crusader or the Nazarene [Christian], should he be killed first because of his religion? Your legal rulings have differed from and don't have any relation to the legal rulings of the other scholars.*

OBL: I will say that these issues have resulted in a lot of legal rulings from the Muslims. In Pakistan, there are a lot of the legal rulings issued by scholars (one of the greatest being *Mufti* Nizamuddin Shamzai),[17] and in the land of the Arabs, more precisely Saudi Arabia, a lot of approved and repeated legal rulings appeared. One of the best of them is that of Sheikh Hamud bin Abdallah bin Uqla al-Shu'aybi,[18] may God bless his life, who is one of the greatest scholars in Saudi Arabia; he urges the duty of fighting the Americans and fighting the Israelis in Palestine, making [attacks on] their blood and wealth permissible. There also appeared a *fatwa* from Sheikh Sulayman

---

15 The "*intifada* of Rajab" refers to the Second Palestinian or "al-Aqsa" *intifada*, which began in Rajab 1421/October 2000 (Rajab is the seventh month in the Islamic calendar, two months before Ramadan).

16 Tabuk is a northern province of Saudi Arabia, close to Jordan.

17 *Mufti* Nizamuddin Shamzai (1952–2004) was a senior Sunni Muslim cleric. He extended support to the Taliban, issuing a *fatwa* against the USA after its invasion of Afghanistan in October 2001. He was killed in a drive-by shooting in Karachi, sparking a riot by Sunni Muslims.

18 Hamud bin Abdallah bin Uqla al-Shu'aybi is a Saudi Arabian cleric whose legal rulings deem the entire American population culpable for attacking the Muslim community.

al-Ulwan,[19] and a book written by one of the students of knowledge, The Truth About the Modern Crusader Wars, in which he denounced those who say that this fighting is invalid, and those who disagree with true Islamic law, and spoke against other wrongdoings. Yes, he wrote well, and we implore God to bless him.

TA: *What about the killing of innocent civilians?*

OBL: It is very strange for Americans and other educated people to talk about the killing of innocent civilians. I mean, who said that our children and civilians are not innocents, and that the shedding of their blood is permissible? Whenever we kill their civilians, the whole world yells at us from east to west, and America starts putting pressure on its allies and puppets. Who said that our blood isn't blood and that their blood is blood? What about the people that have been killed in our lands for decades? More than 1,000,000 children died in Iraq, and they are still dying, so why do we not hear people that cry or protest, or anyone who reassures or anyone who sends condolences? And it is said in truth by our Prophet in the authentic *hadith*: "A woman has entered hell because of a cat she tied up without giving it food or without letting it eat from the blessings of the earth."[20] And that is just because of a cat, so what about the millions of Muslims that are getting killed? Where are the [comments of the] educated? Where are the writers? Where are the scholars? Where are the free? Where are the ones who have one atom of faith in their hearts? How is it that these people are moved when civilians die in America, and not when we are being killed everyday? Everyday in Palestine, children are killed. There is a great misconception in people today, which needs to be corrected by every means possible, and the numbers [who have died] need to be recalculated. There is a strong instinct in humans to lean towards the powerful without knowing it, so when they talk about us, they know we will not answer them, and if they stand in the ranks of the governments and the Americans, they will think that they will feel something that we don't.

A long time ago, one of the kings that ruled ancient Arabs killed an Arab,[21] and people became inured to the idea that kings kill humans. So the brother

19 Sulayman al-Ulwan is a cleric whose legal rulings emphasize the exclusivity of Islam.
20 From the *hadith* collection of Muslim, book 4, no. 1,975.
21 This is a reference to a story from the *hadith* collection of Muslim, book 42, no. 7,148.

of the deceased went to the king and killed him. After this victory, the people were astonished, and said: "You are able to kill a king just because of your brother?" So who permitted the rule of that king?" These are both equal souls, and the blood of Muslims is equal, but in those times some people's blood was more equal than others, so that gentle man replied: "My brother is my king." And today all our brothers in Palestine are our kings, so we kill the kings of disbelief and the kings of the Crusaders, and the civilians among the disbelievers, in response to the amount of our sons they kill: this is correct in both religion and logic.

TA: *So you say that this is an eye for an eye? They kill our innocents, so we kill theirs?*

OBL: Yes, so we kill their innocents—this is valid both religiously and logically. But some of the people who talk about this issue, discuss it from a religious point of view ...

TA: *What is their proof?*

OBL: They say that the killing of innocents is wrong and invalid, and for proof, they say that the Prophet forbade the killing of children and women, and that is true. It is valid and has been laid down by the Prophet in an authentic Tradition ...

TA: *This is precisely what I'm talking about! This is exactly what I'm asking you about!*

OBL: ... but this forbidding of killing children and innocents is not set in stone, and there are other writings that uphold it.

God's saying: "And if you punish (your enemy, O you believers in the Oneness of God), then punish them with the like of that with which you were afflicted ..."[22]

The scholars and people of the knowledge, amongst them Sahib al-Ikhtiyarat [ibn Taymiyya] and ibn al-Qayyim, and Shawaani, and many others, and Qurtubi[23]—may God bless him—in his Qur'an commentary, say that if the

---

22 Qur'an, 16:126. The verse concludes: "but it is best to stand fast."

23 For ibn Taymiyya, see above, p. 5, n. 7. The Syrian ibn al-Qayyim (1292–1350) was a student and disciple of ibn Taymiyya, who wrote a number of Qur'anic commentaries and analyses of the prophetic traditions. For al-Qurtubi, see above, pp. 60–61, n. 8.

disbelievers were to kill our children and women, then we should not feel ashamed to do the same to them, mainly to deter them from trying to kill our children and women again. And that is from a religious perspective, and those who speak without any knowledge of Islamic law, saying that killing a child is not valid and whatnot, and in the full knowledge that those young men, for whom God has cleared the way, didn't set out to kill children, but rather attacked the biggest center of military power in the world, the Pentagon, which contains more than 64,000 workers, a military base which has a big concentration of army and intelligence ... [*interjection by Taysir Alluni*]

TA: *What about the World Trade Center ...?*

OBL: As for the World Trade Center, the ones who were attacked and who died in it were part of a financial power. It wasn't a children's school! Neither was it a residence. And the general consensus is that most of the people who were in the towers were men that backed the biggest financial force in the world, which spreads mischief throughout the world. And those individuals should stand before God, and rethink and redo their calculations. We treat others like they treat us. Those who kill our women and our innocent, we kill their women and innocent, until they stop doing so.

TA: *Moving on, Sheikh Osama, the media and security services say that you lead a network with a very big reach, which some say spreads over 40 or 50 countries, and that the al-Qaeda organization has substantial resources, which you use a lot to order missions. [They say] that you support many Islamic organizations or movements, which some describe as "terrorist". The question that we ask you is, what is the magnitude of the involvement of the al-Qaeda organization, and what is the type of involvement that exists between the al-Qaeda organization and Osama bin Laden?*

OBL: I say in response to this what I have stated before, that this matter isn't about any specific person, and that it is not about the al-Qaeda organization. We are the children of an Islamic Nation, with the Prophet Muhammad as its leader; our Lord is one, our Prophet is one, our direction of prayer is one, we are one *umma*, and our Book [the Qur'an] is one. And this blessed Book, together with the *hadith* of our noble Prophet, has religiously commanded us with the brotherhood of faith, and all the true believers are brothers. So the situation is not as the West portrays it: that there exists an "organization" with a specific name, such as "al-Qaeda", and so on. That particular name is very old, and came about quite independently of me. Brother Abu Ubaida al-Banshiri[24] created a military base to train the young men to fight against the Soviet empire, which was truly vicious, arrogant, brutal, and terrorized the faithful. So this place was called "The Base", as in a training base, and the name grew from this. We aren't separated from the *umma*. We are the children of an *umma*, and an inseparable part of it, from those public demonstrations which spread from the Far East, from the Philippines, to Indonesia, to Malaysia, to India, to Pakistan, reaching Mauritania—and so we are discussing the conscience of our *umma*.

These young men that have sacrificed themselves in New York and Washington, these are the ones that speak the truth about the conscience of our *umma*, and they are its living conscience, which sees that it is imperative to take revenge against the evildoers and transgressors and criminals and terrorists, who terrorize the true believers. So, not all terrorism is restrained or ill-advised. There is terrorism that is ill-advised and there is terrorism that is a good act. So, in their definition of the word, if a criminal or a thief feels that he is terrorized by the police, do we label the police terrorists and say they terrorized the thief? No, the terrorism of the police towards the criminals is a good act, and the terrorism that is being exercised by the criminals against the true believers is wrong and ill-advised. So America and Israel practise ill-advised terrorism, and we practise good terrorism, because it deters those from killing our children in Palestine and other places.

TA: *Now, Sheikh Osama, what is your strategy concerning the Arab states? We have seen that some Arab states have discussed what happened in New York and Washington and have backed the American claims against you, opposing what happened in New York and Washington. Some Arab states were very strong in their criticism. The latest speech of the Saudi Interior Minister, for example, warned against you personally, and warned against the following of your curriculum and what you say. So do you have a specific strategy for Arab nations? And what is your answer to the latest declaration by the Saudi Interior Minister?*

24 Abu Ubaida al-Banshiri was an instructor at the Egyptian-run "al-Farooq" training camp in Khost during the Soviet-Afghan war. A Cairene who made his name fighting against the Northern Alliance and the Soviets, he became bin Laden's military coordinator. He died in 1996 in a boat accident in Africa.

OBL: I assure you that we are a part of this *umma*, that our goal is the victory of the *umma*, and struggle is to remove mischief, inequality, irresponsibility, and to emphasize the importance of avoiding these things, and the removal of the man-made laws that America has forced on its collaborators in the region, so that our *umma* can be ruled by the Book that has been sent down by its Creator, God. So I listened to some of the words of the Interior Minister and he blamed us directly, also saying that "those people call Muslims disbelievers"—we seek God's refuge from this. We think that Muslims are Muslims, and we don't call any Muslims disbelievers unless they specifically commit one of the well-known great sins of Islam, in full knowledge that this is one of the wrongful actions in religion.

So I say that, in general, our concern is that our *umma* unites either under the Words of the Book of God or His Prophet, and that this nation should establish the righteous caliphate[25] of our *umma*, which has been prophesised by our Prophet in his authentic *hadith*:[26] that the righteous caliph will return with the permission of God. The *umma* is asked to unite itself in the face of this Crusaders' campaign, the strongest, most powerful, and most ferocious Crusaders' campaign to fall on the Islamic *umma* since the dawn of Islamic history. There have been past Crusader wars, but there have never been campaigns like this one before.

So Bush has declared in his own words: "Crusade attack."[27] The odd thing about this is that he has taken the words right out of our mouth [that this war is a crusade]. Some people also believe what is said about us, like the [Saudi] Minister's words, that we declare other Muslims to be unbelievers—we seek God's refuge from this. But, when Bush speaks, people make apologies for him and they say that he didn't mean to say that this war is a Crusade, even though he himself said that it was! So the world today is split in two parts, as Bush said: either you are with us, or you are with terrorism. Either you are with the

25 "Caliph" ("successor") is a title indicating the successor to the Prophet Muhammad; an alternative title is "Commander of the Faithful" (amir ul-muminin). The holder of the title claims spiritual and temporal authority over all Muslims. The title has been in abeyance since the abolition of the Ottoman Caliphate in 1924. For many radical Islamist movements, who identify the root cause of the Muslim world's problems as a decline in spirituality and religious observance, the restoration of the Caliphate is a priority.
26 From the *hadith* collection of al-Tirmidhi.
27 Bin Laden pronounced this phrase in English, in referring to President Bush's September 16 2001 speech on the lawn of the White House.

Crusade, or you are with Islam. Bush's image today is of him being in the front of the line, yelling and carrying his big cross. And I swear by God Almighty, that whoever walks behind Bush or his plan has rejected the teachings of Muhammad, and this ruling is one of the clearest rulings in the Book of God and the *hadith* of the Prophet; and I advise, as I and many other scholars have advised before, that the proof for this is the Almighty's words while addressing to the true believers: "O you who believe! Take not the Jews and the Christians as allies, they are but allies to one another. And if any amongst you takes them as allies, then surely he is one of them ..." and this is the ruling: "And if any amongst you takes them as allies, then surely he is one of them ..."[28] "Verily, God guides not those people who are evil-doers."[29]

The scholars of knowledge have said that whoever takes the disbelievers as allies has become a disbeliever, and the biggest sign of alliance is favoring their victory, in speaking, discussing, and writing. So whoever walks behind Bush and his campaign against the Muslims has disbelieved in God and His Prophet. God also says in the verse that follows the previous one:

> Yet you [Prophet] will see the perverse at heart rushing to them for protection, saying, "We are afraid fortune may turn against us." But God may well bring about triumph or some other event of His own making: then they will rue the secrets they harbored in their hearts, and the believers will say, "Are these the men who swore by God using their strongest oaths that they were with you? All they did was in vain: they have lost everything.[30]

Ibn Kathir has said in his commentary:[31] Many companions of the Prophet didn't know that the spearhead of the hypocrites was the disbeliever and hypocrite, Abdallah ibn Ubayy ibn Salul. So when arguments occurred between the Muslims and the Jews, and when the Prophet decided to punish the Jews, the spearhead of hypocrisy [Abdallah ibn Salul] moved and stood with the Jews, in the way of the Prophet, so these verses were handed down for this reason. So

---

28 Qur'an, 5:51.

29 Qur'an, 3:86. The first sentence of the verse reads: "Why would God guide people who deny the truth after they have believed and acknowledged that the Messenger is true, and after they have been shown clear proof?"

30 Qur'an, 5:52–53.

31 See above, p. 93, n. 45.

those who the disbelievers ally themselves with have disbelieved in God and His Prophet. I add the following verse, to stress what I previously stated, because he who allies himself with the disbelievers has become an apostate, as this verse shows:

> You who believe, if any of you go back on your faith, God will soon replace you with people He loves and who love Him, people who are humble towards the believers, hard on the disbelievers, and who strive in God's way without fearing anyone's reproach. Such is God's favor. He grants it to whoever He will. God has endless bounty and knowledge.[32]

So I tell the Muslims to be very wary and careful about befriending Jews and Christians. Whoever helps them do so with one word, let him be devout to God, and to renew his faith so he can repent about what he did ...

TA: *Even one word?*

OBL: Even one word, whoever upholds them with one word ...

TA: *Falls into this apostasy?*

OBL: Falls into apostasy, a terrible apostasy, and there is no might nor power except with God ...

TA: *But Sheikh, a big part of our* umma *falls into this ...*

OBL: No ... No, it is not a big part. This is the rule of God, and a clear statement in His generous Book, and it is one of the clearest of rulings.

TA: *And the Arab and Islamic governments ...?*

OBL: Anyone that ... there is no point naming names. If you know the truth, you will know its followers. You will not know the truth by looking at men; it is in the Book of God, which is one of the constants for us. If the world becomes full of people who want to change things in it, that won't affect us or change our convictions at all. It is either truth or it is mischief. Either it is Islam or either is it disbelief. So these verses ... [*interjection by Taysir Alluni*]

32 Qur'an, 5:54.

TA: *Just to make things clear, if you please. Isn't it possible to forgive those states that are considered to be impotent and weak? Let us take the state of Qatar, for example.[33] The state of Qatar is a small state, whose Foreign Minister once said that he is surrounded by a supreme force that can wipe out his existence with ease. Therefore, he is forced to become an ally of America and others. Isn't it possible to forgive such states? Like Kuwait, for example? Or Bahrain?*

OBL: Concerning these matters, the matters that concern Islam, the matters concerning the killing of true believers and Muslims ... what these aforementioned states do, who use compulsion as an excuse, is not the same compulsion that is allowed by Islamic law. Their type of compulsion is not permitted by religion. Now let's say (for example), if the Emir of Qatar came and he ordered one of his men to kill your son, and we then asked that soldier why he killed the son of brother Taysir, he says: "Well brother, I have been forced to do it! And you know, brother Taysir, you mean a great deal to me, but I have been compelled to kill your son!" So the blood of the Muslims will be shed with these kind of excuses, with this kind of compulsion that isn't backed by Islamic law. The soul of that soldier isn't better than the soul of your son. If he is killed, he will be killed by violation and oppression, but he [the soldier] is not allowed to obey the tyrant by killing your son. So this kind of compulsion isn't permitted by religion.

TA: *What is your opinion about what is being said concerning your analogies and the "Clash of Civilizations?" Your constant use and repetition of the word "Crusade" and "Crusader" shows that you uphold this saying, the "Clash of Civilizations".[34]*

OBL: I say that there is no doubt about this. This [Clash of Civilizations] is a very clear matter, proven in the Qur'an and the traditions of the Prophet, and any true believer who claims to be faithful shouldn't doubt these truths, no matter what anybody says about them. What goes for us is whatever is found

33 The Emir of Qatar, Hamad bin Khalifa al-Thani, founded al-Jazeera in February 1996, providing it with start-up funds of $137 million; the network still receives financial aid from the Qatari government.

34 This phrase was originally coined in an article by Samuel Huntington entitled "The Clash of Civilizations?" (*Foreign Affairs*, 1993), in which he proposed that in years to come: "The clash of civilizations will dominate global politics. The fault lines between civilizations will be the battle lines of the future " a thesis he later expanded into his book *The Clash of Civilizations and the Remaking of World Order* (Usborne, 1996).

in the Book of God and the *hadith* of the Prophet. But the Jews and America have come up with a fairytale that they transmit to the Muslims, and they've unfortunately been followed by the local rulers [of the Muslims] and a lot of people who are close to them, by using "world peace" as an excuse. That is a fairytale that has no substance whatsoever!

TA: ... *Peace?*

OBL: The peace that they foist on Muslims is in order to ready and prepare them to be slaughtered, and still the killing goes on. So, if we try to defend ourselves, they call us "terrorists", and the slaughter still goes on. So it is said that the Prophet observed in truth: "The Hour will not come until the Muslims fight the Jews and kill them. When a Jew hides behind a rock or a tree, it will say: 'O Muslim, O Servant of God! There is a Jew behind me, come and kill him!' All the trees will do this except the boxthorn, because it is the tree of the Jews."[35] And whoever claims that there is permanent peace between us and the Jews has disbelieved what has been sent down through Muhammad; the battle is between us and the enemies of Islam, and it will go on until the Hour—and as for the so-called "Peace" or "Peace award", that is a gimmick that is given to the biggest bloodshedders. That man, Begin, the perpetrator of the Deir Yassin massacre, was awarded the [Nobel] Peace Prize. That traitor Anwar al-Sadat, the one that sold the land and the [Palestinian] issue and the blood of the martyrs, was awarded the Peace Prize.[36]

So we are in a time, as is said in truth by our Prophet in this authentic tradition: "There will come upon the people years of deceit in which the liar will be believed, the truthful disbelieved, the treacherous trusted and the trustworthy held to be treacherous, and the despicable will speak out. It was said: 'Who are the despicable ones?' He said: 'The lowly, ignoble man who speaks out about public affairs.'"[37] And unfortunately, this situation is

---

35 From the *hadith* collection of al-Bukhari, no. 3,593.

36 Yasser Arafat, Shimon Peres, and Yitzhak Rabin were awarded the Nobel Peace Prize for the 1993 Oslo Accords. In 1978, the Egyptian Prime Minister Anwar al-Sadat and Israeli Prime Minister Menachem Begin received the award for negotiating peace between Egypt and Israel. Begin is widely held responsible for an attack on the Palestinian village of Deir Yassin, on April 9 1948, by members of the radical Zionist organizations Irgun and Lehi. Over 100 people were killed.

37 From the *hadith* collection of Ahmad, no. 7,899, and of ibn Majah, no. 4,036. This is a highly suspect saying of the Prophet because of its sources.

prevailing upon the Islamic world today, with its big leaders, and its famous rulers—it is a trick; they [the rulers] trick people and lie to them, but, with the permission of God, God's liberation and release is close, and the promised victory is close—God willing.

TA: *So we can deduce from the words of Sheikh Osama bin Laden that he refers to the ordeal that Afghanistan is going through right now, and the war that America is waging with its allies, that it falls within the compass of a battle between the Crusaders—or those whom you call Crusaders—and Islam. How do you see an exit from this ordeal?*

OBL: As I have mentioned today, we are in a strong and brutal battle, between us and the Jews, with Israel being the spearhead, and its backers among the Zionists and Crusaders. So we have not hesitated to kill the Jews who conquered the sanctuary of our Prophet.[38] And those who kill our children, women, and brothers night and day, and whoever stands in the aggressors' ranks, has only himself to blame. So if you mean: how can we exit from this ordeal, this is in the hands of others. It is like this: we have been violated, so our first duty is to remove this violation. So whoever violated us, let him remove the violation. It appears to us, from the writing of the Prophet, that we will have to fight the Jews under his name and on this land, in this blessed land which contains the sanctuary of our Prophet [Palestine]. And the United States has involved itself and its people again and again for more than 53 years, and recognized and supported Israel, and dispatched a general air supply line in 1393 AH [1973] during the days of Nixon, from America to Tel Aviv, with weapons, aid, and men, which affected the outcome of the battle,[39] so how could we not fight it [America]? It is incumbent upon on every Muslim to fight it. So if it wants to survive, we have offered some simple advice, but America has terrorized and it has erased its own values.

The Americans have made laughable claims. They said that there are hidden messages intended for terrorists in bin Laden's statements. It is as if we are living in a time of carrier-pigeons, without the existence of telephones, without

---

38 Jerusalem, Islam's third holiest site.

39 America kept Israel resupplied during the 1973 Arab-Israeli war (October 6–24 1973), also known as the "Yom Kippur" or "Ramadan" war. Furious at this airlift, which enabled Israel to defeat Egyptian and Syrian forces, the Arab world imposed the 1973 oil embargo against the United States, Western Europe, and Japan.

travelers, without the Internet, without regular mail, without faxes, without email. This is just farcical; words which belittle people's intellects. We swore that America could never dream of safety, until safety becomes a reality for us living in Palestine. That has exposed the American government, and that it exists as an agent of Israel, and puts Israel's needs before the needs of its own people. So the situation is straightforward: America won't be able to leave this ordeal unless it pulls out of the Arabian peninsula, and it ceases its meddling in Palestine, and throughout the Islamic world. If we gave this equation to any child in any American school, he would easily solve it within a second. But, according to Bush's actions, the equation won't be solved unless our swords fall on their heads, with the permission of God.

TA: *Alright, Sheikh Osama, do you have any message you want to address to the viewers?*

OBL: I say: Concerning this ordeal and this battle between Islam and the Crusaders, I want to reiterate that we will continue this *jihad* and the incitement of our *umma* to it, until we bring it about, while blessing us, and the war, as we have been promised, that is going on between us and the Jews. So any nation that joins the Jewish trenches has only itself to blame, as Sheikh Sulaiman Abu-Ghaith[40] has declared in some of his previous statements concerning America and Britain; he did not set this in stone, but indeed gave some of other nations a chance to review their calculations. What is Japan's concern? What is making Japan join this hard, strong, and ferocious war? It is a blatant violation of our children in Palestine, and Japan didn't predict that it would be at war with us, so it should review its position. What is the concern of Australia in the farthest south with the case of these weak Afghans? And these weak Palestinians? What is Germany's concern with this war? Besides disbelief, this is a war which, like previous wars, is reviving the Crusades. Richard the Lionheart, Barbarossa from Germany, and Louis from France— the case is similar today, when they all immediately went forward the day Bush

40 The Kuwaiti Sulaiman Abu Ghaith (1965/6–) is regarded as al-Qaeda's official spokesman. He first came to prominence during the 1990–1 Iraqi occupation of Kuwait, which he denounced. After the Gulf War, he became a vocal critic of the Kuwaiti government and royal family, demanding the institution of *sharia* law, whereupon he was banned from giving sermons. He met bin Laden in Afghanistan in 2000, and came to worldwide attention following the 9/11 attacks, appearing in two widely circulated videos in October 2001, in which he defended the attacks and threatened reprisals for the US invasion of Afghanistan.

lifted the cross. The Crusader nations went forward. What is the concern of the Arab nations in this Crusaders' War? They involved themselves with it openly, without disguise, in broad daylight. They have accepted the rule of the cross. Everyone that supports Bush with one word, even without offering help and aid, and whatever else that is described as facilities, is nothing but a traitor. They change its name, by not calling it military aid, and then join in killing our sons—and they tell us that this is not facilitation and help? How can we believe that this system is collecting aid to help the weak Afghans, all the while openly giving Saudi Arabia to the Americans and their allies? How can we believe these states, when they are one of the main reasons for the deaths of more than one million children?

I say to the people who walk behind these rulers, don't you have hearts? Don't you have faith? How can you declare faith while you are helping those fornicating disbelievers against the children of Islam. You help them against our children in Iraq and Palestine. I say to those who talk about the innocents in America, they haven't tasted yet the heat of the loss of children, and they haven't seen the look on the faces of the children in Palestine and elsewhere. By what right are our families in Palestine denied safety? The helicopters hunt them while they are in their homes, while they are amongst their women and children; everyday the bodies and wounded are removed. So these fools cry about the deaths of Americans, and they don't cry about the deaths of our sons? Don't they fear receiving a similar punishment? And our Prophet said in truth: "He who does not supply the *jihad*, or well look after a warrior's family when he is away, will be smitten by God with a sudden calamity."[41] So let them fear God, and repent, and let them remove the siege from those innocent children. So the Westerners are free to choose. Europe wants to enter the war—that is their prerogative, but our duty is to fight whoever is in the ranks of the Jews. America and the American people are free; they have entered the trench, and they will get what is coming to them.

And concerning us, we are in worship and in *jihad*. It is said in truth about our Prophet: "Verily a man's standing firm in the ranks for one hour (in *jihad*) in the Way of God, the Mighty and Majestic, is more virtuous than 60 years of worship."[42] So what can be better than this? Under the pride of God, we

---

41 From the *hadith* collection of Abu Dawud, 2:2497.
42 From the *hadith* collection of al-Bayhaqi.

ask the Almighty to accept us and you, and concerning the Muslims, I tell them to trust in the victory of God, and to answer the call of God, and the order of His Prophet, with *jihad* against world unbelief. And I swear by God, happy are those who are martyred today, happy are those who are honored to stand under the banner of Muhammad, under the banner of Islam, to fight the world Crusade. So let every person amongst them come forward to fight those Jews and Americans, the killing of whom is among the most important duties and most pressing things, and let them remember the teaching of the Prophet, when he said to the child ibn Abbas: "Young man, I shall teach you some words of advice: Be mindful of God, and God will protect you. Be mindful of God, and you will find Him in front of you. If you ask, ask of God; If you seek help, seek help of God. Know that if the world were to gather together to benefit you with anything, it would benefit you only with something that God had already prescribed for you, and that if they gather together to harm you with anything, they would harm you only with something God had already prescribed for you. The pens have been lifted and the pages have dried."[43] So don't discuss the killing of Americans with anyone, trust in the divine favor of God, and remember your appointment with God in the presence of the Best of Prophets.

And in conclusion, I would like to dedicate a call to the brothers in Pakistan, to the position of the Pakistani government, with much sorrow. Pakistan is one of the biggest pillars of this unlucky alliance, this Crusaders' Alliance. So the movement of our brothers in Pakistan will lead—with the permission of God—to a big attack on this unlucky Crusader Alliance. So whoever has stood with America, by aiding them with material or immaterial things, this constitutes disbelief and the biggest rejection of the creed and teachings of Islam. And it is a duty incumbent on the brothers in Pakistan to make a strong and purposeful move, for the sake of victory of the religion of God, and the victory of the Prophet Muhammad. And the Islam of today is calling them—Oh Islam! Oh Islam! Oh Islam!

---

43 From the *hadith* collection of al-Tirmidhi.

IV

WAR IN AFGHANISTAN 2001–2002

12

CRUSADER WARS

November 3 2001

Delivered as a letter to al-Jazeera's Kabul bureau ten days before the entry of the Northern Alliance into the city, this statement was read out by an al-Jazeera newscaster and videoed for transmission, off-air, to its headquarters in Doha. However, the transmission was intercepted by the Pentagon; when it was broadcast, a US spokesman was on hand to present the American side of the case.[1] US concern was not unfounded, as public support for the war in Afghanistan, always low in the Arab world, was weakening more generally, due in part to al-Jazeera's harrowing broadcasts of airstrikes against civilian targets; by contrast, American television networks lacked pictures with such dramatic impact. Short of fluent Arabic speakers, the Department of State summoned out of retirement Christopher Ross, former US Ambassador to Syria, who read out a long prepared statement in reponse to bin Laden's message, and offered replies to questions posed by the al-Jazeera anchor.[2]

Bin Laden's statement is set against the "enormous media commotion" in the wake of 9/11. His leading argument is that the American response to 9/11 constitutes clear evidence that the war being waged by the United States and its allies is a Crusade against Islam. The onslaught on Afghanistan is not an isolated conflict, but the latest episode in a long chain of aggressions, which started at the end of World War One and the colonial division of the Middle East between European powers. Seeking to muster the widest possible support for resistance to the US attack on the Taliban regime, bin Laden unfolds his most sweeping analysis to date of 20th century history, from the time when "the entire Islamic world fell under the British, French, and Italian governments", to the role of the United Nations—responsible for the partition of Palestine and the fate of Muslims in Bosnia—as a successor to the Crusader states, and the latest vehicle of their designs. For bin Laden, Kashmir and Chechnya are battlefronts as well as Palestine and Iraq. Courting

---

1 See Miles, *Al-Jazeera*, pp. 161–3.
2 Miles, *Al-Jazeera*, pp. 162–3.

official opinion in Khartoum and Jakarta, bin Laden even includes Southern Sudan and East Timor—neither of which have majority Muslim populations—as victims of plots against Islam. "The enmity between us and the infidels is a doctrinal one," states bin Laden, and all Muslims must stand together in resistance to the "war of annihilation" long waged against them.

Praise be to God. We beseech Him for help and forgiveness. We seek refuge in God from the evil of our souls and our bad deeds. He whom God guides will not go astray, and he whom He leads astray can have no guide. I testify that there is no god but God alone, who has no equal.

In the midst of these tumultuous events, after these great attacks that struck America at its heart in New York and in Washington, there was enormous and unprecedented media coverage, which has conveyed people's views on events. People have been divided into two camps: those who support the attacks against American arrogance and tyranny, and those who condemn them. Shortly afterwards, when the United States launched this unjust campaign against the Islamic Emirate of Afghanistan, people were again divided: one section supported these unjust campaigns, and the other condemned and rejected them.

These major events that have divided people into two camps are of great concern to Muslims, since many of the rulings pertain to them, and they are of significant relevance as concerns Islam and acts contrary to it. It is therefore necessary for Muslims to understand the nature and reality of this struggle, in order to decide which side to take.

The mass demonstrations from the easternmost point in the Islamic world to its westernmost point, from Indonesia, the Philippines, Bangladesh, India, and Pakistan to the Arab world and finally to Nigeria and Mauritania, show that this war is fundamentally religious in nature. The Muslims of the East have responded to and sympathized with other Muslims against the Crusader people of the West. Those who try to hide this clear and evident reality, which the entire world knows to be true, are deceiving the Islamic nation and trying to deflect their attention from the real nature of the struggle. This reality is established in the book of God Almighty and in the teachings of our Prophet. We cannot ignore this enmity between us and the infidels, since it is a doctrinal one. We must show loyalty to the believers and those who profess that there is no god but God, and we must renounce the idolaters, infidels, and heretics (against whom I seek God's help). God Almighty said "And the Jews and Christians will not be satisfied with you until you follow their faith."[3] So the issue is one of faith and doctrine, not of a "war on terror," as Bush and Blair depict it. Many thieves belonging to this nation were captured, and no one moved. However, these masses from the furthest east to the furthest west do not move for bin Laden's sake but for the sake of their religion, because they know that they are in the right, and that they are resisting the strongest, fiercest, most dangerous and violent Crusader campaign against Islam since Muhammad was sent. In light of this clear and evident fact Muslims must know where they stand in relation to this war.

After American politicians had spoken, and American newspapers and television channels overflowed with evident Crusader hatred in this campaign against Islam and its people, Bush left no room for the doubts or media opinion. He stated clearly that this war is a Crusader war. He said this in front of the whole world so as to emphasize this fact. Those who maintain that this war is against terrorism, what is this terrorism that they talk about at a time when people of the *umma* have been slaughtered for decades, in response to which we do not hear a single voice or action of resistance? When the victim starts to avenge the innocent children in Palestine, Iraq, southern Sudan, Somalia, Kashmir, and the Philippines, the hypocrites and rulers' jurists stand up and defend this blatant unbelief—I seek God's help against them all. The masses have understood the issue, but some still flatter those who have conspired with the infidels to prevent the Islamic nation from undertaking the duty of *jihad* to reassert the authority of God's word. For the truth is that Bush has fought a Crusade and raised his banner high, and stood at the front of the procession. All those who have stood behind him in this campaign have committed one of the ten contraventions of Islam. The people of knowledge have agreed that allegiance to the infidels and their supporters against the believers is among the biggest contraventions of Islam. There is no strength or power save with God.

Look at this war that began some days ago against Afghanistan. Is it a single, unrelated event, or is it part of a long series of Crusader wars against the Islamic world? Since World War One, which ended over 83 years ago, the

---

3 Qur'an, 2:120. The verse goes on: "Say, 'God's guidance is the only true guidance.' If you were to follow their desires after the knowledge that has come to you, you would find no one to protect you from God or help you."

entire Islamic world has fallen under the Crusader banners, under the British, French, and Italian governments. They divided up the whole world between them, and Palestine fell into the hands of the British. From that day to this, more than 83 years later, our brothers and sons have been tortured in Palestine. Hundreds of thousands of them have been killed, hundreds of thousands detained. Then look at recent events, for example in Chechnya. This Muslim nation has been attacked by the Russian predator, which believes in the Orthodox Christian creed. The Russians have exterminated an entire people and forced them into the mountains, where they have been devoured by disease and freezing winter, and yet no one has done anything about it. Then there is the genocidal war in Bosnia that took place in front of the whole world's eyes and ears. For several years, even in the heart of Europe, our brothers were murdered, our women raped, and our children slaughtered in the safe havens of the United Nations, and with its knowledge and cooperation. Those who refer our tragedies today to the United Nations, and want us to resolve them through it, are hypocrites who are trying to deceive God and His Prophet and those who believe. Aren't our tragedies actually a result of the United Nations' actions? Who issued the decision to partition Palestine in 1947 and gave Islamic lands to the Jews? It was the United Nations. Those who maintain that they are the leaders of the Arabs and are still part of the United Nations are contravening what was revealed to Muhammad. Those who refer to international legitimacy have contravened the legitimacy of the Qur'an and the teachings of the Prophet. For it is at the hands of this same United Nations that we have suffered so much. No Muslim, nor anyone in his right mind, should appeal to it under any circumstances. It is merely an agent of this crime by which we are massacred daily, and which it does nothing to stop. For more than fifty years, our brothers in Kashmir have been tortured, slaughtered, killed, and raped. Their blood has been shed and their houses broken into, and yet still the United Nations has done nothing. And today, without any evidence, the United Nations passes resolutions in support of tyrannical, oppressive America, against these poor people who have emerged from a ruinous war at the hands of the Soviet Union. Look at the second Chechen war that is still going on today. An entire people is once again being subjected to war by this Russian predator. The humanitarian agencies, even the American ones, have called on President Clinton to stop supporting Russia, but Clinton says that this will not serve

American interests. A year ago Putin called on the Crusaders and Jews to stand by him, telling them that they should support him and thank him for waging war against Islam. The enemies are speaking very clearly and yet the leaders of the region hide and are ashamed to support their brothers. And what is worse, they even prevent Muslims from helping their own brothers. Look at the position of the West and the United Nations with regard to events in Indonesia. They moved to partition the most populous nation in the Islamic world. That criminal Kofi Annan publicly put pressure on the Indonesian government, telling it that it had 24 hours to partition and separate East Timor from Indonesia, otherwise he would have to introduce military forces to do it. The Crusader armies of Australia were on the shores of Indonesia and they did in fact intervene and separate East Timor, which is part of the Islamic world.[4]

We should therefore see events not as isolated incidents, but as part of a long chain of conspiracies, a war of annihilation in all senses of the word. On the pretext of reconstruction, 13,000 of our brothers were killed in Somalia. In southern Sudan hundreds of thousands were killed,[5] and as for events in Palestine and Iraq, words cannot do them justice. More than a million children have been killed in Iraq, and the killing continues. As for what is happening these days in Palestine, may God help us. No one, not even animals, would put up with what is going on there. One of my confidants told me that he saw a butcher slaughtering a camel in front of another camel. When it saw the blood coming out of its brother it got so agitated and enraged that it bit the man's hand and tore it right off.

---

4 Along with the Philippines, East Timor is one of only two Roman Catholic-majority countries in Asia. A former Portuguese colony, the territory was invaded and annexed by Indonesia in 1976, with the tacit support of the US government. During Indonesian rule, an estimated 100,000 to 250,000 people were killed, out of an initial population of 600,000 at the time of the invasion. Following a UN-sponsored agreement between Indonesia, Portugal, and the US, on August 30 1999, a UN-supervised popular referendum was held, the East Timorese voted for full independence from Indonesia, but violent clashes, instigated primarily by anti-independence militias (aided by elements of the Indonesian military) broke out soon afterwards. Peacekeepers led by Australia were brought in to restore order. These were later replaced by UN forces. Independence was recognized on May 20 2002.

5 The second Sudanese civil war started in 1983, following President Nimeiry's dissolution of the three federal states in the predominantly Christian South, and the introduction of *sharia* law there. The result was one of the longest lasting and deadly wars of the late 20th century. An estimated 1.9 million civilians were killed in southern Sudan, with another four million displaced.

How can the poor mothers in Palestine bear the murder of their children at the hands of the oppressive Jewish policemen, with American support, American aeroplanes and tanks? Those who distinguish between America and Israel are true enemies of the *umma*. They are traitors who have betrayed God, His Prophet, and their *umma*, who have betrayed its trust and who numb its senses. These battles cannot be seen in isolation from each other, but must be seen as part of the great series of fierce and ugly Crusader wars against Islam.

Every Muslim must stand under the banner that says: "There is no god but God and Muhammad is His Prophet."[6] I would remind you of what our Prophet told ibn Abbas, may God be pleased with him. He said: "Boy, I am going to teach you something. Remember God, and He will protect you. Remember God, and you will find him on your side. If you ask for something, ask God. If you seek help, seek God's help. You should know that if the *umma* comes together to help you in some way, it can only do so with something that God has already decided for you. If it comes together to harm you, the same applies. God decides man's fate."[7]

I tell the Muslims who have given everything in these last weeks to continue along your path. For your stand with us gives strength to us and to your brothers in Afghanistan. Give more efforts in the struggle against this unprecedented global crime.

O Muslims, fear God and help your religion, for Islam is calling you. May God bear witness that I have conveyed the message.

Peace, and all God's mercy and blessings, be upon you.

---

6 This is the *shahada*, the Muslim declaration of belief in the unity of God and the prophethood of Muhammad. Its recitation is one of the five pillars of Islam.

7 From the *hadith* collection of al-Tirmidhi.

13

THE EXAMPLE OF VIETNAM

November 12 2001

Bin Laden's only post-9/11 newspaper interview, this was published in Urdu in the Pakistani daily, Ausaf, on November 7 2001, and in the Arabic-language London newspaper Al-Quds Al-Arabi *on November 12, as Taliban lines collapsed and Kabul lay open to the US-backed Northern Alliance. Reiterating that the attacks of 9/11 were actions of revenge for the deaths of Muslims, and denying that the US had any solid evidence to link him to them, on this occasion bin Laden states that "there are many polite and good people in the West", and that the mission of the Prophet is about "spreading the message of God, not killing people. We ourselves are the victims of murders and massacres. We are only defending ourselves against the United States." But, he continues, the Jewish lobby dominates US foreign policy, and all Americans bear responsibility for atrocities against Muslims, as it is they who elect Congress, which endorses government policy. Bin Laden's monitoring of Western politics is indicated by his reference to a speech given by Bush the previous day, and most strikingly by the historical parallel he makes with Vietnam: "I demand that the American people take note of their government's policy against Muslims. They described the government's policy against Vietnam as wrong. They should now take the same stand as they did before. The onus is on Americans to prevent Muslims being killed at the hands of their government."*

Rejecting the argument that Pakistan had no option but to side with America against the Taliban, he declares Musharraf a "disappointment," who will be punished by God and the Pakistani people. Asked about his own health, he denies media reports that he was suffering from a renal disorder. Despite his dismissal of these claims, a videotape released a month later (Statement 14) shows him to have aged considerably over the past year, and to be possibly suffering from an injury to the left side of his body.[1]

---

1 A biography of bin Laden, published in 1991, stated that he also suffered from low blood pressure and diabetes: Essam Deraz, *Osama bin Laden: Narrating the Greatest Battles of the Pro-Afghani Arabs* (Cairo, 1991) cited in Bergen, *Holy War Inc,* p. 60.

HM: *Within a few hours of the commencement of the American bombing of Afghanistan, the Qatari channel al-Jazeera broadcast a videotape featuring a statement from you, in which you said that the September 11 attacks in the United States were carried out by Muslims.² How did you know that the attackers were Muslim?*

OBL: After September 11, the United States government itself released a list of people who were involved in the attacks. All those on the list were Muslims. Fifteen of them were from Saudi Arabia, two from the Emirates, one from Lebanon and one from Egypt. According to my information, all of them were passengers on the airplanes [that carried out the attacks]. They have been prayed for in their countries. But the United States is saying that they were hijackers.

HM: *On your videotape you demonstrate your approval of the 9/11 events, although many people, among them hundreds of Muslims, were killed in these attacks. Do you think that killing innocent people is consistent with Islamic principles?*

OBL: This is a significant issue in Islamic jurisprudence. According to my information, if the enemy occupies an Islamic land and uses its people as human shields, a person has the right to attack the enemy. In the same way, if some thieves broke into a house and took a child hostage to protect themselves, the father has the right to attack the thieves, even if the child gets hurt. The United States and their allies are killing us in Palestine, Chechnya, Kashmir, Palestine, and Iraq. That's why Muslims have the right to carry out revenge attacks on the US.

Islamic law says that Muslims should not stay long in the land of infidels. The targets of September 11 were not women and children. The main targets were the symbol of the United States: their economic and military power. Our Prophet Muhammad was against the killing of women and children. When he saw the body of a non-Muslim woman during a war, he asked what the reason for killing her was. If a child is older than thirteen and bears arms against Muslims, killing him is permissible. The American people should remember that they pay taxes to their government and that they voted for their president. Their government makes weapons and provides them to Israel, which they use to kill Palestinian Muslims. Given that the American Congress is a committee

2 This is a reference to bin Laden's statement of October 7 2001: see above, pp. 103–05.

140

that represents the people, the fact that it agrees with the actions of the American government proves that America in its entirety is responsible for the atrocities that it is committing against Muslims. I demand the American people to take note of their government's policy against Muslims. They described the government's policy against Vietnam as wrong. They should now take the same stand that they did previously. The onus is on Americans to prevent Muslims from being killed at the hands of their government.

HM: *So can we interpret this as meaning that you are not against the American people, only against their government?*

OBL: Yes, we are following our Prophet's mission. That mission is spreading the message of God, not killing people. We ourselves are the victims of murder and massacres. We are only defending ourselves against the United States. This is a defensive *jihad* to protect our land and people. That's why I have said that if we don't have security, neither will the Americans. It's a very simple equation that any American child could understand: live and let others live.

HM: *The Sheikh of al-Azhar in Egypt has issued a juridical decree to the effect that your views are sacrilegious and have nothing to do with Islam.[3] What is your opinion on that?*

OBL: No official scholar's juridical decrees have any value as far as I'm concerned. History is replete with such scholars who described their own vested interests as just (although this is prohibited in Islam). People like this also describe the Jewish occupation of Palestine and the presence of American forces around the houses in Saudi Arabia, whose sanctity should not be violated, as fair. These people are supporting the infidels for their own personal benefit. You [*addressing HM*], tell me how you would react if Indian forces entered Pakistan? The Israeli forces are occupying our land and the American forces are sitting on our territory. We no longer have any choice but *jihad*.

3 Muhammad Said Tantawy, the Grand *Mufti* of Egypt, head of al-Azhar University and the Imam of the al-Azhar mosque in Cairo, had declared the perpetrators of the 9/11 attacks and suicide bombers to be "heretics", who were not following the true path of Islam. Tantawy, an independent scholar, was appointed by Egyptian President Hosni Mubarak; as a government employee, some radical Muslims consider that his decrees are designed to accommodate the regime.

HM: *Some Western media outlets say that you are trying to find chemical and nuclear weapons. To what extent are these allegations true?*

OBL: I listened to President Bush's speech yesterday, November 7.[4] He was trying to frighten the European countries into thinking that Osama bin Laden is going to attack the whole of Europe with lethal weapons. I want to make it clear that if the United States uses chemical or nuclear weapons against us, we will not perish.[5] The United States is indeed using chemical weapons against us, and has decided to use nuclear weapons too, but our war will continue.

HM: *There were demonstrations in many European countries against the American attacks on Afghanistan. Thousands of the demonstrators in Berlin and Rome were non-Muslims. What do you think of them?*

OBL: Many in the West are polite and good people. The American media are inciting them against Muslims, but some of these good people are demonstrating against the American attacks because human nature is against cruelty and injustice. In Bosnia Muslims were slaughtered on the United Nations' watch. I know that some officials in the American foreign ministry resigned in protest at this behaviour by the United Nations. Some years earlier, the American ambassador to Egypt resigned in protest at President Jimmy Carter's policies.[6]

---

4 On November 7 2001, President Bush and Prime Minister Blair held a meeting at the White House to discuss a number of issues, including military strategy in Afghanistan and building a global coalition against all forms of terrorism. When Bush was asked if he had decided on a figure for the reduction of the US nuclear weapons stockpile, he responded by saying that "We don't need an arms control agreement to convince us to reduce our nuclear weapons down substantially … But our nation and this terrorist war says to me more than ever that we need to develop defenses to protect ourselves against weapons of mass destruction that might fall in the hands of terrorist nations. If Afghanistan or if the Taliban had a weapon that was able to deliver a weapon of mass destruction, we might be talking a little different tune about our progress against al-Qaeda than we are today. So it's important for us to be able to develop defenses that work. And the ABM Treaty prevents us from doing that."

5 The English-language Karachi newspaper, *Dawn*, replaces the phrase "We will not perish" with "We might respond with chemical and nuclear weapons. We possess these weapons as a deterrent," an interpolation that looks plainly apocryphal.

6 On August 15 1979, the American ambassador to the UN, Andrew Young, resigned after a private meeting with a representative of the Palestinian Liberation Organization. A year later, the Secretary of State Cyrus Vance resigned over the decision to proceed with a secret military mission (which subsequently failed) to rescue 53 American hostages in Iran. However, Hermann Eilts, who was the ambassador to Egypt from 1970–79, remained at his post, working with Carter to broker the 1978 Camp David Accords.

So good people are everywhere, but the pro-Jewish lobby has taken the United States and the West hostage.

HM: *Some people think that war is not the answer. Do you believe that it is possible to reach a political solution to put a stop to the current war?*

OBL: This question should be put to those who started the war. We are only protecting ourselves.

HM: *Are you going to offer yourself for trial in an Islamic country if the American forces withdraw from Saudi Arabia and the Aqsa Mosque is liberated?*

OBL: Afghanistan is the only Islamic country [in the world]. In Pakistan they use English laws, and I don't recognize the Saudi government as Islamic. In any case, if the Americans have charges against us, we have a long list of charges against them.

HM: *After the 9/11 attacks the Pakistani government decided to cooperate with the US. This is something you consider unacceptable. Can you tell us what Pakistan should have done instead?*

OBL: The Pakistani government should have respected its people's views. It should not merely have deferred to the unjust position taken by the US. The US does not have solid evidence against us, just some threads and indications. To begin bombing on the basis of such guesswork is injustice.

HM: *What could we have done if the United States chose to attack us in Pakistan in cooperation with India and Israel?*

OBL: What damage has the US done to Afghanistan in the end? We will not let Pakistan and its people stand alone. We will protect Pakistan. But General Musharraf has disappointed us.[7] He says that the majority supports him; I say that they oppose him. He is standing in the enemy ranks. President Bush has

7 General Pervez Musharraf seized power in Pakistan on October 12 1999, assuming the Presidency on June 20 2001. The Taliban's ascendancy in Afghanistan had owed much to support provided by the Pakistan Inter-Services Intelligence (ISI) agency, but in a 180-degree turn Musharraf's speech of September 19 2001 pledged Pakistani support to the USA in its War on Terror. Musharraf's speech provoked widespread demonstrations and riots throughout Pakistan.

used the word "Crusade," and the reality is that the Crusader war is still going on. President Bush was the one who started the war. There is no logic in offering Afghan blood to save Pakistan. General Musharraf wants to improve the Pakistani economy by selling Afghanis.[8] He will receive his punishment from God and the Pakistani people. What is unfolding now in Afghanistan is one of the great wars of Islamic history. The great powers are united against Muslims, so taking part in this war is something that deserves a reward from God.

HM: *A French newspaper has alleged that you have kidney failure and that you went to Dubai last year for treatment. Is that true?*

OBL: My kidneys are all right. I did not go to Dubai last year. One British newspaper has published an imaginary interview with an Islamabad dateline with one of my sons who lives in Saudi Arabia. All this is false.

HM: *Is it correct that a daughter of Mullah Omar is your wife, or that your daughter is Mullah Omar's wife?*

OBL: [*Laughing*] All my wives are Arabs, and all my daughters are married to Arab mujahids. My relationship with Mullah Omar is one of faith.[9] He is the greatest, the most honest and the happiest Muslim at this time, for he doesn't fear anyone except God. He does not have a personal relationship with me. He just acts according to his religious commitment; the kind of life I have chosen is ultimately not for personal gain.

8 Since 9/11, America has provided Pakistan $788 million in budget support, and two separate tranches of debt relief that have allowed Pakistan to cut in half its official debt to the US, from $3 billion to $1.5 billion. The remaining $1.5 billion debt is less burdensome to the Pakistani government thanks to the bilateral rescheduling of Pakistan's Paris Club debt. "Statement on the Recommendations of the 9/11 Commission Report," www.state.gov/p/sa/rls/rm/35611.html/

9 Peter Bergen writes that "There were widely circulated rumours of a marital alliance between their families: perhaps bin Laden had married one of Omar's daughter's. Every Taliban official I spoke to denies this. (In 2000, bin Laden married the fourth and last wife allowed to him under Islamic law; she is a Yemeni.)" *Holy War Inc*, p. 166.

14

NINETEEN STUDENTS

December 26 2001

By December 2001, when this statement was recorded for release to al-Jazeera, to be shown on or near Christmas Day, bin Laden was a fugitive, hunted by American-led forces in an assault on the cave complex in the Tora Bora mountains, the former mujahidin *base in eastern Afghanistan. The rapid US conquest of Afghanistan had put an end to the concentration of radical Islamic leadership, volunteers, and infrastructure in the country that had developed in the late 1990s. Physical assets were destroyed and personnel scattered; it was at this point that bin Laden seems to have told his associates to disperse, and money was given to anyone with a viable plan to launch attacks on Western interests.*

While still denying that the US had any evidence against him to warrant the attack on Afghanistan, bin Laden now delivered his most extended and passionate celebration of the hijackers of 9/11. It was "not nineteen Arab states," but "nineteen post-secondary students who shook America's throne;" they had struck a mighty blow at the destructive and usurious global economy controlled by America, deployed along with military force to impose unbelief and humiliation on the poor. Their feat, says bin Laden, was a response to daily injustice and oppression, the killing of children in Palestine that is a modern version of the Pharaoh's killing of Jewish children in Egypt. He states that the attackers have shown the way to a struggle against America that is both financial and military, since it is just as important to strike at the US economy by all means available as it is to fight US troops and those allied with them. The coming fight, he warns, will be another, greater Vietnam for the USA. Its downfall will come, not through bin Laden's agencies, dead or alive, but through the spiritual awakening of the umma, *manifest in the victorious* jihad *against the Soviet army, and now inspiring its sequel against America.*

Praise be to God. We beseech Him for help and forgiveness. We seek refuge in God from the evil of our souls and our bad deeds. He whom God guides will not go astray, and he whom He leads astray can have no guide. I testify that there is no god but God alone, Who has no partners, and I testify that Muhammad is His servant and messenger.

Three months after the blessed strikes against global unbelief and its leader America, and approximately two months after the beginning of this vicious Crusader campaign against Islam, we should discuss the meaning of these events, which have revealed things of the greatest importance to Muslims. It has become all too clear that the West in general, with America at its head, carries an unspeakable Crusader hatred for Islam. Those who have endured the continuous bombing from American aeroplanes these last months know this only too well.

How many innocent villages have been destroyed, how many millions forced out into the freezing cold, these poor innocent men, women, and children who are now taking shelter in refugee camps in Pakistan while America launches a vicious campaign based on mere suspicion?[1]

If America had evidence that could prove with a degree of certainty who did this deed [9/11], then it would attribute it to Europe, to the IRA, for example. There were many ways in which it could have dealt with the problem, but even though it was merely a matter of suspicion, the real, ugly face of Crusader hatred for the Islamic world immediately manifested itself in all its clarity.

At this point I would like to emphasize the fact that the struggle between us and America is of the utmost gravity and importance, not only to Muslims but to the entire world. On what basis does America accuse this group of emigrants[2] who wage *jihad* for God's sake, against whom there is no evidence other than that of injustice, oppression, and hostility?

---

1 According to the United Nations High Commission for Refugees (UNHCR), an estimated 200,000 Afghans fled their country in 2001, joining the 3.5 million already outside the country.

2 The emigration (*hijra*) of Muhammad and his followers from Mecca to Medina in 622 is a concept of profound significance in Islam. After the *hijra*, Muhammad prevailed, defeating the Meccans at the battle of Badr in 624, and winning over the people of Medina, returning home to Mecca in triumph in 630. Radical Islamists have consciously imitated the *hijra*, withdrawing to a society that allows them to live as "true" Muslims, and launching a campaign that they believe will, like Muhammad's, eventually be successful. Like Muhammad, they will endure periods of oppression and difficulty but, as they follow God's will, and the injunctions of Muhammad and the "righteous predecessors" (*salaf*), they will eventually prevail.

The history of the Arab *mujahidin* who waged *jihad* for the grace of God Almighty is as clear as can be. In the face of the Soviet Union's despicable terrorism against children and innocents in Afghanistan twenty years ago, these Arab *mujahidin* rose up and left their jobs, universities, families, and tribes to earn the pleasure of God, to help God's religion and to help these poor Muslims.

It is inconceivable that those who came to help the poor people today came to kill innocents, as is being alleged. History recounts that America supported everyone who waged *jihad* and fought against Russia,[3] but when God blessed these Arab *mujahidin* with going to help those poor innocent women and children in Palestine, America became angry and turned its back, betraying all those who had fought in Afghanistan.

What is happening in Palestine today is extremely clear, and something about which all of humanity since Adam can agree. Some may get corrupted, and people differ on many issues, but there are some whom God Almighty keeps from corruption, in contrast to those whose souls have become deviant and have reached an excessive degree of oppression and hostility. But one issue on which people are agreed, even if they themselves have been the victims of oppression and hostility, is that you cannot kill innocent children.

The deliberate killing of innocent children in Palestine today is the ugliest, most oppressive, and hostile act, and something that threatens all of humanity.

History knows that one who kills children, even if rarely, is a follower of Pharaoh. God Almighty favoured the sons of Israel when He helped them escape from Pharaoh. "Remember when We saved you from Pharaoh's people, who subjected you to terrible torment, slaughtering your sons and sparing only your women."[4] Slaughtering children was something for which the head of oppression, unbelief, and hostility, Pharaoh, was famous, yet the sons of Israel have done the same thing to our sons in Palestine. The whole world has witnessed Israeli soldiers killing Muhammad al-Durreh and many others like him.[5]

---

3 Bin Laden had previously denied the idea that America contributed significantly to the Afghan resistance against the USSR; see above, p. 86.

4 Qur'an, 2:49.

5 On September 30 2000, a French cameraman caught on film Israeli security forces shooting and killing 12-year-old Muhammad al-Durreh in Gaza. An Israeli inquiry into the incident found no fault with their security forces, despite the testimony of the cameraman and the video showing the event, for which see www.ramallahonline.com/modules.php?name=News&file=article&sid=8.

People across the entire world, both in East and West, are contravening their faiths by denying these deeds, but America goes on supporting those oppressors and enemies of our sons in Palestine. God Almighty has decreed that if someone reaches such an excessive degree of hostility that he kills another unlawfully, this is the most abhorrent deed, but it is yet more abhorrent to kill innocent children. God Almighty says: "On account of [his deed], We decreed to the Children of Israel that if anyone kills a person—unless in retribution for murder or spreading corruption in the land—it is as if he kills all mankind, while if any saves a life it is as if he saves the lives of all mankind."[6]

So in fact it is as if Israel—and those backing it in America—have killed all the children in the world. What will stop Israel killing our sons tomorrow in Tabuk, al-Jauf and other areas?[7] What would the rulers do if Israel broadened its territory according to what they allege is written in their false, oppressive, unjust books, which said that "Our borders extend as far as Medina"?[8] What will rulers do except submit to this American Zionist lobby?

Rational people must wake up, or what befell Muhammad al-Durreh and his brothers will happen tomorrow to their sons and women. There is no strength or power save in God.

The matter is extremely serious. This disgraceful terrorism is practised by America in its most abhorrent form in Palestine and in Iraq. This terrible man, Bush Sr, was the reason for the murder of over a million children in Iraq, besides all the other men and women [who have been killed].

The events of 22nd Jumada al-Thani, or Aylul [September 11] are merely a response to the continuous injustice inflicted upon our sons in Palestine, Iraq,

6 Qur'an, 5:32. This is in the Qur'anic story of Cain and Abel, with reference to Cain's deed. The verse concludes, "Our messengers came to them with clear signs, but many of them continued to commit excesses in the land."

7 Tabuk and al-Jauf are the names of cities in northwest Saudi Arabia and the provinces that surround them, bordering Jordan and the Gulf of Aqaba. Tabuk is also home to a major Saudi air force base; a large US-operated joint-training base is located just outside the town.

8 The Torah defines the borders of the Promised Land as follows: "In that day the Lord made a covenant with Abram, saying: 'Unto thy seed have I given this land, from the river of Egypt unto the great river, the river Euphrates." (Genesis 15:18–21). Current maps of the projected "Eretz Israel", the land that made up the ancient kingdoms of Israel and Judah, show its borders extending into present-day Iraq, Egypt, and Saudi Arabia, north of Medina. See for example http://www.ahavat-israel.com/eretz/future.php; http://www.globalsecurity.org/military/world/israel/greater-israel-maps.htm

Somalia, southern Sudan, and other places, like Kashmir. The matter concerns the entire *umma*. People need to wake up from their sleep and try to find a solution to this catastrophe that is threatening all of humanity.

Those who condemn these operations [9/11] have viewed the event in isolation and have failed to connect it to previous events or to the reasons behind it. Their view is blinkered and lacks either a legitimate or a rational basis. They merely saw others in America and the media decrying these operations, so they did the same themselves.

These people remind me of the wolf who, seeing a lamb, said to it: "You were the one who polluted my water last year." The lamb replied: "It wasn't me," but the wolf insisted: "Yes it was." The lamb said: "I was only born this year." The wolf replied: "Then it was your mother who polluted my water", and he ate the lamb. When the poor ewe saw her son being torn by the wolf's teeth, her maternal feelings drove her to give the wolf a hard butt. The wolf cried out: "Look at this terrorism!" And all the parrots repeated what he said, saying "Yes, we condemn the ewe's butting of the wolf." What do you think about the wolf eating the ewe's lamb?

These blessed, successful strikes are merely a reaction to events in our land in Palestine, in Iraq, and in other places. America has continued this policy with the coming of George Bush Jr, who began his term with violent airstrikes on Iraq to emphasize the policy of oppression and hostility, and to show that the blood of Muslims has no value.[9]

This blessed reaction came by the grace of God Almighty, showing very clearly that this haughty, domineering power, America, the Hubal of the age, is based on great economic power, but it is soft.[10] How quickly it fell from the sky, by the grace of God Almighty.

It was not nineteen Arab states that did this deed [9/11]. It was not Arab armies or ministries who humbled the oppressor who harms us in Palestine and elsewhere. It was nineteen post-secondary students—I beg God Almighty to accept them—who shook America's throne, struck its economy right in the heart, and dealt the biggest military power a mighty blow, by the grace of God Almighty.

9 The February 26 2001 bombings included a large sortie of US and UK planes attacking sites near Baghdad; the raids were almost universally condemned.

10 Hubal is the name of a pagan idol whose followers were defeated by early Muslim forces. Bin Laden also uses this name for America in Statement 10 (see above, p. 105).

Here we have clear proof that this destructive, usurious global economy that America uses, together with its military force, to impose unbelief and humiliation on poor peoples, can easily collapse. Those blessed strikes in New York and the other places forced it to acknowledge the loss of more than a trillion dollars, by the grace of God Almighty. And they used simple means—the enemy's aeroplanes and schools—without even the need for training camps. God gave them the chance to teach a harsh lesson to these arrogant people who think that freedom only has meaning for the white race, and that other peoples should be humiliated and subservient, not even rising up when they strike us, as they did previously in Iraq.

I say that American military power, as demonstrated recently in Afghanistan, where it poured down all its anger on these poor people, has taught us great and important lessons in how to resist this arrogant force, by the grace of God Almighty.

By way of example, if the front line with the enemy is 100km long, this line should also be deep. In other words, it is not enough for us to have a defense line 100, 200, or 300 metres deep. It should be a few kilometres deep, with trenches dug all the way along and through it, so that the intensity of the American bombing is exhausted before it destroys these lines, and so that light, quick forces can move from one line to another and from one defense position to another.

We made use of this tactic after the intense American bombardment on the northern and Kabul lines,[11] and in this way the years pass and, with the will of God Almighty, America will not break the *mujahidin* lines.

Furthermore, it is well known that there are two elements to fighting; there is the fighting itself and then there is the financial element, such as buying weapons. This is emphasized in many verses of the Qur'an, such as the following: "God has purchased the persons and possessions of the believers in return for the Garden."[12]

11 On October 7 2001, American and British forces began an aerial bombing campaign, targeting Taliban forces and al-Qaeda. Two weeks into the campaign, the Taliban line facing the Northern Alliance held; at this stage, the US began using cluster bombs and 15,000-pound daisy cutters. By November 2, Taliban lines were decimated; Kabul fell on November 13.

12 Qur'an, 9:111. The verse goes on: "... they fight in God's way: they kill and are killed—this is a true promise given by Him in the Torah, the Gospel, and the Qur'an. Who could be more faithful to his promise than God? So be happy with the bargain you have made: that is the supreme triumph."

150

So the struggle is both financial and physical. Even if the distance between us and the American military base is very great, and our weapons do not match up to their planes, we are able to soak up the pressure of these strikes with our broad defense lines. And in another way it is possible to strike the economic base that is the foundation of the military base, so when their economy is depleted they will be too busy with each other to be able to enslave poor peoples.

So I say that it is very important to focus on attacking the American economy by any means available. Here we have seen the real crime of those who claim to call for humanity and freedom. Just a tiny quantity [of explosives]—7 grams' worth—is more than enough to account for anyone. But America, in her hatred for the Taliban and for Muslims, drops bombs weighing 7 tons on our brothers in the front lines. That is equivalent to seven thousand kilograms, or seven million grams, even though 7 grams is more than enough for one person.

When the young men—we beg God to accept them—exploded less than two tons [of explosive] in Nairobi, America said that this was a terrorist strike, and that this is a weapon of mass destruction. But they have no qualms about using two bombs weighing seven million grams each.

After the Americans bombed entire villages[13] for no reason other than to terrify people and make them afraid of hosting Arabs or going near them, their minister of defense got up and said that that was their right, meaning effectively that they had the right to annihilate people so long as they were Muslim and not American. This is the clearest and most blatant crime. Everyone who hears them saying that they did such things "by mistake" knows that this is the clearest and most brazen lie.

Some days ago, the Americans announced that they had hit al-Qaeda positions in Khost and had dropped a bomb on a mosque, which they said was a mistake. After investigations it became clear that scientists in Khost were saying their Ramadan evening prayers and had a meeting afterwards with the hero *mujahid* sheikh Jalal al-Din Haqqani, one of the foremost leaders of the *jihad* against the Soviets, who has resisted this American occupation of Afghan land. So they bombed the mosque and the Muslims while they were at

---

13 By mid-December 2001, US bombs had killed an estimated 3,767 civilians. See Seumas Milne, "The innocent dead in a coward's war," *Guardian*, December 20 2001, and more generally, Michael Mann, *Incoherent Empire* (Verso, 2003), p. 30. Mann notes that during the US bombing of Afghanistan, "Overall civilian losses must have been close to 10,000—triple the deaths inflicted by 9/11." (Ibid.)

prayers, killing 105 of them. God save Sheikh Jalal, we hope that He blesses his life.[14]

This is Crusader hatred. So those who speak out and say that they condemn terrorism, but do not pay attention to the consequences, should take note. Our terrorism against America is a praiseworthy terrorism in defense against the oppressor, in order that America will stop supporting Israel, who kills our sons. Can you not understand this? It is very clear.

America and the western leaders always say that Hamas and Islamic Jihad in Palestine, and other such militias, are terrorist organizations. If self-defense is terrorism, what is legitimate? Our defense and our fight is no different to that of our brothers in Palestine like Hamas. We fight for "There is no God but God." The word of God is the highest and that of God's enemies is the lowest. So let us relieve the oppression of the poor people in Palestine and elsewhere.

Every possible analysis clearly shows all sensible Muslims should stand in the trenches,[15] because this is the most dangerous, aggressive, violent, and fierce Crusader war against Islam. With God's will, America's end will not be far off. This will be nothing to do with the poor slave bin Laden, whether dead or alive. With God's grace, the awakening has begun, which is one of the benefits of these operations. I hope that God Almighty will take those young men to martyrdom and bring them together with the Prophet, the martyrs, and the righteous.

---

14 On November 16–17, US planes bombed a mosque and the attached religious seminary on the outskirts of Khost, as part of a campaign targeted at Jalaluddin Haqqani, seen as a key link between the Taliban and al-Qaeda. Local officials were quoted as saying that a total of 62 people were killed in the mosque, and 34 in the religious school. The Deobandi cleric Maulvi Jalaluddin Haqqani rose to prominence in the 1980s as a military leader of the radical Islamic group Hezb-i-Islami, led by Gulbuddin Hekmatyar. He enjoyed close ties with the Pakistani military and the Gulf States. He joined the Taliban in 1996, and two years later was appointed Minister of Tribal and Border affairs. Bin Laden contacted Haqqani before his departure to Afghanistan in May 1996, and was his guest there.

15 The word "trench," employed by bin Laden throughout his statements, has particular significance in Islam. The Qur'an (85:4) reads "Damned were the makers of the Trench", referring to a fiery trench into which Muslims, refusing to renounce Islam, were cast for their faith. It also alludes to the Battle of the Trench in 627, one of Muhammad's early victories against considerable odds. A Meccan army of 10,000, comprising Muslims and Jews, mounted a campaign against the Muslims in Medina, defended by Muhammad and 3,000 followers. All the defenders joined to dig a trench north of Medina to protect the city; when the Meccan cavalry arrived, they tried for three days to cross the trench, but were unsuccessful; on the third day, a strong hurricane forced them to retreat, and admit defeat.

Those young men did a very great deed, a glorious deed. God rewarded them and we pray that their parents will be proud of them, because they raised Muslims' heads high and taught America a lesson it won't forget, with God's will.

As I warned previously in an interview on the ABC channel, by involving itself in a struggle with the sons of Saudi Arabia, America will forget the Vietnam crisis, with the grace of God Almighty. What is yet to come will be even greater.

From Saudi Arabia fifteen young men set out—we pray to God to accept them as martyrs. They set out from the land of faith, where lies the Muslims' greatest treasure, where faith returns, as our Prophet rightly said, to Medina, just as the snake returns to its hole. Another two came from the Eastern Peninsula, from the Emirates, another from the Levant, Ziad al-Jarrah, and another from the land of Egypt, Mohammed Atta, may God accept all of them as martyrs.

With their actions they provided a very great sign, showing that it was this faith in their hearts that urged them to do these things, to give their soul to "There is no god but God". By these deeds they opened a great door for good and truth. Those we hear in the media saying that martyrdom operations should not be carried out are merely repeating the desires of the tyrants, America and its collaborators.

Every day, from east to west, our *umma* of 1200 million Muslims is being slaughtered, in Palestine, in Iraq, Somalia, Western Sudan, Kashmir, the Philippines, Bosnia, Chechnya, and Assam. We do not hear their voices, yet as soon as the victim rises up and offers himself on behalf of his religion, people are outraged. 1200 million Muslims are being slaughtered without anyone even knowing, but if anyone comes to their defense, those people just repeat whatever the tyrants want them to say. They have neither common sense nor authority.

There is a clear moral in the story of the boy, the king, the magician, and the monk, of people offering themselves for "There is no god but God". There is also another meaning, which is that victory is not only a question of winning, which is how most people see it, but of sticking to your principles.

God mentioned the people of the trench and immortalized their memory by praising them for being resolute in their faith. They were given a choice between faith and being thrown into the fire. They refused not to believe in God, and so they were thrown into hell. At the end of the story of the boy, when the tyrant king ordered that the believers should be thrown in the pit, a poor mother came carrying her son. When she saw the fire she was afraid that harm would befall her son, so she went back. But as the Prophet relates, her son told her: "be patient, mother, for you are in the right."

No Muslim would ever possibly ask: what did they benefit? The fact is that they were killed—but this is total ignorance. They were victorious, with the blessings of God Almighty, and with the immortal heavens that God promised them. Victory is not material gain; it is about sticking to your principles.

And in the sayings of our Prophet, there is the story about the uneducated boy, the magician and the monk.[16] One day, an animal was blocking the road, and the boy said, "Today, I'll find out who is better, the monk or the magician." Because he was lacking in knowledge, he did not as yet understand which one was better, so he asked God to show him. If the monk was more beloved to God Almighty, then he would be able to kill the animal. So the boy picked up the rock and threw it at the animal, and it dropped dead. The monk turned to him and said: "My son, today you are better than me,"[17] even though he was far more knowledgeable than this ignorant young boy. Nevertheless, God Almighty lit up this boy's heart with the light of faith, and he began to make sacrifices for the sake of "There is no god but God".

This is a unique and valuable story which the youth of Islam are waiting for their scholars to tell them, which would show the youth that these [the 9/11 attackers] are the people who have given up everything for the sake of "There is no god but God", and would tell them what the scholar told the boy: "Today, you are better than us."

This is the truth. The measure of virtue in this religion is, as the saying of our Prophet goes, the measure of faith—not only collecting knowledge but

16 This refers to a parable told by the Prophet, recorded in the *hadith* collection of Muslim, book 42, no. 7,148. In the parable, a boy is chosen by the king to receive training to be the new court magician, but the boy is captivated by a monk who is devoted to Islam. At one point a wild animal blocks the road, and the boy invokes God, saying that if the monk's business is more important then he should be able to kill the wild animal by throwing a stone at it, and if the magician's business is more important, the stone should not kill the beast. The animal dies at his throw, and the boy becomes utterly devoted to God. This irks the king, who then executes the monk and attempts several times to execute the boy, but the boy survives because of his continual affirmation of Islam. When he finally assents to die in the name of Islam, the members of the public who converted because of his testimony are threatened with being thrown into a trench of fire unless they repent. None of them do.

17 Quoted from the *hadith* collection of Muslim, book 42, no. 7,148 (see above, n. 25).

using it. According to this yardstick, whoever fights them [the unbelievers] physically is a believer, whoever fights them verbally is a believer, and whoever fights them with his heart is a believer. Nothing can be more essentially faithful than this. These people fought the great unbelief with their hands and their souls, and we pray to God to accept them as martyrs.

The lord of martyrs Hamza bin Abd al-Muttalib, said that God illuminated a unknown man's heart with faith, and he stood up against an unjust imam, who rebuked him and killed him, as is written in the *al-Jami al-Sahih*.[18]

He won a great victory that not one of the noble followers or companions could achieve. God Almighty raised him up to the status of lord of the martyrs. This is something that our Prophet emphasized. So how could any sane Muslim say, "What did he benefit from it?" This is clear error and we ask God for good health.

God opened the way for these young men to tell America, the head of global unbelief, and its allies, that they are living in falsehood. They sacrificed themselves for "There is no god but God."

We have spoken much about these great events, but I will sum things up by emphasizing the importance of continuing *jihadi* action against America, both militarily and economically. America has been set back, with the help of God Almighty, and the economic bleeding still goes on today. Yet still we need more strikes. The youth should strive to find the weak points of the American economy and strike the enemy there.

Before I finish, I should mention these heroes, these true men, these great giants who erased the shame from the forehead of our *umma*. I should like to recite some poetry in praise of them and all those who follow the same path as Muhammad.

But before that, I would like to stress one point, which is that these battles going on round the clock today in Afghanistan against the Arab *mujahidin*, and particularly the Taliban, have clearly shown just how powerless the American government and its soldiers really are. Despite the great develop-

---

18 Hamza ibn al-Muttalib, was the uncle of the Prophet Muhammad. He converted to Islam in the sixth year of Muhammad's prophecy, and was the first military commander of Islam. The *al-Jami al-Sahih*, a collection of 7,275 tested prophetic traditions, was written by the Persian Muhammad al-Bukhari (810–70), who travelled all over the Islamic world in order to compile the book, learning over 600,000 traditions, true and false.

ments in military technology, they can't do anything without relying on apostates and hypocrites.[19] So what is the difference today between Babrak Karmal,[20] who brought in the Russians to occupy his country, and the deposed president Burhan al-Din (and *din* has nothing to do with him)?[21] What difference is there between the two? One brought Russians to occupy the land of Islam and the other brought Americans. As I said, this clearly shows the weakness of the American soldier, by the grace of God Almighty. So you should seize this chance, and the youth should continue the *jihad* and work against the Americans. I'll finish with some lines of poetry in memory of those heroes from the land of Hijaz, the land of faith, from Ghamid and Zahran, from Bani Shahr, from Harb, from Najd,[22] and we pray to God to accept them all, and in memory of those who came from Holy Mecca, Salem and Nawaf al-Hazmi, Khaled al-Mihdhar, or those who came from Medina, the radiant, who left life and its comforts for the sake of "There is no god but God".[23]

I testify that these men, as sharp as a sword,

Have persevered through all trials.

How special they are who sold their souls to God,

Who smiled at Death when his sword gazed ominously at them,

Who willingly bared their chests as shields.

Though the clothes of darkness enveloped us and the poisoned tooth bit us,

Though our homes overflowed with blood and the assailant desecrated our land,

19 Bin Laden is referring to the government of Pakistan, which was cooperating fully with the American invasion of Afghanistan.

20 Babrak Karmal was the USSR-backed Communist president of Afghanistan from December 1979 until 1986, when he resigned as a scapegoat for Soviet reverses during the war.

21 In 1992, following the Soviet withdrawal from Afghanistan, Burhanuddin Rabbani was appointed President of the Islamic Council of Afghanistan until Kabul fell to the Taliban in 1996. He became head of the Northern Alliance against the Taliban, and was still recognized by the West as Afghanistan's head of state until formally handing over to Hamid Karzai on December 22 2001. Bin Laden makes a play on words in Arabic. The element "al-Din" is a common feature in Arabic names, *din* meaning religious. Bin Laden's pun is ironic; for him, Rabbani is not remotely religious.

22 These are various tribes and locations from the Arabian peninsula.

23 Nawaf al-Hazmi and Khaled al-Mihdhar were the two Meccans suspected of being the chief organizers of 9/11, along with the pilots; Nawaf's brother Salem was also one of the hijackers.

Though from the squares the shining of swords and horses vanished,
And sound of drums was growing
The fighters' winds blew, striking their towers and telling them:
We will not cease our raids until you leave our fields.[24]

Peace be with you and all God's mercy and blessings.

24 The author of the poem recited by bin Laden is Yusuf Abu Hilala, a professor of Islamic law at a Jordanian University, and longstanding member of the Muslim Brotherhood. Abu Hilala was a close friend of bin Laden's mentor Abdallah Azzam, and apparently dedicated a poem to bin Laden entitled "The Fighting Eagle". Bin Laden made two small but significant changes to the last lines of the poem, which originally read: "The fighters' winds blew, striking their castles, and telling the assailants: / Our swords will not be thrown down until you leave our fields." Bin Laden altered "castles" to "towers", and replaced "swords will not be thrown down", with "raids will not cease".

15

TO THE PEOPLE OF AFGHANISTAN

August 25 2002

This brief handwritten letter was scanned and posted on the website islamonline.net.[1] *By now, the Karzai government had been installed by the US, and NATO troops were patrolling Afghanistan to suppress resistance to it. Taliban guerrillas had yet to regroup. But despite apparent defeat, bin Laden calls on the Afghan people to rise up against these Western armies and drive them from the land, as their ancestors had expelled Mongol invaders and British colonialists, and the* mujahidin *had broken Russian armies a decade before. The Afghans have always been 'lions of the holy law', and their courage and fortitude will mete out to the Americans the fate that overtook the Russians.*

Praise be to God, almighty lord of the heavens and earth, beloved and omnipotent. Prayers and peace upon the imam of the *mujahidin*, our leader and master Muhammad, upon all his family and followers, and upon those who follow them in righteousness until the day of judgment.

This letter is sent to you by your brother in religion and belief, Osama bin Muhammad bin Awad bin Laden.

Peace be upon you and all God's mercy and blessings.

I send this letter to the steadfast, resilient people who wage *jihad* with the sword in one hand and the holy Qur'an in the other. You lions of the holy law, you guardians of the religion, know that God Almighty has said in His book: "God has made a promise to those among you who believe and do good deeds: He will make them successors to the land, as He did those before them."[2]

---

1 Sourced at http://www.islamonline.net/English/News/2002-08/26/article19.shtml. The letter was obtained from an anonymous Afghan source.

2 Qur'an, 24:55. The rest of the verse and omits the majority, which reads, "He will strengthen the religion He has chosen for them; He will grant them security to replace their fear.

Oh people of Afghanistan, you know that *jihad* is of the utmost value in Islam, and that with it we can gain pride and eminence in this world and the next. You know that it saves our lands, protects our sanctity, spreads justice, security, and prosperity, and plants fear in the enemies' hearts. Through it kingdoms are built, and the banner of truth flies high above all others. Oh people of Afghanistan, I am convinced that you understand these words of mine more than anyone else, since throughout the ages no invader ever settled in your lands, since you are distinguished for your strength, defiance and fortitude in the fight, and since your doors are open only to Islam. That is because Muslims never came as colonizers or out of worldly self-interest, but as missionaries bringing us back to God.

Oh people of Afghanistan, God has given you the blessing of sacrificing yourselves for Him, and you have sacrificed what is dear and precious in order to make the great words "There is no god but God and Muhammad is his messenger" a reality in your land. You didn't let global unbelief—that is, Britain, Russia, and America—penetrate your land and challenge the Muslims' pride in east and west. From my position, I can say that the great spheres [of influence] being drawn around these big countries amount to not even a mosquito's wing. Indeed, they are worthless when compared to God's power and support for the faithful *mujahidin*. Whoever doubts this should learn from the Russians how the blessed *jihad* destroyed their myth. And before them, neither the Tartars nor the English could defy the holy warriors, because the peaks of this blessed land's mountains resisted every stubborn infidel.[3]

And by the will of God Almighty, we will soon see the fall of the unbelievers' states, at whose forefront is America, the tyrant, which has destroyed all human values and transgressed all limits, and which only understands the logic of power and war.

Power to Islam and victory to the Muslims

Abi Abdallah[3]

'They worship Me and do not join anything with Me.' Whoever still chooses to disbelieve is truly rebellious."

3 This name is used here for the first time in one of bin Laden's formal statements, but is a normal Arabic method of address. Arab men begin life carrying a title as the "son of X" (bin X or ibn X) and after fathering a child can assume the title "father of Y" (Abu Y). Bin Laden's oldest son is named Abdallah; he has fathered at least 24 children.

16

TO THE AMERICANS

October 6 2002

This letter was posted on the internet in Arabic on October 14 2002, and later in English trans-lation; it was issued in response to unidentified articles by American writers examining the reasons behind radical Islamic attacks, and responses to them.[1] The letter proceeds to pose, and answer two questions: "Why are we fighting you?"; and "What are we calling you to do, and what do we want from you?" In a feature of the Arab fatwa tradition, opinions are here couched as detailed responses to specific questions, broken down into sections and subsections in such a way as to emphasize the irrefutable logic of jihad. *Unusual aspects of the style, and in part the content, of the document suggest that associates may have contributed to its composition, although there can be no certainty of this.*

Two features mark the letter out. The first is its succinct but wide-ranging summary of what bin Laden holds to be the political misdeeds of the United States across the Muslim world: in Palestine, Somalia, Chechnya, Kashmir, the Lebanon, Iraq, Afghanistan, and not least in the Arab states that act as its willing agents. The second is a moral and cultural denunciation of American society as a sink of usury, debauchery, drug addiction, gambling, prostitution, and environmental destruction, a result of America's apostasy in separating church and state, and choosing to live by man-made laws rather than those of God. This portrait of the US follows a call to the American people to convert to Islam. Fantastical as the prospect of such a conversion must be—as the letter itself implies ("I doubt you will do so")—the appeal has a practical function within the umma. *Its purpose is to answer Muslim critics of 9/11 who argued that al-Qaeda did not offer Americans an opportunity to convert to Islam before attacking them, thereby*

---

1   The full text of this letter was published in English translation in the London *Observer* on November 24 2002, after being posted on the Al-Qala'h website on October 14 2002; this website, a forum for radical Islamists, was used by "The Secret Organization Group of al-Qaeda of *Jihad* Organization in Europe" to claim responsibility for the London attacks on July 7 2005. It has since been shut down.

violating God's ruling: "We never punish until we have sent a messenger."² The exhaustive detail of the letter is bin Laden's proof to Muslims that he has explored every avenue to resolve this war by peaceful means, and given proper warning of the destruction that will be visited upon Americans if they refuse to listen to his advice.

Another novel aspect of this statement is the extent to which it uses arguments against the American state circulating widely in the West itself, in effect taunting the United States with not living up to its own rhetoric. The corruption of the American political system by money, suspension of civil liberties with the Patriot Act, rejection of the Kyoto Accords, connivance with the cancellation of democracy in Algeria, support for Israeli flouting of UN resolutions, cover-up of the massacre in Qunduz, and—last but not least—the detention without trial of prisoners in Guantanamo, "a historical embarrassment to America and its values", all become part of a general indictment. Americans have chosen the governments that have pursued these policies. They have the ability to change these, but have not done so; that, states bin Laden, is why they are not innocent of the crimes committed in its name. Bin Laden's concluding advice to them is blunt. "Pack your luggage and get out of our lands".

In the Name of God, the Most Gracious, the Most Merciful,

> Those who have been attacked are permitted to take up arms because they have been wronged—God has the power to help them [believers] victory.³

> The believers fight for God's cause, while those who reject faith fight for an unjust cause. Fight for the allies of Satan: Satan's plays are truly weak.⁴

Some American writers have published articles under the title "On what basis are we fighting?"⁴ These articles have generated a number of responses, some of which adhered to the truth and were based on Islamic Law, and others which have not. Here we wanted to outline the truth as an explanation and warning, hoping for God's reward, seeking success and support from Him. While seeking God's help, we form our reply based on two questions directed at the Americans:

---

2 See Scheuer, *Imperial Hubris*, p. 153; citing John Kelsay, "Religion, Morality and the Governance of War: The Case of Classical Islam," *Journal of Religious Ethics*, vol. 18, no. 2 (Fall 1990), p. 125.

3 Qur'an, 22:39.

4 Qur'an, 4:76.

1) Why are we fighting and opposing you?

2) What are we calling you to, and what do we want from you?

As for the first question: Why are we fighting and opposing you? The answer is very simple:

(1) Because you attacked us and continue to attack us.

(a) You attacked us in Palestine:

(i) Palestine, which has foundered under military occupation for more than 80 years. The British handed over Palestine, with your help and your support, to the Jews, who have occupied it for more than 50 years; years overflowing with oppression, tyranny, crimes, killing, expulsion, destruction, and devastation. The creation and continuation of Israel is one of the greatest crimes, and you are the leaders of its criminals. And of course there is no need to explain and prove the degree of American support for Israel. The creation of Israel is a crime which must be erased. Each and every person whose hands have become polluted in the contribution towards this crime must pay its price, and pay for it heavily.

(ii) It brings us both laughter and tears to see that you have not yet tired of repeating your fabricated lies that the Jews have a historical right to Palestine, as it was promised to them in the Torah. Anyone who disputes with them on this alleged fact is accused of anti-semitism. This is one of the most fallacious, widely-circulated fabrications in history. The people of Palestine are pure Arabs and original Semites. It is the Muslims who are the inheritors of Moses (peace be upon him) and the inheritors of the real Torah that has not been changed. Muslims believe in all of the Prophets, including Abraham, Moses, Jesus, and Muhammad. If the followers of Moses have been promised a right to Palestine in the Torah, then the Muslims are the most worthy nation of this.

When the Muslims conquered Palestine and drove out the Romans, Palestine and Jerusalem returned to Islam, the religion of all the Prophets. Therefore, the call to a historical right to Palestine cannot be raised against the Islamic *umma* that believes in all the Prophets of God— and we make no distinction between them.

(iii) The blood pouring out of Palestine must be equally avenged. You must know that the Palestinians do not cry alone; their women are not widowed alone; their sons are not orphaned alone.

(b) You attacked us in Somalia; you supported the Russian atrocities against us in Chechnya, the Indian oppression against us in Kashmir, and the Jewish aggression against us in Lebanon.[5]

(c) Under your supervision, consent, and orders, the governments of our countries which act as your collaborators, attack us on a daily basis;

(i) These governments prevent our people from establishing the Islamic *sharia*, using violence and lies to do so.

(ii) These governments give us a taste of humiliation, and place us in a great prison of fear and subjugation.

(iii) These governments steal our *umma*'s wealth and sell it to you at a paltry price.

(iv) These governments have surrendered to the Jews, and handed them most of Palestine, acknowledging the existence of their state over the dismembered limbs of their own people.

(v) The removal of these governments is an obligation upon us, and a necessary step to free the *umma*, to make the *sharia* the supreme law and to regain Palestine. And our fight against these governments is not separate from our fight against you.

(d) You steal our wealth and oil at paltry prices because of your international influence and military threats. This theft is indeed the biggest theft ever witnessed by mankind in the history of the world.

(e) Your forces occupy our countries; you spread your military bases throughout them; you corrupt our lands, and you besiege our sanctuaries,

5 Israel invaded Lebanon in June 1982, with the objective of destroying Palestine Liberation Organization (PLO) forces based there. When it completed its withdrawal from south Lebanon on May 22 2000, an estimated 10,000 had been killed and another 10,000 injured. During the occupation, Israel's allies, Phalangist Christian Militia carried out massacres of Palestinians at the Sabra and Shatila refugee camps in Israeli-occupied Beirut, which Israeli forces made no efforts to prevent. Between 3,000–3,500 people were killed, including women and children. In its investigation into the massacre, published in Spring 1983, the Israeli Kahan commission found that Defense Minister Ariel Sharon, later Prime Minister of Israel, bore "personal indirect responsibility," recommending that he be dismissed from his post, and concluding that he should never hold public office again.

to protect the security of the Jews and to ensure the continuity of your pillage of our treasures.

(f) You have starved the Muslims of Iraq, where children die every day. It is a wonder that more than 1.5 million Iraqi children have died as a result of your sanctions, and that you have not shown concern. Yet when 3,000 of your people died, the entire world rises up and has not yet sat down.[6]

(g) You have supported the Jews in their idea that Jerusalem is their eternal capital, and have agreed to move your embassy there. With your help and under your protection, the Israelis are planning to destroy the al-Aqsa mosque. Under the protection of your weapons, Sharon entered the al-Aqsa mosque, to pollute it as a preparation to capture and destroy it.[7]

(2) These tragedies and calamities are only a few examples of your oppression and aggression against us. It is commanded by our religion and intellect that the oppressed have a right to respond to aggression. Do not expect anything from us but *jihad*, resistance, and revenge. Is it in any way rational to expect that after America has attacked us for more than half a century, that we will then leave her to live in security and peace?

(3) You may then dispute that all the above does not justify aggression against civilians, for crimes they did not commit and offenses in which they did not participate:

(a) This argument contradicts your continuous repetition that America is the land of freedom, and freedom's leaders in this world. If this is so, the American people are the ones who choose their government through their own free will; a choice which stems from their agreement to its

6 Between 1991 and 1999 an estimated 500,000 children died as a result of the UN-imposed economic sanctions on Iraq. See, *inter alia*, Mohamed M Ali, John Blacker, and Gareth Jones, "Annual mortality rates and excess deaths of children under five in Iraq, 1991–98," *Population Studies*, 2003. 2,595 people died in the attacks on the World Trade Center on September 11 2001; 125 in the Pentagon attacks; 265 died on the four hijacked planes. In total, at least 2,985 people died on 9/11.
7 On September 28 2000, Ariel Sharon, then leader of the opposition in the Israeli parliament, visited the Haram as-Sharif (Temple Mount) in Jerusalem, site of the Dome of the Rock and al-Aqsa mosque, accompanied by several hundred Israeli policemen and declared that the complex would remain under Israeli control in perpetuity.

policies. Thus the American people have chosen, consented to, and affirmed their support for Israel's oppression of the Palestinians, the occupation and usurpation of their land, and its continuous killing, torture, punishment, and expulsion of the Palestinians. The American people have the ability and choice to refuse the policies of their government, and even to change it if they want.

(b) The American people are the ones who pay the taxes which fund the planes that bomb us in Afghanistan, the tanks that strike and destroy our homes in Palestine, the armies which occupy our lands in the Arabian Gulf, and the fleets which ensure the blockade of Iraq. These tax dollars are given to Israel for it to continue attacking us and invade our lands. So the American people are the ones who fund the attacks against us, and they are the ones who oversee the expenditure of these monies in the way they wish, through their elected candidates.

(c) Also, the American army is part of the American people. It is this very same people who are shamelessly helping the Jews fight against us.

(d) The American people are the ones who employ both their men and their women in the American Forces which attack us.

(e) This is why the American people cannot be innocent of all the crimes committed by the Americans and Jews against us.

(f) God, the Almighty, legislated the permission and the option to avenge this oppression. Thus, if we are attacked, then we have the right to strike back. If people destroy our villages and towns, then we have the right to do the same in return. If people steal our wealth, then we have the right to destroy their economy. And whoever kills our civilians, then we have the right to kill theirs.

The American Government and press still refuses to answer the question: Why did they attack us in New York and Washington?

If Sharon is a man of peace in the eyes of Bush, then we are also men of peace. America does not understand the language of manners and principles, so we are addressing it using the language it understands.

(2) As for the second question that we want to answer: What are we calling you to, and what do we want from you?

165

(1) The first thing that we are calling you to is Islam.

(a) The religion of the Unity of God; of freedom from and rejection of the association of equals with Him; of complete love of Him, the Exalted; of complete submission to His Laws; and of the discarding of all the opinions, orders, theories, and religions which contradict the religion He sent down to His Prophet Muhammad. Islam is the religion of all the Prophets, and makes no distinction between them—peace be upon them all.

It is to this religion that we call you; the seal of all the previous religions. It is the religion of the Unity of God, sincerity, the best of manners, righteousness, mercy, honor, purity, and piety. It is the religion of showing kindness to others, establishing justice between them, granting them their rights, and defending the oppressed and the persecuted. It is the religion of enjoining the good and forbidding the evil with the hand, tongue, and heart. It is the religion of *jihad* in the way of God so that God's Word and religion reign supreme. And it is the religion of unity and agreement on the obedience to God, and total equality between all people, without regard to their colour, sex, or language.

(b) It is the religion whose book—the Qur'an—will remain preserved and unchanged, after the other Divine books and messages have been changed. The Qur'an is the miracle until the Day of Judgment. God has challenged anyone to bring a book like the Qur'an or even ten verses like it.

(2) The second thing we call you to, is to stop your oppression, lies, immorality, and debauchery that has spread among you.

(a) We call you to be a people of manners, principles, honor, and purity; to reject the immoral acts of fornication, homosexuality, intoxicants, gambling, and usury.

We call you to all of this, in order that you may be freed from that which you have become caught up in; that you may be freed from the self-deception that you are a great nation, the self-deception your leaders spread amongst you to conceal from you the despicable state that you have reached.

(b) It is saddening to tell you that you are the worst civilization witnessed in the history of mankind:

166

(i) You are the nation who, rather than ruling by the *sharia* of God in its Constitution and Laws, choose to invent your own laws as you will and desire. You separate religion from your policies, contradicting the pure nature which affirms Absolute Authority to the Lord and your Creator. You flee from the embarrassing question posed to you: How is it possible for God the Almighty to fashion His creation, grant men power over all creatures and land, grant them all the amenities of life, and then deny them that which they are most in need of: knowledge of the laws which govern their lives?

(ii) You are the nation that permits usury, which has been forbidden by all the religions. Yet you build your economy and investments on usury. As a result of this, in all their different forms and guises, the Jews have taken control of your economy, through which they have then taken control of your media, and now control all aspects of your life making you their servants and achieving their aims at your expense; precisely what Benjamin Franklin warned you against.[8]

(iii) You are a nation that permits the production, trading, and usage of intoxicants. You also permit drugs, and only forbid the trade of them, even though your nation is the largest consumer of them.

(iv) You are a nation that permits acts of immorality, and you consider these acts to be pillars of personal freedom. You have continued to sink down this abyss from level to level until incest has spread amongst you, in the face of which neither your sense of honor nor your laws object.

Who can forget your President Clinton's immoral acts committed in the official Oval office? After that you did not even bring him to account, other than that he "made a mistake", after which everything passed with no punishment. Is there a worse kind of event for which your name will go down in history and be remembered by nations?

(v) You are a nation that permits gambling in its all forms. The companies practice this as well, resulting in investments becoming active and the criminals becoming rich.

(vi) You are a nation that exploits women like consumer products or advertising tools, calling upon customers to purchase them. You use women to

8 The reference here is to comments attributed to Franklin in a "Chit Chat Around the Table During Intermission," at the Constitutional Convention in Philadelphia in 1787—long known to be a fabrication by an American Nazi sympathizer, William Dudley Pelley, in 1934.

serve passengers, visitors, and strangers to increase your profit margins. You then rant that you support the liberation of women.

(vii) You are a nation that practices the trade of sex in all its forms, directly and indirectly. Giant corporations and establishments are established on this, under the name of art, entertainment, tourism, and freedom, and other deceptive names that you attribute to it.

(viii) And because of all this, you have been described in history as a nation that spreads diseases that were unknown to man in the past. Go ahead and boast to the nations of man, that you brought them AIDS as a Satanic American Invention.[9]

(xi) You have destroyed nature with your industrial waste and gases, more than any other nation in history. Despite this, you refuse to sign the Kyoto agreement so that you can secure the profit of your greedy companies and industries.[10]

(x) Your law is the law of the rich and wealthy, who hold sway in their political parties, and fund their election campaigns with their gifts. Behind them stand the Jews, who control your policies, media, and economy.

(xi) That which you are singled out for in the history of mankind, is that you have used your force to destroy mankind, more than any other nation in history; not to defend principles and values, but to hasten to secure your interests and profits. You dropped a nuclear bomb on Japan, even though Japan was ready to negotiate an end to the war.[11] How many acts of oppression, tyranny, and injustice have you carried out, O callers to freedom?

(xii) Let us not forget one of your major characteristics: your duality in both manners and values; your hypocrisy in manners and principles. All

9 AIDS originated in sub-Saharan Africa during the twentieth century. The estimated prevalence of HIV infection in North America is among the lowest in the world, at between 0.3 and 0.6 per cent of the population.

10 Although a signatory to the Kyoto protocol to the UN Framework Convention on Climate Change, the USA has not ratified the protocol, which is non-binding. The present administration has indicated that it does not intend to submit the treaty for ratification.

11 Several high-ranking US military commanders, including Eisenhower and MacArthur, Supreme Allied Commander in the Southwest Pacific, felt that there was no military justification for the bombings. In a 1946 report, the United States Strategic Bombing Survey noted that Japan would in all probability have surrendered even if the atomic bombs had not been dropped.

manners, principles, and values have two scales: one for you and one for everybody else.

(a) The freedom and democracy that you call for is for yourselves and for the white race only; as for the rest of the world, you impose upon it your monstrous, destructive policies and governments, which you call "friends of America". Yet you prevent them from establishing democracies. When the Islamic party in Algeria wanted to practice democracy and they won the election, you unleashed your collaborators in the Algerian army on them, and attacked them with tanks and guns, imprisoned them and tortured them—a new lesson from the "American book of democracy".

(b) Your policy on prohibiting and forcibly removing weapons of mass destruction to ensure world peace only applies to those countries which you do not permit to possess such weapons. As for the countries to which you gave consent, such as Israel, they are allowed to keep and use such weapons to defend their security. Anyone else who you suspect might be manufacturing or keeping these kinds of weapons, you call criminals and you take military action against them.

(c) You are the last ones to respect the resolutions and policies of International Law, yet you claim to want to selectively punish anyone else who does the same. Israel has for more than 50 years been pushing UN resolutions and rules to the wall with the full support of America.[12]

(d) As for the war criminals whom you censure and form criminal courts for—you shamelessly ask that your own are granted immunity.[13] However, history will not forget the war crimes that you committed against the Muslims and the rest of the world; those you have killed in Japan, Afghanistan, Somalia, Lebanon, and Iraq will remain a disgrace that you will never be able to escape. It will suffice to remind you of your latest war crimes in Afghanistan, in which densely populated innocent

12 For a list of US vetoes cast against UN Security Council Resolutions on Palestine, see http://www.caabu.org/press/documents/vetoes.html.
13 Established in 2002, the International Criminal Court (ICCt) is a permanent tribunal set up to prosecute individuals for genocide, crimes against humanity, and war crimes. The USA signed, but did not ratify the treaty establishing the court, and is not legally bound by it.

civilian villages were destroyed, bombs were dropped on mosques, causing the roof of the mosque to collapse on the heads of the Muslims praying inside.[23] You are the ones who broke the agreement with the *mujahidin* when they left Qunduz, bombing them in Jangi fort, and killing more than 1,000 of your prisoners through suffocation and thirst.[14] God alone knows how many people have died by torture at the hands of you and your collaborators. Your planes remain in the Afghan skies, looking for anyone remotely suspicious.

(e) You have claimed to be the vanguards of Human Rights, and your Ministry of Foreign affairs issues annual reports containing statistics of those countries that violate any Human Rights. However, all these values vanished when the *mujahidin* hit you [on 9/11], and you then implemented the methods of the same documented governments that you used to curse. In America, you arrested thousands of Muslims and Arabs, took them into custody with no reason, court trial, nor did you disclose their names. You issued newer, harsher laws.[15]

What happens in Guantanamo is a historical embarrassment to America and its values, and it screams into your hypocritical faces: What is the value of your signature on any agreement or treaty?[16]

(3) What we call you to thirdly is to take an honest stance with yourselves—and I doubt you will do so—in order to discover that you are a nation without principles or manners, and that, to you, values and principles are something which you merely demand from others, not that which you yourself must adhere to.

---

14 On November 25 2001, Taliban fighters holding the town of Qunduz surrendered to Northern Alliance forces. They were taken to the Qala-e-Jangi prison complex near Mazar-i-Sharif; en route, many hundreds of prisoners died of asphyxiation in the shipping containers used to transport them. Later, some 230 prisoners and one CIA officer died in an uprising at Qala-e-Jangi. See Babak Dehghanpisheh, John Barry, and Roy Gutman, "The Death Convoy of Afghanistan," *Newsweek*, August 26 2002.

15 The US Patriot Act (Uniting and Strengthening America by Providing Appropriate Tools Required to Intercept and Obstruct Terrorism Act of 2001) was signed into law on October 26 2001.

16 Prisoners held in the US naval base at Guantanamo Bay, southeast Cuba, are accorded neither rights as enemy combatants under the Geneva Convention, nor constitutional rights in the US, since the Justice Department argues that Guantanamo is not legally inside US territory.

(4) We also advise you to stop supporting Israel, and to end your support of the Indians in Kashmir, the Russians against the Chechens, and also to cease supporting the Manila Government against the Muslims in the southern Philippines.[17]

(5) We also advise you to pack your luggage and get out of our lands. We only desire this for your goodness, guidance, and righteousness, so do not force us to send you back as cargo in coffins.

(6) Sixthly, we call upon you to end your support of the corrupt leaders in our countries. Do not interfere in our politics and method of education. Leave us alone, or else expect us in New York and Washington.

(7) We also call you to deal with us and interact with us on the basis of mutual interests and benefits, rather than the policies of subjugation, theft, and occupation, and not to continue your policy of supporting the Jews because this will result in more disasters for you.

If you fail to respond to all these conditions, then prepare to fight with the *umma*, the Nation of Monotheism, which puts complete trust on God and fears none other than Him. The *umma*, which is addressed by its Qur'an with the words:

> Do you fear them? It is God you should fear if you are true believers. Fight them: God will punish them at your hands, He will disgrace them, He will help you conquer them, He will heal the believers' feelings and remove the rage from their hearts. God turns to whoever He will in His mercy; God is all knowing and wise.[17]

The Nation of honor and respect:

> But power belongs to God, to His Messenger and to the believers.[18]

> Do not lose heart or despair—if you are the true believers you have the upper hand.[19]

17 Qur'an, 9:13–14.
18 Qur'an, 63:8.
19 Qur'an, 3:139.

The Nation of Martyrdom; the Nation that desires death more than you desire life:

> [Prophet], do not think of those who have been killed in God's way as dead. They are alive with their Lord, well provided for, happy with what God has given them of His favor; rejoicing that for those they have left behind who have yet to join them there is no fear, nor will they grieve; [rejoicing] in God's blessing and favor, and that God will not let the reward of the believers be lost.[20]

The Nation of victory and success that God has promised:

> It is He who has sent His Messenger with guidance and the religion of truth to show that it is above all [other] religions, even though the idolators hate it.[21]

> God has written: "I shall most certainly win, I and My messengers." God is powerful and almighty.[22]

The Islamic Nation that was able to dismiss and destroy the previous evil Empires like yourself; the Nation that rejects your attacks, wishes to remove your evils, and is prepared to fight you. You are well aware that the Islamic Nation, from the very core of its soul, despises your haughtiness and arrogance.

If you Americans refuse to listen to our advice and the goodness, guidance, and righteousness that we call them to, then be aware that you will lose this Crusade Bush began, just like the other previous Crusades in which you were humiliated at the hands of the *mujahidin*, fleeing to your home in great silence and disgrace. If you Americans do not respond, then your fate will be that of the Soviets who fled from Afghanistan to deal with their military defeat, political breakup, ideological downfall, and economic bankruptcy.

This is our message to the Americans, as an answer to theirs. Do they now know why we fight them and over which form of ignorance, by the permission of God, we shall be victorious?

20 Qur'an, 3:169–71.
21 Qur'an, 61:9.
22 Qur'an, 58:21.

17

TO THE ALLIES OF AMERICA

November 12 2002

One of the briefest of bin Laden's messages, this was delivered as an audiotape to al-Jazeera, and is designed as a commentary on six attacks, all but one involving civilian targets—in Tunisia, Pakistan, Yemen, Kuwait, Bali, and Moscow—carried out by different Muslim groups in the course of 2002. Four of these occurred in the month of October, the most ruthless being the terror bombings in Bali, which left 202 dead, mainly Australian and British tourists. The message has sharp words of rebuke for all the nationalities that suffered casualties in these attacks, invoking a single juridical principle: reciprocity. What you have done to us we will do to you. Bin Laden details the ledger of loss, due to violent death and destruction, which includes Palestine and Iraq, a wedding party bombed in Khost, Afghanistan, and the carnage of Chechnya. "Just as you kill, so you shall be killed; just as you bomb, so you shall be bombed. And there will be more to come."

Ironically, this message also includes use of the basmala. *The invocation of God as at once the source and channel of mercy is the most frequent formula for Muslims. It is used before meals, before travel, before public addresses as well as in prayer. Bin Laden invokes it here to begin his rebuke of American allies, as if condemning them to witness how far they are from the mercy of the Almighty.*

Peace be upon those who follow true guidance.

The road to safety begins with the cessation of hostilities, and reciprocal treatment is a part of justice. The events that have taken place since the attacks on Washington and New York, like the killing of the Germans in Tunisia,[1] the

---

1 On April 11 2002, a huge truck bomb was detonated at the 2,000-year-old Ghriba synagogue on the Tunisian island of Djerba, killing fourteen German tourists, six Tunisians, and a Frenchman, and wounding 30 others. The suicide bomber was a local 24-year-old middle-class Tunisian, Nizar Nouar, who apparently spent time in Afghanistan in 2000–01.

French in Karachi,[2] the bombing of the giant French tanker in Yemen,[3] the killing of marines in Failaka[4] and of the British and Australians in the Bali explosions,[5] the recent operation in Moscow,[6] and various other operations here and there: these are all reactions in kind perpetrated by the zealous sons of Islam in defense of their religion and in response to the order of their Lord and their Prophet.

What Bush—the pharaoh of the age—is doing, killing our sons in Iraq, and what America's ally Israel is doing, using American aeroplanes to bomb houses in Palestine with old men, women, and children in them, was enough for the sane leaders among you to distance themselves from this criminal gang. Our people have suffered murder and torture in Palestine for nearly a century. But as soon as we defend them the world gets agitated and joins forces against the Muslims under the false and unjust pretext of fighting terrorism.

Why are your governments allying themselves against the Muslims with the criminal gang in the White House? Don't they know that this gang is the biggest murderer of our age?

This Rumsfeld, the butcher of Vietnam, is responsible for the deaths of two million, as well as injuries to many others. And as for Cheney and Powell, they have reaped more murder and destruction in Baghdad than Hulagu the Tatar.[7]

Why are your governments, especially those of Britain, France, Italy, Canada, Germany, and Australia, allying themselves with America in its attacks on us in Afghanistan?

2 In Karachi, on May 8 2002, a suicide bomber detonated a car bomb next to a bus, killing himself, eleven Frenchmen, and two Pakistanis; 40 others were wounded. The eleven Frenchmen were engineers working with Pakistan to design a submarine for the Pakistani navy.

3 On October 6 2002, the French oil tanker *Limburg*, filled with 397,000 barrels of crude oil, was rammed by an explosive-laden boat in the Gulf of Aden. One (Bulgarian) crew member was killed, 12 others were injured, and 90,000 barrels of oil were released into the Gulf of Aden.

4 On October 8 2002, during a US-marine training exercise on the Kuwaiti island of Failaka, two Kuwaiti nationals walked up to American troops and opened fire, killing one and injuring two more.

5 On October 12 2002, three bombs were detonated on the Indonesian island of Bali, killing 202 people and injuring 209, including 88 Australians, 38 Indonesians, and 26 British. A group of around a dozen local Indonesian Islamic activists were behind the attack.

6 On October 23 2002, 40 armed Chechen rebels took control of the crowded Dubrovka theater in Moscow, holding hostage 700 people. On the morning of October 26, Russian special forces pumped an aerosol anaesthetic gas into the theater before storming the building. All 40 rebels and 128 hostages died during the raid or in the following days. The rebel Chechen commander Shamil Basayev claimed responsibility for the attack.

7 Grandson of Genghis Khan, the Mongol ruler Hulagu Khan (1217–65) conquered much of southwest Asia, destroying many of the remaining Muslim states. He sacked Baghdad in 1258, killing some 250,000 inhabitants.

We warned Australia beforehand not to take part in the war in Afghanistan, as well as about its disgraceful attempts to separate East Timor, but it ignored the warning until it woke up to the sound of explosions in Bali. Its government then falsely contended that Australians had not been targeted.[8]

If it pains you to see your victims and your allies' victims in Tunisia, Karachi, Failaka, and Oman, then remember that our children are murdered daily in Palestine and Iraq. Remember our victims in the mosques of Khost, and the deliberate murder of our people at weddings in Afghanistan.[9] If it pains you to see your victims in Moscow, then remember ours in Chechnya.

How long will fear, killing, destruction, displacement, orphaning, and widowing be our sole destiny, while security, stability, and happiness is yours?

This is injustice. The time has come to settle accounts. Just as you kill, so you shall be killed; just as you bomb, so you shall be bombed. And there will be more to come.

With God's will, the Islamic *umma* has started to strike back with its own sons, who have given their pledge to God that they will continue the *jihad* with word and deed so long as they have eyes to see or blood in their veins, in order to establish truth and eradicate falsehood.

Finally, I call upon God to help us achieve the victory of His religion and to continue the *jihad* for Him until we meet Him and He is content with us. For He is the guarantor of that and well capable of it.

Our final prayer is thanks to God, Lord of the Worlds.

8 In the wake of the Bali bombings, Australian Prime Minister John Howard talked of a general warning, but said that intelligence was at no time specific about the attack in Bali.

9 On July 1 2002 a US plane mistakenly targeted a house full of wedding guests in Oruzgan, central Afghanistan. 30 guests were killed, and at least 40 injured.

V

WAR IN IRAQ 2003–2004

18

TO THE PEOPLE OF IRAQ

February 11 2003

From the autumn of 2002 onwards, it became increasingly clear that the United States was preparing to invade Iraq and overthrow the Ba'ath regime, and that it would be seconded by Britain. Five weeks before the assault was finally launched, the first of three messages from bin Laden to the Iraqi people, consisting of a sixteen minute-long audiotape, was delivered to al-Jazeera, and immediately broadcast. It appears to have been issued in response to appearances on al-Jazeera by leading figures of the Bush administration, including Condoleezza Rice, Colin Powell and Donald Rumsfeld. Although al-Jazeera broadcast the message within hours of receiving it, Washington seems to have known about the tape in advance, for shortly before the letter was aired, Secretary of State Powell told a Senate panel that a tape that al-Jazeera was about to broadcast was evidence of bin Laden's partnership with Iraq.[1]

Condemning in advance the invasion of Iraq, which he predicts will combine massive air strikes and a non-stop propaganda campaign, bin Laden encourages the population to resist by recounting in detail the defensive tactics that enabled him and his fellow-fighters to survive the saturation bombing of their redoubts in the Tora Bora mountains in December 2001. But in Iraq, he writes, "what the enemy fears most is urban and street warfare, in which heavy and costly human losses can be expected". Insisting on "the importance of dragging the enemy into a protracted, exhausting, close combat, making the most of camouflaged defense positions in plains, farms, hills, and cities", he also stresses the capacity of "martyrdom operations" to inflict "unprecedented harm" on the enemy. These prescriptions describe with remarkable accuracy the tactics that would be successfully adopted by much of the Iraqi resistance from the summer of 2003 onwards.

In the great new battle that is imminent, bin Laden excoriates the Arab leaders who act as accomplices to America, declaring them hypocrites and apostates who have put themselves outside the community of Islam: "It is permissible to take their money and their blood." The Saudi rulers,

---

1 Miles, *Al-Jazeera*, p. 232.

though nervous of the upcoming war, had in fact already closed a number of airports near the Iraqi border to civilian aircraft so they could be secretly used by the US military. Muslims must rise up and free themselves from such traitorous tyrants. Bin Laden singles out six countries as most urgently in need of liberation—three monarchies, Jordan, Morocco, and Saudi Arabia, and three military dictatorships—Pakistan, Nigeria, and Yemen. His reasons for excluding Egypt and the Gulf sheikhdoms, for him equally logical targets, are unclear. In Iraq itself, Muslims can fight with a good conscience alongside Ba'athists, however atheist they may be, against the common enemy—since socialist rulers are finished anyway, whether in Aden or Baghdad. Just as there was once a convergence of interests, which did no harm to the faith, between Muslims and Persians in fighting Byzantines, so the resistance of the devout to Americans in Iraq should have no compunction in joining forces with loyalists of the fallen regime to expel them.

Peace be with you and all God's mercy and blessings.

"You who believe, be mindful of God, as is His due, and make sure you devote yourselves to Him, to your dying moment."[2]

We are following with intense interest and concern the Crusaders' preparations for war to occupy one of Islam's former capitals,[3] loot Muslims' riches, and install a stooge government to follow its masters in Washington and Tel Aviv, like the other treacherous puppet Arab governments, to pave the way for the establishment of Greater Israel. "God is enough for us; He is the best protector."[4] In the midst of this corrupt, unjust war that the infidels of America are waging with their agents and allies, we would like to emphasize a number of important values:

First, sincerity of will, and fighting for the one God, who has no equal, rather than for any particular ethnic group or any of the pagan regimes so common in the Arab countries, including Iraq. God Almighty said: "The believers fight for God's cause, while those who reject faith fight for an unjust cause. Fight the allies of Satan: Satan's strategies are truly weak."[5]

2 Qur'an, 3:102.

3 Baghdad was founded on July 30 762 by the Abbasids, replacing Damascus as the capital of a Muslim Empire stretching from North Africa to Persia. Within a generation, it was one of the largest, most cosmopolitan cities in the world; by the 9th century, its population was between 300,000–500,000.

4 Qur'an, 3:173.

5 Qur'an, 4:76.

Second, we remind you that victory comes only with God. All we need to do is prepare and motivate for *jihad*. God Almighty said: "You who believe! If you help God, He will help you and make you stand firm."[6] We must be quick to seek repentance from God for our sins, especially the grave ones. As God's Prophet said: "Avoid the seven deadly sins: associating others with God, sorcery, killing others, which God has forbidden unless it is just, usury, taking money from orphans, desertion, defaming innocent women believers,"[7] as well as the other grave sins such as drinking alcohol, adultery, disobeying parents, and committing perjury.[8] In general, we must always be quick to obey God, and remember especially to repeat His name when joining battle. Abu al-Darda said: "Do a good deed before battle, for you fight with your deeds."[9]

Third, it has become clear to us during our defensive *jihad* against the American enemy and its enormous propaganda machine, that it depends for the most part on psychological warfare. It also depends on intense air strikes, which hide its most conspicuous weak points: fear, cowardice, and lack of fighting spirit among its troops. These troops are utterly convinced of their government's tyranny and lies, and they know the cause they are defending is not just. They merely fight for capitalists, takers of usury, and arms and oil merchants, including the criminal gang in the White House. Add to that Bush Senior's personal grudges and Crusader hatred. It has also become clear to us that one of the most effective and readily available means of neutralizing the Crusader enemy's air force is to dig large numbers of roofed and disguised trenches, something I pointed out in a previous statement last year during the battle of Tora Bora. In that great battle, the forces of faith triumphed over all the evil forces of materialism by remaining true to their principles. I will recount a part of it to you to prove both how cowardly they are and how effective trenches are at wearing the enemy down. Our number was something approaching three hundred *mujahidin*. We dug one hundred trenches, spread across an area no more than one square mile—one trench for every three brothers—so as to avoid heavy human casualties from the bombing. From the

---

6 Qur'an, 47:7.

7 From the *hadith* collection of al-Bukhari, vol. 4, book 51, no. 28.

8 Although these are all discouraged in Islam, they are not a part of the *hadith* record that outlines the most destructive sins.

9 Quoted in ibn Qutiba al-Dinuri, *Ayun al-Akhbar*, p. 144. Abu Darda was one of the Prophet Muhammad's nominated transcribers of the Qur'an, who would record each passage of the Qur'an as it was revealed to him. 42 different transcribers were used.

first hour of the American campaign on 20th Rajab 1422 AH [October 7 2001], our positions came under intensive bombardment. This continued on and off until the middle of Ramadan, and on the morning of Ramadan 17th [December 3 2001] very heavy bombing began, especially after the American command had confirmed that some of the al-Qaeda command, such as the humble servant and the brother and *mujahid* Dr Ayman al-Zawahiri were still in Tora Bora. The bombing continued around the clock—not a second went by without warplanes flying over our heads, day and night. The American defense ministry command room, with all its allies, put everything they had into blowing up and destroying this small area. They tried to eradicate it altogether. The planes poured down their fire on us, especially after they had completed their standard missions in Afghanistan. The American forces barraged us with smart bombs, bombs weighing a thousand pounds, cluster bombs, and bunker busters. Bombers like the B-52 circled above us, one of them for more than two hours, dropping twenty to thirty bombs at a time. Modified C-130 planes attacked us all night with carpet bombs and other kinds of modern firepower. Despite the unprecedented scale of this bombardment and the terrible propaganda, all focusing on one small, besieged spot, as well as the hypocrites' forces, which they got to fight against us for over two weeks, non-stop, and whose daily attacks we resisted by the will of God Almighty, we pushed them back in defeat every time, carrying their dead and injured. Despite all this, the American forces dared not storm our positions. What clearer evidence could there be of their cowardice, of their fear and lies, of the myths about their alleged power? The battle culminated with the resounding, devastating failure of the global alliance of evil, with all its supposed power, to overcome a small group of *mujahidin*, numbering no more than three hundred, in their trenches within one square mile, at temperatures as low as ten degrees below zero. We suffered only about 6 per cent casualties in the battle, and we ask God to accept them as martyrs. As for those in the trenches, we lost only about 2 per cent, thank God. If all the forces of global evil could not even achieve their objective over one square mile against a small number of *mujahidin* with such modest capabilities, how could they expect to triumph over the entire Islamic world? This is impossible, with God's will, as long as people stay true to their religion and insist on waging *jihad* for it. So, brother *mujahidin* in Iraq, do not be frightened by the lies propagated by America about its power, and about its smart or laser-guided bombs. These have no significant effect in hills, trenches, plains, or forests, as they require clear targets. Neither smart nor stupid bombs can penetrate well-disguised trenches in anything better than a random way that wastes the enemy's ammunition and resources. So use trenches as much as you can: as the Caliph Umar, may God be pleased with him, said: "Use the ground as a shield." In other words, take the earth as a shield, for with God's grace and will it ensures the total exhaustion of the enemy's bomb supply within a few months. Their daily production is small enough to be easily endured, with God's will. We also underline the importance of dragging the enemy forces into a protracted, exhausting, close combat, making the most of camouflaged defense positions in plains, farms, hills, and cities. What the enemy fears most is urban and street warfare, in which heavy and costly human losses can be expected. Further, we emphasize the importance of martyrdom operations, which have inflicted unprecedented harm on America and Israel, thanks to God Almighty.

We also decree that any of the hypocrites in Iraq, or Arab rulers who have helped America in their murder of Muslims in Iraq, anyone who approved of their actions and followed them into this Crusader war by fighting with them or providing bases or administrative support, or any other kind of backing, should be aware that they are apostates who are outside the community of Islam; it is therefore permitted to take their money and their blood. God Almighty said: "You who believe, do not take the Jews and the Christians as allies: they are allies only to each other. Anyone who takes them as an ally becomes one of them—God does not guide such wrongdoers."[10] We also stress to true Muslims that, amid such momentous events and such a heated atmosphere, they must motivate and mobilize the *umma* to liberate themselves from their enslavement to these oppressive, tyrannical, apostate ruling regimes who are supported by America, and to establish God's rule on earth. The areas most in need of liberation are Jordan, Morocco, Nigeria, Pakistan, Saudi Arabia, and Yemen. It is also no secret that this Crusader war is directed primarily against the people of Islam, regardless of whether the socialist party, or Saddam, remains [in power] or not.[11] So, Muslims in general and in Iraq in

10 Qur'an, 5:51.

11 By the socialist party, bin Laden means the Ba'ath ("resurrection") party. Ba'athist ideology combined Arab socialism, nationalism, and Pan-Arabism. Originally a pan-Arab organization, it split in 1966 into two branches, one based in Syria, the other in Iraq. In Iraq, the Ba'athists held power from 1963 until 2003; in Syria they are still in power.

particular must prepare themselves for *jihad* against this unjust campaign and make sure to acquire ammunition and weapons. This is their prescribed duty. God Almighty said: "[Let them be] on their guard and armed with their weapons: the disbelievers would dearly like you to be heedless of your weapons and baggage, so that they can take you in a single assault."[12] It is well known that fighting under pagan banners is not allowed, and that the Muslim's belief and banner must be clear when fighting for God. As the Prophet, said: "Only he whose aim in fighting is to keep God's word supreme fights in God's cause."[13] There is no harm in such circumstances if the Muslims' interests coincide with those of the socialists in fighting the Crusaders, despite our firm conviction that they are infidels. The time of these socialist rulers is long past. The socialists are infidels, wherever they may be, whether in Baghdad or Aden.[14] The current fighting and the fighting that will take place in the coming days can be very much compared to the Muslims' previous battles. There is nothing wrong with a convergence of interests here, just as the Muslims' struggle against Byzantium suited the Persians but did not harm the Prophet's companions, may God be pleased with them.

Before concluding, we should also emphasize the importance of good morale and of guarding against false rumours, defeatism, uncertainty, and discouragement. God's Prophet, said: "Bring good news and do not discourage others."[15] He also said: "Abu Talha's voice in the army is better than a thousand men."[16] At the battle of Yarmuk,[17] a man said to Khaled ibn Walid: "How many the Byzantines are, and how few the Muslims." Khaled, may God be pleased with him, replied: "Nonsense. Armies do not triumph by having large

12 Qur'an, 4:102. Bin Laden does not quote the whole verse, so the context is lost. In its entirety, verse 102 describes a system for prayer in rotations so that part of the Muslims will remained armed at all times.

13 From the *hadith* collection of al-Bukhari, vol. 1, book 3, no. 125.

14 Before 1990, when North and South Yemen merged to become the Republic of Yemen, the People's Democratic Republic of Yemen, whose capital was Aden, was the only Communist state to exist in the Middle East.

15 Quoted in ibn Manzur, *Lisan al-Arab*, p. 5,079.

16 Quoted in ibn Manzur, *Makhtasar Tarikh Damashq*, p. 1,234.

17 The Battle of Yarmuk (Syria) was fought between the Muslim Arabs and Byzantines, four years after the death of the prophet Muhammad, in August 636. It marked the first great wave of Muslim conquests outside Arabia, and heralded the rapid advance of Islam into Christian Palestine, Syria, and Mesopotamia. The Muslim forces were led by the celebrated general Khalid ibn Walid (584–642); though outnumbered, the Muslim forces were victorious, and Damascus was captured within a month of the battle.

numbers. They are only conquered by their own defeatism," or something along those lines. May the words of God Almighty stay in your mind: "A prophet should not take prisoners until he has ensured his dominance in the land."[18] And "When you meet the disbelievers in battle, strike them in the necks."[19] Your reprimand to the Crusaders should be just as the poet said: "All there is between you and me is the piercing of kidneys and smiting of necks."

In conclusion, I enjoin us all to fear God both covertly and overtly, and to be patient in the *jihad*, for victory requires patience. I enjoin us all to pray and to repeat God's name. God Almighty said: "Believers, when you meet a force in battle, stand firm and keep God firmly in mind, so that you may prosper."[20]

Oh God, revealer of the book, director of the clouds, defeater of factions, defeat them and give us victory over them.

Oh God, revealer of the book, director of the clouds, defeater of factions, defeat them and give us victory over them.

Oh God, revealer of the book, director of the clouds, defeater of factions, defeat them and give us victory over them.

"Our Lord, give us good in this world and in the Hereafter, and protect us from the torment of the Fire."[21] May God's prayers and blessings be upon Muhammad and upon all his family and companions.

18 Qur'an, 8:67.
19 Qur'an, 47:4.
20 Qur'an, 8:45.
21 Qur'an, 2:201. This is noted in the following Qur'anic verse as being an effective prayer of righteous believers.

19

AMONG A BAND OF KNIGHTS

February 14 2003

This is the first and only statement of bin Laden that is framed as a sermon. It was delivered three days after his Letter to the Iraqi People, on February 14, the holiest day of the Islamic calendar, Eid al-Adha, the Feast of the Sacrifice. A 53-minute audiotape, it was circulated on various websites, and excerpts were published by the Saudi-owned newspaper al-Hayat. Although warning once more of the imminent attack on Iraq, the sermon seeks to retell the entire story of Western aggressions in the Arab world, from the Sykes-Picot agreement for the division of the Middle East between British and French spheres of control to its latter-day sequel in the Bush-Blair axis for domination of the region. In this, bin Laden maintains, Saudi Arabia is also scheduled for division, in the interests of the United States and Greater Israel alike, schemes already afoot in 1973, when Nixon contemplated invading the peninsula.

Scriptural authority and contemporary deeds are invoked for a virulent denunciation of the role of the Jews in the region, going back to the time of Muhammad. But, continues bin Laden, accomplices in Zionist-American aggression are the client Arab states, who have permitted "the hegemony of the infidels" to be established over the Muslim umma. *In Afghanistan the puppet Karzai is an embodiment of this system, but the Saudi, Kuwaiti, Bahraini, Qatari, and Pakistani rulers are so many Arab or Punjabi Karzais too, and Muslims must dissociate themselves from such tyrants. Turning to the* jihad *against infidel power in Afghanistan, now in its third year, bin Laden reports that it is going well. Russia was defeated in Afghanistan and Chechnya, the United States in the Lebanon and Somalia: scripture and history offer many such examples of Muslim victories against exceptional odds. The 9/11 attacks showed the world that the United States is not invincible: although America is a vast military and economic superpower, if its weak points are targeted, then "the whole edifice will totter and sway." The sacrifices of all warriors for Islam will be rewarded, and he counts himself among the lucky who may enjoy a martyr's death—the "band of knights" portrayed in his concluding poem, "dwelling in a high mountain pass", who "descend to face armies."*

Praise be to God, who revealed the Verse of the Sword to His servant and Messenger in order to establish Truth and eradicate falsehood. Praise be to God, who has said: "When the forbidden months are over, wherever you find the polytheists, kill them, seize them, besiege them, ambush them—but if they turn [to God], maintain the prayer, and pay the prescribed alms, let them go on their way, for God is most forgiving and merciful."[1] Praise be to God, who has said: "Fight them: God will punish them at your hands, He will disgrace them, He will help you to conquer them, He will heal the believer's feelings."[2] And prayers and peace and blessings be upon our Prophet Muhammad, who said, "I was sent with a sword in my hands so that only God Almighty is worshipped without equal. He put my sustenance in the shadow of my spear, and disgraced and humiliated those who oppose my order. He who imitates another is no better than them."[3] He also said: "Banish the polytheists from the Arabian peninsula."[4]

As I speak, the blood of Muslims continues to be shed in vain in Palestine, Chechnya, Philippines, Kashmir, and Sudan, and our children are dying because of the American sanctions in Iraq. As I speak, our wounds have yet to heal from the Crusader wars of the last century against the Islamic world, or from the Sykes-Picot Agreement of 1916 between France and Britain, which brought about the dissection of the Islamic world into fragments.[5] The Crusaders' agents are still in power to this day, in light of a new Sykes-Picot agreement, the Bush-Blair axis, which has the same banner and objective, namely the banner of the Cross and the objective of destroying and looting of our beloved Prophet's *umma*.

1 Qur'an, 9:5.
2 Qur'an, 9:14.
3 From the *hadith* collection of ibn Hanbal, vol. 5, book 3, no. 5,409.
4 From the *hadith* collection of al-Bukhari, vol. 4, book 52, no. 288. This was one of three requests Muhammad made on his deathbed. This *hadith* forms part of the title of Statement 3 (see above, p. 23).
5 The Sykes-Picot agreement of May 16 1916 was a secret understanding between the governments of Britain and France, defining their spheres of post-World War One influence and control in the Middle East. The boundaries of the agreement are still apparent in the border between Syria and Iraq. Britain gained control of areas roughly comprising Jordan, Iraq, and an area around Haifa in what is now Israel. France was allocated southeast Turkey, northern Iraq, Syria, and Lebanon. The area that came to be called Palestine was scheduled for international administration pending consultation with other international powers. The agreement's principal terms became League of Nations mandates, and were ratified by the Council of the League of Nations on July 24 1922.

The Bush-Blair axis claims that it wants to annihilate terrorism, but it is no longer a secret—even to the masses—that it really wants to annihilate Islam. Furthermore, in their speeches and statements, the rulers of the region affirm their support for Bush in his "war on terror", i.e. his war on Islam and Muslims.[6] This is clear treachery against our religious community and our *umma*, relying on the blessing of the government-backed scholars and corrupt ministers. Nor can there be any doubt that the current preparation for an attack on Iraq is anything other than the latest in a continuous series of aggressions on the countries of the region, including Syria, Iran, Egypt, and Sudan. However, the focus on dividing up Saudi Arabia takes up the lion's share of their plan. It is well known that this is an old strategic aim of theirs, ever since Saudi Arabia's client status was transferred from Britain to the United States sixty years ago. America tried to fulfil this aim three decades ago in the aftermath of the war of Ramadan 10th, when President Nixon threatened to invade Saudi Arabia in its entirety, although by the grace of God he wasn't able to do so at the time.[7] However, with the onset of the second Gulf War America has established seriously important military bases all over Saudi Arabia, and near the capital in particular. Their only remaining task was to divide the country up, and it seems as if the time for that has now arrived. "God is sufficient for us and He is a great guardian."[8] The conclusion is that America's objective of general control over the region, and of division of Saudi Arabia in particular, is no passing summer cloud but a

6 No Gulf Cooperation Council state (Bahrain, Kuwait, Oman, Qatar, Saudi Arabia, and the United Arab Emirates [UAE]) "openly" supported the overthrow of the government of Iraq in 2003, but there is little question that the states of the GCC assisted US military operations in Iraq in ways that ranged from the UAE and Oman allowing over-flight or basing rights, to the stationing of thousands of sailors, troops, and combat aircraft in Bahrain, Oman, and Saudi Arabia. While GCC governments expressed opposition to the war in the weeks leading up to mid-March, official criticism of the United States became increasingly muted, as the war became a foregone conclusion. Sean Foley, "The Gulf Arabs and the new Iraq: the most to gain and the most to lose?" *Middle East Review of International Affairs*, June 2003, vol. 7, no. 2.

7 The reference is the 1973 Arab-Israeli War, in which Saudi Arabia did not participate, although it was crucial to the ensuing oil embargo. Secret intelligence documents brought to light in 2004 revealed that the Nixon administration contemplated an invasion of several Gulf states to seize their oil fields and end the embargo, although this plan was never fully developed. See *Washington Post*, January 1 2004, pA1 (http://www.washingtonpost.com/ac2/wp-dyn?pagename=article&node=&contentId=A46321-2003Dec31&notFound=true).

8 Qur'an, 3:173.

strategic goal of America's cunning policy that cannot be ignored. And what have the governments of the region done to resist this hostile strategic goal? Nothing, except to increase their client status towards the Crusaders, in addition to regular meetings of Arab interior ministers to fight against the *mujahidin* and to make life difficult for the honorable preachers and scholars who are trying to alert our *umma* to the need to defend itself. One of the most important objectives of this new Crusader campaign, after dividing up the region, is to prepare it for the establishment of what is called the state of Greater Israel, which would incorporate large parts of Iraq and Egypt within its borders, as well as Syria, Lebanon, and Jordan, the whole of Palestine, and a large part of Saudi Arabia. Do you know what harm and suffering Greater Israel will bring down upon the region? What is happening to our people in Palestine is just a small example of what they want to repeat in the rest of the region courtesy of the Zionist-American alliance: murder of men, women, and children, incarceration, terrorism, destruction of houses, bulldozing of fields and razing of factories. People are living in constant fear and alarm, expecting death to come at any moment from a missile or bomb destroying their house and killing their womenfolk. How will we respond to our Lord on the Day of Judgment?

Not even valiant fighting men could put up with what is happening there, so how can poor mothers stand by watching their children killed in front of them? "We belong to God, and to Him we shall return."[9] "He is sufficient for us and He is a great guardian."[10] Oh Lord, I declare You innocent of [i.e., not responsible for] the actions of these Jews, Christians, treacherous rulers, and those under their rule, and I apologize to You for these men who are failing to support our religion. The creation of Greater Israel will entail Jewish domination over the countries of the region. What will explain to you who the Jews are?[11] The Jews are those who slandered the Creator, so how do you think they deal with God's creation? They killed the Prophets and broke their promises. Of them God has said: "How is it that whenever they made a covenant or a pledge, some of them throw it away? In fact, most of them do

---

9 Qur'an, 2:156. In the context of the verse, this is a saying for those facing calamity.
10 Qur'an, 3:173.
11 The form of this question is a standard rhetorical form from the Qur'an; see, for example, Qur'an, 97:2.

not believe."[12] These Jews are masters of usury and leaders in treachery. They will leave you nothing, either in this world or the next. Of them God said: "Do they have any share of what He possesses? If they did they would not give away so much as the groove of a date stone."[13] These Jews believe as part of their religion that people are their slaves, and whoever denies their religion deserves to be killed. Of them God said: "[That is] because they say 'We are under no obligation toward the gentiles'—they tell a lie against God and they know it."[14]

These are some of the characteristics of the Jews, so beware of them. These, too, are some of the features of the Crusader plan, so resist it. Now how can we stop the infidels' evil and save the Muslim lands? To answer this question I say—and success is with God—what the righteous servant and Prophet of God, Shu'aib, said: "I only want to put things right as far as I can. I cannot succeed without God's help: I trust in Him, and always turn to Him."[15] And so the way to stop the infidels' evil is *jihad* for the sake of God. As He said: "So [Prophet] fight in God's way. You are accountable only for yourself. Urge the believers on. God may well curb the power of the disbelievers, for He is stronger in might and more terrible in punishment."[16] To begin with I bring you the good news that today, by the grace of God, our *umma* possesses enormous powers, sufficient to rescue Palestine and the rest of the Muslim lands. However, these powers have been fettered and we must work to release them. For our *umma* has been promised victory. If it has been delayed, that is only because of our sins and our failure to help God. As God said: "You who believe! If you help God, He will help you, and make you stand firm."[17] Our *umma* has also been promised victory over the Jews, as our Prophet told us: "The Day of Judgment will not come until the Muslims fight and kill the Jews.

12 Qur'an, 2:100.
13 Qur'an, 4:53.
14 Qur'an, 3:75.
15 Qur'an, 11:88. The verse begins, "He [Shu'aib] answered, 'My people, can you not see? What if I am acting on clear evidence from my Lord? He Himself has given me good provision: I do not want to do what I am forbidding you to do.'" Shu'aib (meaning "one who shows the right path") was appointed by God to be a prophet to those who lived in the lands east of Mount Sinai, the people of Mudyan and Aykah, who were notorious for cheating. Shu'aib warned them against this; they ignored him, and both lands were destroyed by the wrath of God.
16 Qur'an, 4:84.
17 Qur'an, 47:7.

They [the Jews] will hide behind rocks and trees, and the rocks and trees will say: Oh Muslim, oh servant of God, there is a Jew behind me, so come and kill him. This is except for the boxthorn tree, which is the tree of the Jews."[18]

This *hadith* of the Prophet also contains a warning that the struggle against the enemy will be decided by fighting and killing, not by paralysis of the powers of our *umma* for decades through other means, like the deceptive idea of democracy. Along with this good news, I should tell you about something to help us in our *jihad* for the sake of God. Among them are stories of the battles and wars during the last two decades in which the Muslims were victorious, raising the self-confidence of the sons of our *umma*. This is because it is very important to mobilize our *umma* to defend itself against the Zionist-Crusader alliance. In fact, the Islamic *umma* is the greatest human power, if only the religion were properly established. History has shown in recent centuries that it is able to fight and resist the so-called superpowers. But before discussing this I should mention an incident which is relevant to the subject of fighting the superpowers. Historians tell us that al-Muthanna al-Shaibani came to Medina seeking the Caliph Umar's support in fighting the Persians. For three days Umar petitioned people's help, but not a single person came forward. Realizing the fear in people's hearts at the difficulty of fighting a superpower, Umar told al-Muthanna to describe how God had granted him victory against the Persians in order to rid them of their fear. So al-Muthanna began to tell them what had happened and to motivate them, saying: "O you people, don't let them frighten you, for we have defeated and humiliated the Persians, capturing the best parts of the agricultural region of Iraq. We outwitted them and gained ascendancy over them."

So the people were inspired. Abu Ubeid al-Thaqafi stood up and was given the banner by Umar, and the people followed him into battle. And I say, like these noble men: O you people, don't let America and its army frighten you, for by God we have struck them and defeated them time and again. They are the most cowardly people in battle. We have seen while fighting to defend ourselves against the American enemy that it depends mainly on psychological warfare, in light of the huge propaganda machine that it possesses, as well as on intense aerial bombardment, which hides its most conspicuous Achilles heel, namely the fear, cowardice, and lack of fighting spirit of the American

18 From the *hadith* collection of al-Bukhari, no. 3,593.

soldiers. If I had longer, I would tell you some almost unbelievable things that happened when we fought them in Tora Bora in Afghanistan, and I pray to God that He will give us time to discuss them in detail.

To begin with, I could remind you of the defeat of some of the superpowers at the hands of the *mujahidin*, in particular the defeat of the former Soviet Union, which took place, by the grace of God, after ten years of fierce fighting at the hands of the sons of Afghanistan and their Muslim supporters. Likewise the defeat of the Russians in Chechnya, where the *mujahidin* provided the most amazing examples of self-sacrifice and, with their Arab brothers and helpers, smashed the arrogance of the Russians and inflicted upon them defeat after defeat. The Russians withdrew in disarray after the first war, and then came back with American support.[19] But still they are suffering crushing defeats at the hands of a small group of believers, and we pray to God to help them stand firm and be victorious.

I could also remind you of the defeat of the American forces in the year 1982, when the sons of Israel destroyed Lebanon, and the Lebanese resisted. They sent a truck loaded with explosives into a US marine base in Beirut, sending more than 240 of them to Hell, the worst possible fate.[20] Then, after the Second Gulf War, America put her armies into Somalia and killed 13,000 Muslims there, and there is no strength or power save in God. But then the lions of Islam, the Afghan Arabs and their brothers leapt on them and rubbed their arrogance in the mud, killing many of them, destroying their tanks and downing their planes. So America and her allies fled in the dark of night, without disturbing anyone, praise and glory be to God. During that time, the youth of *jihad* prepared explosives against the Americans in Aden, and when they went off all the coward Americans could do was run away in less than

19 Bin Laden is here referring to the ongoing Second Chechen War, over whether Chechnya should remain within the Russian Federation or become an independent nation. Major combat took place between 1999 and 2002, although sporadic fighting continues today. The estimated death toll varies from 11,000–50,000 Russian servicemen, and 20,000–100,000 civilians. Between 230,000–400,000 people have been displaced. Following 9/11, Russian President Vladimir Putin attracted more Western support for the war in Chechnya, portraying Chechen militants as Islamic terrorists. For stated US policy on Chechnya as of May 2002, see http://www.state.gov/p/eur/rls/rm/2002/10034.htm.

20 On October 23 1983, a truck filled with explosives was detonated at the US Marine Barracks, Beirut International Airport. The attack killed 220 US Marines and 21 other US service personnel. Many believe that the Hezbollah organization was behind the bombing; several Shia militant groups claimed responsibility.

24 hours. Then in the year 1995 there was an explosion in Riyadh that killed four Americans, the clear message of which was that the sons of the region objected to the American policy of supporting the Jews and occupying Saudi Arabia. Then in the following year, another explosion in Khobar killed 19 Americans and wounded more than 400, and the Americans were forced to move their biggest bases from the cities to the desert. Then after that, in 1998, the *mujahidin* gave America a clear warning to stop supporting the Jews and to leave Saudi Arabia, but the enemy rejected it and the *mujahidin* were able, by the grace of God, to deal them two mighty blows in East Africa. After that, America was warned once again and failed to respond, so God helped the *mujahidin* to successfully implement a great martyrdom operation, demolishing the American destroyer USS *Cole* in Aden.[21] This operation was a solid blow in the face of the American military and also exposed the fact that the Yemeni government was a collaborator, like the rest of the region's governments.

Then when they saw the gang of criminals in the White House misrepresenting the truth, whose idiotic leader claims that we despise their way of life—although the truth that the Pharaoh of the age is hiding is that we strike them because of their injustice towards us in the Islamic world, especially in Palestine and Iraq, and their occupation of Saudi Arabia—the *mujahidin* decided to overcome this obfuscation and to bring the battle right into their heartland. And on that blessed Tuesday, the 23rd of Jumada ath-thani 1422, which corresponds to September 11 2001, the Zionist-American alliance was mowing down our sons and our people in the blessed land of al-Aqsa, at the hands of the Jews but with American planes and tanks, and our sons in Iraq were dying as a result of the oppressive sanctions of America and its agents, while the Islamic world was a very long way from properly establishing Islam.

21 On the morning October 12 2000, the destroyer USS *Cole* moored at the port of Aden, Yemen, to refuel. A small boat drew up alongside and between 500 and 700 pounds of explosive were detonated, blowing a large hole in the steel hull of the USS *Cole*. Seventeen American sailors were killed, and 39 injured. Six men, all veterans of the Afghanistan war, were arrested in connection with the attack. Of them, Abd al-Rahman al-Nashiri (alias Mohammed Omar al-Harazi) first met bin Laden in Afghanistan in 1996; in 1998 he conceived the attack on the *Cole*, which bin Laden approved and funded. The Yemeni Jamal al-Badawi (1969–) was captured and sentenced to death on September 29 2004. Al-Nashiri (currently being held by the USA at an undisclosed location) was also tried and sentenced in absentia. The other four conspirators were sentenced to terms of between five to ten years for their involvement in the attack. For bin Laden's poem on the attack, read out at his second son's wedding in January 2001, see Burke, *Al-Qaeda*, p. 213.

Amidst all this frustration, despair, and procrastination among Muslims—except for those upon whom God had been merciful—and amidst all this injustice, arrogance, and aggression on the part of the Zionist-American alliance, while "Uncle Sam" was committing these reckless transgressions and terrible oppression in contempt of everyone, going through the world without paying attention to anyone else and thinking that nothing could attack it, disaster struck it. What will explain to you what disaster is? There came a group of young believers with dishevelled hair and dusty feet, who had been chased all over the world. But God had guided them, firmed up their belief and "inscribed faith into their hearts,"[22] so they "did not fear anyone's reproach."[23] They sought to be with God, and deprived themselves of sleep while injustice was being done. They poured out the water of life, not the water of shame.[24] So they attacked the enemy with their own planes in a brave and beautiful operation, the like of which humanity has never seen before, destroying the idols of America. They struck at the very heart of the Ministry of Defense, and they hit the American economy right at its heart, too. They rubbed America's nose in the dirt, and wiped its arrogance in the mud. As the twin towers of New York collapsed, something even greater and more enormous collapsed with them: the myth of the great America and the myth of democracy. It became clear to all that America's values are the lowest, and the myth of the "land of the free" was destroyed, as was the myth of American national security and the CIA, all praise and glory to God. One of the most important positive effects of our attacks on New York and Washington was to expose the reality of the struggle between the Crusaders and the Muslims, and to demonstrate the enormous hostility that the Crusaders feel towards us. The attacks revealed the American wolf in its true ugliness. The entire world woke up from its slumber, and the Muslims realized the importance of the doctrine of friendship and enmity in God. The spirit of brotherhood in faith amongst Muslims was strengthened, which can be considered a great step towards unification of the Muslims under the word of God and establishing the rightly guided Caliphate with the permission of

22 Qur'an, 58:22.
23 Qur'an, 5:54.
24 This is a play on words in Arabic; "ma' al-hayat" ("water of life") and "ma' al-mahya" ("water of shame") use variations on the same root.

God.[25] It also became clear to people that America, this unjust power, can be struck down and humiliated. And for the first time, most of the American population is aware of the reality of the Palestinian issue, and that what happened to them in Manhattan was a result of the unjust policies of their government.

We can conclude that America is a superpower, with enormous military strength and vast economic power, but that all this is built on foundations of straw. So it is possible to target those foundations and focus on their weakest points which, even if you strike only one-tenth of them, then the whole edifice will totter and sway, and relinquish its unjust leadership of the world. This group of young Muslims, despite the fact that the international alliance stands against them, were able to prove to the world that it is possible to resist and to fight the so-called superpowers. They were able to defend their religion and to promote the causes of their *umma* more than the governments and peoples of fifty countries in the Islamic world have done. For they took the path of *jihad* to help their religion, as Abu Hilala said:

> For victory there are reasons, and also for defeat
> And all who inherit eternity have profited.
> The paths of nobility are many, but the shortest
> Is the one that sheds blood far and wide.[26]

There are many examples like these young heroes in our *umma* today, by the grace of God, but they are restrained, and we must all pull together to unfetter them so they can become true *mujahidin* for the sake of God, because *jihad* is the way to honor our *umma* and [preserve] its security.

There are many shackles and obstacles preventing the youth of our *umma* from setting off on the *jihad*, but we will only discuss the most important ones. Let me mention the authentic Prophetic *hadith* that benefits whoever is

---

25 The Four Rightly Guided Caliphs were the first four caliphs in the Sunni tradition of Islam, who are viewed as model leaders. They were all close companions of Muhammad. The first, Abu Bakr (c.573–634) ruled from 632–634, succeeding Muhammad. Bakr nominated Umar as his successor (c.581–644); Uthman ibn Affan (c.574–656); and Ali ibn Ali Talib (598–661). In Shia tradition, Ali is seen as the first imam of Islam, and the first Caliph.

26 Yusuf Abu Hilala is the contemporary Jordanian scholar and poet whom bin Laden quotes at the end of Statement 14 (see above, p. 157).

guided by it and destroys whoever strays from it. The Prophet said: "Those who came before you perished because when one of their nobles stole, they let him go, and when one of their weak men stole, they punished him."[27] So think about it, people of insight, for this is one of the reasons for our predicament, and there is no strength or power save in God. I should also mention the story of how Khalid ibn Walid converted to Islam, so that minds can be freed from following the blind.[28] After he had converted late in life, Khalid was asked: "Where was your mind, that you did not see the light of Prophecy right before you for twenty years?" And he replied: "There were men in front of us whose dreams were like mountains." Imam Ahmad [ibn Hanbal] said: "It is only from a lack of understanding that a man would blindly follow other men and their religion."

The most significant of these shackles and obstacles in our present time are the rulers, the false witnesses among the scholars of evil, the corrupt court ministers, the writers-for-hire and others like them. As for the rulers, everyone is already agreed on their impotence and their treachery. But as for those who ask people to put themselves in the hands of these rulers, despite everything, we say to them: when did the peoples of these countries actually remove their support from these rulers, so that they could be advised to renew their support? The fact is that it never happened, and the result, as you can see, is the hegemony of the infidels over us. For it has been said:

> Those who betray when the going is good
> Will be unable to manage when the going is bad.

Our dispute with these rulers is not one that can be resolved piecemeal. No, we are talking about the central point of Islam, the testimony that there is no god but God and that Muhammad is His Prophet. These rulers have contravened this testimony from its very root through their client status towards the infidels, through their imposition of man-made legislation, as well as through

27 From the *hadith* collection of al-Bukhari, vol. 8, book 81, no. 778.

28 Khalid ibn Walid (584–642) was an Arab Muslim soldier and general. Like Muhammad, a member of the Quraish tribe (against whom Muhammad fought for much of his life), he led the Quraish to victory against the Muslims in the Battle of Uhud, before converting to Islam and apologizing to Muhammad for his previous actions. He became a commander of Muslim armies, conquering Damascus. See also above, p. 184, n. 17.

their acceptance of, and appeals to, the heretical United Nations. Their authority has fallen foul of Islamic law for some time, and there is no way we should remain under it. There isn't enough time to discuss this issue properly here, but in any case we have mentioned what religious scholars have said in Communiqué 17 of the Committee for Advice and Reform. Following this we say: can a Muslim tell other Muslims to pledge themselves to Karzai and cooperate with him to establish Islam, to remove injustice and to foil America in its designs? Impossible and inconceivable, since Karzai is a quisling brought in by America, and supporting him against Muslims is one of the ten acts contradictory to Islam that puts the perpetrator beyond the pale of his religious community.[29] And here we should ask ourselves: what is the difference between a Persian Karzai and an Arab Karzai? Who was it that installed the rulers of the Gulf States? It was the Crusaders, the same people who installed the Karzai of Pakistan, who installed the Karzai of Kuwait, the Karzai of Bahrain, Qatar, and others. Who was it that installed the Karzai of Riyadh and brought him in, even though he had been a refugee from Kuwait a century earlier, to fight on their side against the Ottoman state and its governor, ibn Rashid?[30] It was the Crusaders, and they are still holding us prisoner today. There is no difference between the Karzai of Riyadh and the Karzai of Kabul, "Learn from this, all you with insight."[31] God Almighty said: "Are your disbelievers any better than these? Were you given an exemption in the Scripture?"[32]

---

29 Hamid Karzai (1957–) was selected by the US as President of Afghanistan after the overthrow of the Taliban. He had worked for much of the 1980s as a fundraiser for the Afghan war against the Soviets, becoming a minister in the postwar government of Burhanuddin Rabbani. Initially a supporter of the Taliban, Karzai mistrusted their links with Pakistan, turning down the post of UN ambassador in the newly formed Taliban government in 1996. He then worked to reinstate his cousin, Zahir Shah.

30 Ibn Saud (c.1880–1953) was the first king of Saudi Arabia. On becoming leader of his dynasty in 1901, ibn Saud set out to reconquer family lands from ibn Rashid. He recaptured Riyadh in 1902 and almost half of the Najd region. In 1904 ibn Rashid appealed to the Ottoman Empire for assistance in defeating the House of Saud. Despite reverses, ibn Saud established control over the Najd by 1912, founding a militant religious organization, the Ikhwan ("Brotherhood") and reviving the Saud dynasty's traditional alliance with Wahhabism. In December 1915, he entered into a treaty with the British, making the lands of Saud a protectorate, and pledged to make war against the Ottoman ally ibn Rashid. He defeated the Rashidis in 1922, doubling the territory of the House of Saud, and continued to receive British subsidies until 1924. He captured in Mecca in 1925, and proclaimed himself King of Saudi Arabia in 1932, with British support.

31 Qur'an, 59:2.

32 Qur'an, 54:43.

These rulers who want to solve our issues—the most important of which is Palestine—through the United Nations or by the orders of the United States, as happened with Prince Abdallah's initiative in Beirut,[33] on which all Arabs agreed, which sold the blood of the martyrs and the land of Palestine to please the Jews and Americans and support them against the Muslims— these rulers have betrayed God and His Prophet, and they have gone beyond the pale of the religious community and betrayed our *umma*. I also say that those who want to solve our issues through these weak and treacherous leaders are guilty of self-deception and have also deceived our *umma*. They have come to rely on those who are unjust and in clear error. The best you can say of them is that they are weak and profligate. All Muslims should try to advise them, but if this advice is not accepted, then they should warn them and beware of them. Muslims also have a duty to dissociate themselves from these tyrants, for it is no secret that to do so is not just a gratuitous action but one of the pillars of monotheism without which there can be no faith. For God said: "Whoever rejects false gods and believes in God has grasped the firmest handhold, one that will never break. God is all hearing and all knowing."[34]

As for scholars of evil, corrupt court ministers, writers-for-hire and the like, it has been said: in every era there is a state and there will be men—and these are the followers of the state—who distort the truth and make false testimony, even in the sacred land, in the sacred house, and in the sacred month. They claim that the treacherous rulers are our righteous guardians and they say this in order to strengthen the pillars of the state. These people have erred from the path, so we must reject them and warn them. Indeed, the state focuses on its own scholars and gives them coverage on religious programs where they give juridical decrees on minor issues which the state requires to increase its legitimacy. That is what happened on the day when the King of Saudi Arabia allowed the Americans into the country. He ordered his scholars to give their calamitous juridical decrees that contravened Islam and insulted

---

33 At a summit meeting of the Arab League in Beirut, Lebanon, on March 28 2002, acting Saudi regent Crown Prince Abdullah floated an initiative calling for Israel to withdraw all forces from the Occupied Territories and to recognize the Palestinian Authority as a sovereign nation, with its capital in East Jerusalem. In exchange, Arab states would recognize the state of Israel within borders comprising 78 per cent of Palestine, and establish normal relations with it.

34 Qur'an, 2:256.

the intelligence of Muslims while supporting his treacherous deed in that great disaster. They duly issued them. Our *umma* is still suffering today from that disastrous decision and those deceitful, sycophantic rulings. Whoever has read about the righteous imams in previous times of strife, like Imam Ahmad ibn Hanbal and others, would know the difference between genuine scholars and sycophants, as can be read in the Biographies of the Distinguished Righteous Men and elsewhere. As the poet said:

> If we stitch together this life by tearing apart the next,
> Then neither the next life nor this will be ours.

As for the second obstacle, this constitutes the scholars and preachers who love the truth and hate falsehood, yet refrain from *jihad*. So they chose to prevent the youth from *jihad*, and there is no strength or power save in God. They saw falsehood spreading and increasing, so they summoned each other to undertake their duty of helping the truth, enjoining good and forbidding evil. Many were guided by them, and they have become knowledgeable—may God reward them well for this—but falsehood never thrives in the presence of truth and those who represent it. So it was made legal for them to be persecuted, terrorized, and prevented from speaking in public or giving lessons. They were fired from their jobs and then those who insisted on continuing to enjoin good and forbid evil were imprisoned. This strong pressure gradually led to a deviation from the path—except among those upon whom God was merciful—which is only to be expected, since no one can take the right decision in such circumstances, especially from the point of view of personal security. God's Prophet said: "A judge cannot make a judgment between two people when he is angry."[35] That is when he is angry, so what about when he is frightened? The intimidation practised by Arab states on their peoples has destroyed life in all its dimensions, including religious affairs. Religion is advice, but there can be no advice without security. This fear has divided people into groups, some of whom we will discuss here. One group relapsed and joined the side of the state, becoming its client. Another group thought it would not be able to continue preaching and teaching, or that it would no longer be safe—and nor would their persons, their honor, and their

---

35 From the *hadith* collection of al-Bukhari, vol. 9, book 89, no. 282.

property, if they did not praise and extol the tyrant. So they made a corrupt choice, going into manifest error and leading many others the same way.

And another organization was protected by God from conforming with and praising the traitorous leaders. They made sure to stay under the banner of enjoining good and forbidding evil, and made laudable efforts in calling people to God. But they were not fully prepared for the aforementioned pressures, which were very great indeed, particularly the costs of emigration and *jihad*. The opportunity was available to them more than two decades ago but they didn't take it, thus reducing their ability to take the right decisions—except for those on whom God was merciful—in those tense times. That is why, even now, we see some of them still refraining from taking up *jihad* and resistance. Helping to establish our religion incurs great costs, as is clearly illustrated in God's Book, and in the life of His Messenger and his noble companions. Whoever cannot live up to this will not be able to help Islam, as was mentioned by God in His Holy Book: "You who believe, if any of you renounce your faith, God will soon replace you with people He loves and who love Him, people who are humble towards the believers, and hard on the infidels, people who strive for the sake of God without fearing reproach from anyone."[36] In the incident that occurred between the Prophet and Waraqa bin Nawfal, Waraqa said: "How I hope that I will be alive when your people banish you." The Prophet said: "Would they really do that?" and Waraqa said: "Yes, since no one like you has appeared without facing hostility. If I see the day when that happens, I will give you full support."[37] So, one who wants to embrace his religion fully ends up criticizing the people of falsehood, rather than coexisting—as we can see—with them, while he who wants to support his religion ends up striving to help himself and others, as Waraqa said: "If I see the day when that happens, I will give you full support." This was the case on the day of the pledge of Aqaba,[38] for the victory of religion cannot be covered by lessons alone, but through time and money, as God's commodity is expensive. There is a world of difference between sitting and giving lessons on

36 Qur'an, 5:54.
37 From the *hadith* collection of al-Bukhari, vol. 1, book 1, no. 3. This is part of the story of the first revelation of the Qur'an. Waraqa bin Nawfal was the cousin of Muhammad's wife Khadija, and was the second person (after Khadija) to whom Muhammad recounted his vision.
38 See above, p. 81. n. 22.

the one hand, and giving our souls and heads for the victory of God. That is why al-Abbas bin Abd al-Muttalib, who still followed the religion of his people,[39] wanted to be sure of his nephew Muhammad's position with the Helpers. So he said to them: "If you really are a people of power, endurance, vision in war, and independence, with hostility toward the Arabs, one and all, then they will unite against you." So I tell you: these characteristics were required for the people of faith to protect the Messenger of God, just as they are required today to protect his religion. When al-Abbas had finished speaking, al-Bara bin Ma'rur, who was one of the Helpers, said: "We have heard what you said, and by God if there was anything in our hearts other than what we say, then we would have said it, but we want to be faithful and true and to give our lives to protect the Messenger of God."[40] So I tell you that this is how religion should be. It is based on loyalty, truthfulness and giving up your life to follow a certain path. When the people got up to pledge their allegiance, As'ad bin Zarara said: "Just a minute, people of Yathrib. We should not pledge our lives in obedience before we know that he is the Messenger of God. If we do not expel him today, it would mean a parting of the ways with all Arabs; it would mean that you and some of your best men would be killed. If you are ready to do this, then take him, and may your reward be with God. If you are afraid for yourselves, then expel him, for he has more excuse than you before God." So they said: "Stretch out your hand, for by God we will never break or forsake this pledge."[41]

These are the traits of those who want to protect and establish the religion of Islam. And today, this is what the *mujahidin* say to the scholars and preachers who love the truth and do not appease falsehood. You have raised the banner of Islam, and you know that it is in truth the religion of God's Messenger. Your doing so means opposition to all Arab and non-Arab governments on earth; it means that your best men will be killed and that you will constantly be at war. If you can bear this patiently, then protect the banner and may your reward be with God. But if you fear for yourselves at all, then leave the banner of defense and resistance, but you will be more forgiveable before God if you do not come between the youth of our *umma* and their *jihad* for the sake of God.

39 For al-Muttalib, see above, p. 155, n. 18.
40 Quoted in ibn Juzay, *Safa al-Sufua*, p. 90.
41 Quoted in the ibn Sayijid al-Nas, *Ayun al-Athar ji al-Mujhazi al-Sayyir*, p. 105.

We will now discuss what are the duties of Muslims in the face of this Zionist-Crusader war against our Islamic *umma*. God Almighty said: "So [Prophet] fight in God's way. You are accountable only for yourself. Urge the believers on. God may well curb the power of the disbelievers, for He is stronger in might and more terrible in punishment."[42] Today the most important duty after faith is to repel and fight the enemy aggressor. The Sheikh of Islam [ibn Taymiyya] said: "As for repelling the enemy aggressor who corrupts religion and the world, there is no greater duty after faith than uncompromising struggle against him." So *jihad* is obligatory today on our entire *umma*, for our *umma* will stand in sin until her sons, her money, and her energies provide what it takes to establish a *jihad* that repels the evil of the infidels from [harming] all the Muslims in Palestine and elsewhere. So it is a duty for Muslims to wage *jihad* to the best of their abilities, to confirm the truth and to lay bare falsehood. God's Messenger said in the Sahih of Muslim: "Whoever fights them with his hand is a believer, whoever does so with his tongue is a believer, whoever does so with his heart is a believer, and beyond that there is not so much as a mustard seed's worth of faith."[43]

This great tradition of the Prophet applies to all believers, for inasmuch as we are believers then we are also *mujahidin* for the sake of God and our religion. The believer who cannot wage *jihad* with his hand or his tongue, must do so with his heart, which entails continuing to hate the enemies of God and calling for *jihad* against them, continuing to be friends with the believers and the *mujahidin* and praying for them, and helping them to feel the brotherhood of faith that joins Muslims everywhere from east to west. He must help them to feel that faith lies in one single tent, and that the infidels are in another tent, so that God blesses our *umma* with a state that includes all Muslims under its authority, with His permission. He should give himself for the sake of God with both his hand and his tongue, although this is only the weakest part of faith. He should boycott the goods of America and her allies, and he should be very wary that he does not support falsehood, for helping the infidels over Muslims—even with a single word—is clear unbelief, as the religious scholars have decreed. He must also be wary not to end up among those about whom God said: "They are miserly, and they order others to be

42 Qur'an, 4:84.
43 From the *hadith* collection of Muslim, book 1, n. 81.

the same,"[44] or those of whom He said: "God knows exactly who among you hinder others, who say to their brothers 'Come and join us', who hardly ever come out to fight,"[45] for he should not combine the sin of refraining from *jihad* with that of betrayal.

If individual *jihad* is an obligation upon our entire *umma* today, then it is even more so for the youth than it is for the old. Financial *jihad*, likewise, is an obligation today, particularly for those who have the resources, rather than those who don't. It is part of God's grace to our *umma* today that He has opened the hearts of many of the youth to pursue *jihad* for His sake, and to provide for His religion and His servants. So our *umma* has a duty to assist and encourage them, and to facilitate their affairs so that they can defend it from injustice, shame, and sin. It also has a duty to maintain the *jihad* that exists today and to help it with all its might, for this *jihad* is very dear to us in Palestine, Chechnya, Afghanistan, Kashmir, Indonesia, the Philippines, and other lands of Islam. The banner of *jihad* will only remain aloft in these states, despite the enemies' fierce attacks, by the grace of God and by the indescribable dedication of the *mujahidin*, giving their blood, sweat, and tears. We pray to God to accept them as martyrs.

I bring you the good news that the *jihad* in Afghanistan is going well today, and that things are improving for the *mujahidin*, by the grace of God. Here we are in the third year of fighting, and America has not been able to achieve its goals. Instead it has become embroiled in an Afghan quagmire. And as for what America considered to be victories in the first months of the war, after they captured some cities as a result of the withdrawal of the *mujahidin*, it is no secret to military experts generally, and to those who know Afghanistan particularly, that this was a tactical withdrawal in line with the nature of the Taliban state and the Afghans generally throughout their long history of guerrilla warfare. For the Taliban had no official army with which it could defend these cities, and that is why the Afghans resorted to their hidden powers of guerrilla warfare from the depths of their rugged mountains. This is the same tactic by which they previously conquered, by the grace of God, the army of the USSR, [a victory] which was ensured after they began to use guerrilla warfare and

44 Qur'an, 4:37.
45 Qur'an, 33:18.

increased the rate of operations to two a day. So the Americans are in a sorry plight today, unable either to protect their forces or to form a government that can protect its own leader, let alone others. And by the grace of God, all the *mujahidin* have been organized together this past year, all of them eager for the *jihad* and recognizing it as their duty. If it were not for a lack of resources, it would have been easy for them to increase the amount of daily operations to the previous level in the *jihad* against the Russians, which would be unbearable for the Americans. So the *umma* has a duty today to support the *jihad* generally, while Palestine and Afghanistan are the most important axes that should be focused on, to bleed the Jews, the allies of America, and to bleed the Americans, the allies of the Jews. America's defeat in Afghanistan, with God's permission, will be the beginning of the end for it. With God's will, you will not suffer any harm from us, nor from our brothers the Afghan *mujahidin*, and we hope we will not suffer any harm from you.

The *umma* today is at a crucial point, and it must not show weakness or transgress. The ranks of Muslims in it should unite against the ranks of infidels, and it should show repentance for all its sins. At this tense and important time, it should also forsake the life of frivolity and decadence, and stand up and prepare for the real life of killing, fighting, striking, and injuring. You have the words of the Sheikh of Islam at a time of strife similar to that which we are in now: "You should know, may God reform you, that the Prophet is widely reputed to have said: 'Until the Day of Judgment there will always be a group among my *umma* that manifests the truth, unharmed by those who have abandoned or quarrelled with them.'[46] This dispute divides people into three groups: the victorious party, who are the *mujahidin* against these corrupt people; the opposing party, and those biased towards them, who show contempt for Muslims; and the disloyal party, who refrain from *jihad*, even if they otherwise follow Islam correctly. So every man should decide whether he is with the victorious party, or with either of the other two, since there is no fourth party." The Sheikh went on to say: "By God, even if the first generation of Emigrants and Helpers, like Abu Bakr, Umar, Uthman, Ali,[47] and others, were here at this time, their greatest deed would be *jihad* against this criminal people. Such a raid as this is only missed by those whose trade has lost

46 From the *hadith* collection of Murdin.
47 The four Rightly Guided Caliphs; see above, p. 195, n. 25.

out and who have been humiliated and deprived of great fortune in this life and the next." And here he ended his speech.

So, then, I urge the youth to think for themselves about *jihad*, for they are the first of those obliged to pursue it today, as al-Shatbi has pointed out.

And know that targeting Americans and Jews the length and breadth of the earth is one of the greatest duties and one of the best ways to be close to God Almighty. I also urge the youth to pay attention to the truthful scholars and dedicated preachers, and to make use of their need for secrecy, especially in the military operations of *jihad*.

I bring you all—and those in Palestine particularly—the good news that your *mujahidin* brothers are sticking to the path of *jihad* to target the Jews and Americans, and that with the permission of God Almighty, the Mombasa operation was just the beginning of the deluge.[48] We will not forsake you, so keep fighting for the blessing of God. We are with you, fighting with God's permission. Before I finish, I will urge myself and my brothers in faith to *jihad* for the sake of God with these words:

> I shall lead my steed
> and hurl us both at the target.
> Oh Lord, if my end is nigh,
> may my tomb not be draped
> in green mantles.
> No, let it be the belly of an eagle,
> perched up on high with his kin.
> So let me be a martyr,
> dwelling in a high mountain pass
> among a band of knights who,
> united in devotion to God,
> descend to face armies.
> When they leave this world,
> they leave trouble behind,
> and meet their Day of Judgment,
> as told in the Scriptures.[49]

48 On November 28 2002, a car bomb exploded at the Israeli-owned Paradise Hotel on Mombasa's beachfront; ten Kenyans and three Israelis were killed. Twenty minutes earlier, two surface-to-air missiles were fired at an Israeli-chartered passenger jet taking off from the nearby Moi International Aiport, but missed and the plane landed safely at Tel Aviv.

49 This verse appears to be of bin Laden's own composition.

In conclusion, I urge my Muslim brothers and myself to be devoted to God Almighty both outwardly and inwardly, to keep praying and to be humble before Him. "Lord, give us good in this world and in the Hereafter, and protect us from the torment of the Fire."[50] We ask God Almighty to free our prisoners, especially the two Sheikhs Omar Abdul Rahman[51] and Sa'id bin Zu'air,[52] from the hands of the Americans and their collaborators and to free our brothers from Guantanamo Bay. We ask Him to help the *mujahidin* in Palestine stand firm and give them victory. We ask him to help them and all other Muslim lands against our enemy, and I urge both you and myself always to have God in our minds, and to read and reflect upon the Qur'an, for it contains moral lessons, cures, guidance, and mercy. God said: "People, a teaching from your Lord has come to you, a healing for what is in [your] hearts, and guidance and mercy for the believers."[53] "God always prevails in His purpose, though most people do not realize it."[54] Our final prayer is praise be to God, Lord of the worlds.

50 Qur'an, 2:201.
51 For Omar Abdel Rahman, see above, p. 26, n. 13.
52 Sa'id bin Zu'air is a Saudi Arabian university professor who was imprisoned without charge, for criticizing the Saudi government. He was released in March 2003, only to be incarcerated again in April 2004 for allegedly seditious statements during a debate on the al-Jazeera television network.
53 Qur'an, 10:57.
54 Qur'an, 12:21.

20

QUAGMIRES OF THE TIGRIS AND EUPHRATES

October 19 2003

Eight months elapsed between bin Laden's sermon on the eve of Shock and Awe, and his second message to the people of Iraq, a videotape delivered to al-Jazeera in mid-October. The initial easy success of the Anglo-American invasion had soon been followed by fierce Sunni resistance, bearing out bin Laden's predictions, but catching the invaders by surprise. By the autumn, it had become clear that the US occupation was bogged down in "the quagmires of the Tigris and Euphrates," suffering mounting casualties at the hands of guerrillas, operating in both cities and countryside. Having anticipated only a quick victory, bin Laden notes, America was now begging for help from "mercenaries and scum," presumably a reference to the various lesser states and private security organizations summoned to provide backup to US troops in Iraq.

Congratulating the warriors of the Iraqi resistance, in the frontline of jihad *in the defense of the* umma, *bin Laden tells them "you are descendants of the great knights who brought Islam as far east as China" when the Abbasid Caliphate was based in Baghdad. Warning them to have nothing to do with proposals for peaceful solutions emanating from renegade Arab regimes or the Jewish-Crusader alliance, he also proscribes collaboration with infidel organizations like the Ba'ath socialist party or the Kurdistan Democratic Party. In Palestine, the so-called "road map" is merely a device to stifle the* intifada, *and Abbas—not yet Chairman of the PLO, but already the US choice for the post—another Karzai.*

This is the second letter to our Muslim brothers in Iraq.

Descendants of Sa'd and Muthanna, Khaled and Ma'na, descendants of Salah al-Din!

Peace be with you and all God's mercy and blessings.

I salute you and your blessed *jihad*, for by God you have massacred the enemy and brought joy to the hearts of Muslims everywhere, especially in

Palestine. God has given you the best reward, and your *jihad* is appreciated. God has made you stand firm and guided your fire.

I am rejoicing in the fact that America has become embroiled in the quagmires of the Tigris and Euphrates. Bush thought that Iraq and its oil would be easy prey, and now here he is, stuck in dire straits, by the grace of God Almighty. Here is America today, screaming at the top of its voice as it falls apart in front of the whole world. Praise be to God, who has resisted America's deceitful strategies to the point where it is begging for help from mercenaries and scum from east to west.

It is little wonder that you have managed to do what you have done to America, bringing this shame down upon it, for you are descendants of the great knights who brought Islam as far east as China.

You should know that this war is a new Crusader campaign against the Islamic world, and it is a war of destiny for the entire *umma*. God only knows what serious ramifications it might have for Islam and its people.

So, youth of Islam, wherever you are, and especially in the neighbouring countries and Yemen: You must roll up your sleeves, prepare for *jihad*, and follow the truth. Be sure not to follow those who are victims of their own desires and are a burden on the land, or those who submit to the oppressors, spread lies about you, and hold you back from the blessed *jihad*.

Voices have been raised in Iraq—as previously in Palestine, Egypt, Jordan, Yemen and others—calling for a peaceful democratic solution in cooperation with apostate governments, or with the Jewish and Crusader invaders, instead of fighting for God. We should therefore make note, briefly, of the danger of this wrong-headed, errant idea which contravenes God's law and stands in the way of fighting for Him.

How can you obey those who never fought for God, while remaining true to the duty of *jihad*? Are you not thinking? These are the people who sapped the energies of the *umma* from the righteous men and followed human desires instead; these are the ones who followed democracy, the religion of ignorance. By entering the legislative councils these men have strayed far from truth, as well as leading many others astray.

How can these men enter the council of polytheism, the legislative council of representatives, which Islam has destroyed? Such an action destroys the head of faith, and what else do they have? And then they even claim that they are in the right. They are making a big mistake, and God knows that Islam has nothing to do with them.

Islam is the religion of God, and the legislative councils of representatives are the religion of ignorance. Those who have obeyed the commanders and scholars in making permissible what is forbidden—like entering the legislative councils—or making forbidden what is permissible (like *jihad* for His sake) has taken gods other than God, and there is no strength or power save in God.

I direct my call to Muslims generally and to the people of Iraq specifically, and I say to them: Make sure you do not collaborate with the Crusader forces of America and their supporters. Whoever cooperates with America—under whatever name or title—is an apostate and an infidel.

The same goes for those who collaborate with infidel parties, like the Arab Ba'ath Socialist Party and the Kurdish democratic parties and others like them.

It is no secret that any government formed by America is a traitorous, puppet government, like the rest of the governments in the region, like those of Karzai and Mahmoud Abbas,[1] which have been established in order to put a stop to *jihad*.

The Road Map is merely the latest in a series of conspiracies to end the blessed *intifada*.[2] *Jihad* must go on until an Islamic government is formed that rules according to the law of God.

Muslims, this is no joke; it is a serious matter. Anyone who can muster any effort, anyone who has an opinion, who has principles, strength, or money: now is the time for it. In situations like these, you find out people's true nature. The righteous man learns who is a liar, and the zealot learns who is lazy. And the free, noble, strong Muslim women are expected to play their role too.

And I say to my brother holy warriors in Iraq:
I swear by God that I share your concerns; I feel the same as you do, and I am glad that you are engaged in *jihad*. God knows, if I could find a way to get to your battlefields, I would not hesitate.

And how could I, when we know that our Prophet, our model and example, said: "This is the path of our Prophet Muhammad; it is the path of victory for

1 Often known as Abu Mazen, Mahmoud Abbas (1935–) was elected President of the Palestinian National Authority in January 2005. A leading politician in Fatah (the Movement for the National Liberation of Palestine), he served as Chairman of the PLO after the death of Yasser Arafat on November 11 2004.
2 The "road map for peace" is a plan to resolve the Israel-Palestine conflict, whose principles were first outlined by President Bush in a speech on June 24 2002.

our religion, and the path to the establishment of the state of Muslims. Stick to it, for only the righteous do so."

Muslims, people of Rabi'a[3] and Mudirr, and Kurds: raise your banner, and may God raise you up high. Those infidels will not scare you with their weapons, for God has weakened their schemes and stopped their progress. Don't let their numbers frighten you, for their hearts are empty and they are falling into military and economic disarray, especially after the blessed day in New York, by the grace of God.

After the attack and its repercussions, their losses reached over a trillion dollars—that is, a thousand thousand million dollars—and they have recorded a budget deficit for the third year running, breaking the record this year with more than 450 thousand million dollars in deficit, thanks and blessings to God.

In conclusion:

To my brother holy warriors in Iraq, to the heroes in Baghdad, the house of the caliphate—and all around:

To the Ansar al-Islam,[4] the descendants of Salah al-Din:

To the free men of Ba'qouba, Mosul and al-Anbar:[5]

To those who have emigrated for the sake of God to fight for the victory of their religion, leaving their fathers and sons, leaving their family and homeland:

To all of these: I send my greetings, and say to you: You are the soldiers of God, you are the arrows of Islam, and you are the first line of defense for this *umma* today.

The Romans have gathered under the banner of the cross to fight the nation of beloved Muhammad, prayers and peace be upon him, so think of the rewards

3 Rabi'a al-Adawiyya (717–801), from Basra in modern-day Iraq, first set forth the doctrine of mystical love, and is considered the most important of the early Sufi poets.

4 Formed in 2001, Ansar al-Islam ("Supporters or Partisans of Islam") is an Islamist group which at the beginning of the invasion of Iraq,controlled an area of territory in northern Iraq near the Iranian border. It has been accused of providing a safe haven to Abu Musab al-Zarqawi, who in December 2004 was appointed al-Qaeda's representative in Iraq by bin Laden.

5 The capital of Diyala province in Iraq, Baquba is around 50 kilometres north of Baghdad, within Iraq's so-called "Sunni Triangle". It was the scene of heavy fighting during the invasion of Iraq, and again on June 24 2004. Iraq's third largest city, Mosul, in northern Iraq, has a mainly Arab population in a region populated largely by Kurds. Al-Anbar is Iraq's largest province, sharing borders with Syria, Jordan, and Saudi Arabia, and containing the cities of Ramadi and Fallujah. The Iraqi insurgency is held to be stronger in this province than any other in Iraq.

210

of your *jihad*. I hope that the Muslims will not be harmed by you, for you have asked for God's protection, and placed great hope in Him. So do not shame the Muslims today, but act as Sa'd, may God be pleased with him, did at the Battle of the Trench, where he said:

> He lingered awhile—the lamb follows the camel.
> Death is no matter, if my time has come.

Yes, death is no matter if the time has come.

Lord, this is one of your days, so take the hearts of the youth of Islam and commit them to *jihad* for Your sake.

Lord, keep them to their belief and make them stand firm. Guide their fire and unite their hearts in harmony.

Lord, bring victory to Your servants, the holy warriors, wherever they may be, in Palestine, Iraq, Chechnya, Kashmir, the Philippines, and Afghanistan.

Lord, give comfort to our brothers who are imprisoned in tyrants' jails, in America, Guantanamo, in Occupied Palestine, in Riyadh, everywhere. You have power over everything.

Lord, give us patience, make us stand firm and help us struggle against the infidels. "God is victorious, although most people do not know it."

Pray to God and peace be upon our Prophet Muhammad, his family, and all his companions.

Finally, all praise to God, lord of the worlds.

21

RESIST THE NEW ROME[1]

January 4 2004

Following closely on his second letter to the Iraqis, this is the complete transcript of an audiotape delivered to the al-Jazeera television network and broadcast by it on January 4 2004. Like many of its predecessors, it was initially excerpted, al-Jazeera airing only 14 minutes of the full 47-minute tape.[2] On this occasion, the reason for such drastic abbreviation is clear. This message was bin Laden's most outspoken attack on the rulers of the Arabian peninsula, not least those of the Gulf states, including Qatar itself, where al-Jazeera is based.[3] Less than two months earlier, the US-run Coalition Provisional Authority in Baghdad had announced plans to hand over sovereignty to an Iraqi Interim Government, made in Washington, by mid-2004; it is in this context that bin Laden reiterates that the occupation of Iraq is only one stage in America's plans for the Middle East, in which the "region's ideology" is to be changed.

Bin Laden once again emphasizes the critical nature of the struggle for Iraq by placing it within an epic historical trajectory, from Muhammad's early victories to those of Saladin; the treachery of the Hashemite and Saudi families in allying with the West against the Ottoman Caliphate; the betrayal of Palestine; and the rise of earthly doctrines in the region: pan-Arabism, socialism,

1   Throughout his statements, bin Laden refers both to early Islamic battles against the Byzantine Empire, and to the "Romans"—that is Roman Catholics, or Western Christians—as a synonym for Crusaders. In the Arabic, the terms for "Byzantine" and "Roman" are very similar: "Al-Rum" denotes Byzantines and Byzantium, adherents of the Greek Orthodox Church. The adjective "Rumi" means Byzantine, Greek Orthodox. "Ruma" denotes Rome, and "al-Ruman" (marginally different from "al-Rum" in Arabic) refers to the Romans. Here, bin Laden uses both the Byzantines and the "Romans" to denote a hostile, aggressive enemy empire.

2   An Arabic-language transcript of the full text was posted on the Islamic Studies and Research center, at www.pages4free.biz/image333/index.htm. The website no longer exists at this address. This English translation was taken directly from that posted on www.whywar.com/news/2004/03/04fulltext.html; spelling and syntax have been altered for consistency and clarity.

3   Al-Jazeera continues to depend on support from the state of Qatar (see Miles, *Al-Qaeda*, pp. 346–7).

communism, and democracy. All these ideologies, says bin Laden, have failed, and the present governments in the Muslim world have proved themselves incapable of defending Islam and the umma. After dismissing the Road Map and the Geneva Initiative, and denouncing the infamy of the Saudi Prince (now King) Abdallah in preventing succour from reaching widows of Palestinian martyrs, bin Laden turns to the situation in Arabia itself.

Examining in detail the history of the Gulf States' collaboration with America over Iraq since 1990, he pours scorn on the flight of the Sabah family from Kuwait, and their complete submission to the will of the US. The assorted Emirs and Sheikhs of the Gulf have not only proved utterly incapable of opposing American aggression, he says—they have actively assisted it. In opening their air, land, and sea bases to the Crusader invasion of Iraq in March 2003, they have behaved no better than the Saudi dynasty; indeed, throughout the Arab world, no rulers are accountable, which is why all preside over economies that are less prosperous than al-Andalus today, which Muslims long ago lost to the Crusaders. Bin Laden calls on the people to oust these usurpers. In their place, for the first time he outlines a political alternative—the creation of temporary councils governing by sharia and offering tough leadership to the nation, mobilizing the faithful to defend Islam and giving them easy access to RPGs and tank mines. Jihad is a pressing need for the umma's survival and glory, since "fighting in the cause of God is the peak of religion". Although the enemy overtly preaches peace, it teaches its children the contrary. "The raid of the Romans started in Iraq; no one knows where it will end." After sixty years of uninterrupted wars, the system of American power will disintegrate when it stops fighting.

Thanksgiving and praise are due to God alone, we seek aid from Him alone; and we beseech forgiveness of our sins from Him only; and consign ourselves to the protection of God against the evil of our souls and against all offenses. Truly, whomsoever God guides on the straight path—and He puts him only on the straight path who sincerely desires to walk along that way—no one can lead him astray. And whoever God deflects—and He deflects only him who yearns to be deflected—no one can put him on the straight path. And I bear witness that there is no god except God and I testify that Muhammad is the bondman of God and His Messenger

"You who believe, be mindful of God, as is His due, and make sure you devote yourselves to Him, to your dying moment."[4]

4 Qur'an, 3:102.

From Osama bin Muhammad bin Laden to his brothers and sisters in the Islamic nation, God's peace, prayers, and blessings be upon you.

My message to you concerns inciting and continuing to urge for *jihad* to repulse the grand plots that have been hatched against our nation, some of which have been made particularly evident, such as the occupation of the Crusaders, with the help of the apostates, of Baghdad, the house of the caliphate, under the pretext [that it possesses] weapons of mass destruction.[5] There is also the savage attempt to destroy the al-Aqsa Mosque and destroy *jihad* and the *mujahidin* in beloved Palestine, by employing the pretext of the road map and the Geneva peace initiative.[6]

This is in addition to the crusader media campaigns against the Islamic nation. These campaigns show how malicious are the evils they harbor against the nation in general and against the people of Saudi Arabia in particular. The Americans' intentions have also become clear in their statements about the need to change the beliefs, curricula, and morals of Muslims in order to become more tolerant, as they put it. In clearer terms, it is a religious-economic war. They want the believers to desist from worshipping God so that they can enslave them, occupy their countries, and loot their wealth. It is strange that they want to dictate democracy and Americanize our culture through their jet bombers. Therefore, what is yet to come [from them] is even more malicious and devilish. The occupation of Iraq is a link in the Zionist-Crusader chain of evil. Then comes the full occupation of the rest of the Gulf states to set the stage for controlling and dominating the whole world. For the big powers believe that the Gulf and the Gulf states are the key to controlling the world, due to the presence of the largest oil reserves there.

5 The officially stated reason for the US- and UK-led 2003 invasion of Iraq was that Iraq possessed, and was continuing to develop, weapons of mass destruction (WMD), and had not fully cooperated with UN inspections. Before the invasion, the head UN weapons inspector, Hans Blix, stated that his teams had been unable to find any evidence of nuclear, biological, or chemical weapons in Iraq. Following the invasion David Kay, appointed by President Bush as head of the Iraq Survey Group, resigned his post in January 2004 , saying of the supposed WMD stockpiles in Iraq: "I don't think they existed ... we were all wrong and that is most disturbing." US forces formally abandoned the search for WMD on January 12 2005; on June 8 2005, former US Secretary of State Colin Powell said in a television interview that "where we got the intelligence wrong, dead wrong, is that we thought he also had existing stockpiles, and now we know that those are not there."

6 Launched on December 1 2003 at a ceremony in Geneva, Switzerland, the Geneva Initiative was an extra-governmental peace proposal compatible with moderate Zionist opinion.

The occupation of Baghdad is only one practical stage in what the United States has already thought through and planned. The entire region was targeted in the past, it is being targeted now, and will remain targeted in the future.

What have we prepared for that? The current Zionist-Crusader campaign against the *umma* is the most dangerous and rabid ever, since it threatens the entire *umma*, its religion, and presence. Did Bush not say that it is a Crusader war? Did he not say that the war will continue for many years and target 60 states?[7] Is the Islamic world not around 60 states? Do you not realize this? Did they not say that they want to change the region's ideology, which vents hatred against the Americans? What they mean by this is Islam and its peak. They know full well that they will not enjoy our wealth and land as long as we remain *mujahid* Muslims. So, learn this and keep it in your mind.

O Muslims: The situation is serious, and the misfortune is momentous. By God, my highest wish is to safeguard your religion and your worldly life. You are my brothers in religion and my family in kinship. An honest person would not cheat his people. So, lend me your ears and open up your hearts to me in order that we may examine these pitch-black misfortunes, and so that we may consider how we can find a way out of these adversities and calamities.

To talk about that, let me tell you what God's messenger Shu'ayb—may God's peace and prayers be upon him—told his people: "I only want to put things right as far as I can. I cannot succeed without God's help: I trust Him, and always turn to Him."[8]

In so doing, I seek God's assistance and trust to enforce His will, no matter what the consequences are. I seek the truth and fear nobody in championing rightfulness. I seek the approval of God, even if this angers some people. Our life's term will come to an end and our sustenance is predestined by God. So, why should one fear telling the truth and championing rightfulness? No one should desist from championing *jihad* when it becomes obligatory, except those who have lost their direction, humiliated themselves, and deprived

---

7 In a November 8 2001 address in Atlanta, Georgia, President Bush said "We wage a war to save civilization itself. We did not seek it, but we must fight it—and we will prevail. This is a different war from any our nation has ever faced, a war on many fronts, against terrorists who operate in more than 60 different countries."

8 Qur'an, 11:88. Shu'ayb was one of the prophets appointed by God.

themselves of unmatched reward. Therefore, the first step to emerge from this dilemma is to return to God Almighty, pray for His forgiveness, turn in repentance to Him, and follow the path of his great Qur'an and the tradition of his faithful messenger, may God's peace and prayers be upon him.

We should also look for the main reasons that diverted from within the march along the straight path, and identify the active forces that caused this deviation. We will find, without much effort, that these reasons are the princes, *ulema*, and preachers of evil, and those who have done injustice to the Islamic action, as well as the media persons of these states and those who followed them. The bitter truth is that the princes have managed to seduce many of the individuals in these groups, and have muffled the voices of those who refused to join them.

Since telling the truth and differentiating between right and falsehood are part of the teachings of the Qur'an and the Prophet's *hadith*, in order that people would not confuse falsehood and truth and thus stray from the right path, God said: "Do not mix truth with falsehood, or hide the truth when you know it."[9]

To remove any ambiguity, things have to be called by their true names and described by their religious terms, especially when we talk about the forces that impact upon the *umma*'s progress. This helps us gain a clear image of these forces and their actions, and makes it easier for us to deal with them, since judging things comes after knowing about them. Therefore, religious terms should be used when describing the ruler who does not follow God's revelations and path, and champions the infidels by extending military facilities to them, or implements United Nations resolutions against Islam and Muslims. Those should be called infidels and renegades. Those forces that consciously support tyrants through their own free will are partners in the injustice being done to Muslims. I appeal to the people of the Islamic action to oust their leaders who supported those tyrants, and select strong and honest leaders who can shoulder their duties under the current difficult circumstances and defend the Islamic nation. The media people who belittle religious duties such as *jihad* and other rituals are atheists and renegades. This is as far as concerns those forces that have diverted the course of our march from within.

As to how to resist these enemy forces from outside, we must look back at the previous Crusader wars against our countries to learn lessons that will help

9 Qur'an, 2:42.

us confront this onslaught, understand the most important causes of these attacks, and learn how they were repulsed and resisted.

I say that the West's occupation of our country is old, yet new, and that the confrontation and conflict between us and them started centuries ago. This confrontation and conflict will go on because the conflict between right and falsehood will continue until Judgment Day. Such a confrontation is good for both the countries and peoples. God says: "If God did not drive some back by means of others, the earth would be completely corrupt ..."[10] Those who interpret the Qur'an say that this verse means that had the believers not fought the infidels, the latter would have defeated the believers and the earth would have been corrupted by their ill deeds. So, pay attention to the importance of conflict.

There can be no dialogue with the occupiers except with weapons. If we look at the nature of the conflict between us and the West, we find that when they invaded our countries more than 2,500 years ago they did not have a sound religion or ethics. Their motive was to steal and plunder. Our ancestors in Bilad al-Sham remained under occupation for more than ten decades.[11] We defeated them only after the mission of our Prophet Muhammad. It was the true commitment to Islam that reshaped the Arab character, liberated it from pre-Islamic concepts, enlightened hearts and minds, and released energies. At that time, neither the Arabs nor anybody else could stand in the way of the battalions of faith. The Persians, Tartars, Turks, Romans, and Berbers collapsed in front of the shouts of "God is great". We were the pioneers of the world. We rescued the people from the worship of human beings, for the worship of the God of people.

When our adherence to our religion weakened and our rulers became corrupt, we became weak and the Romans returned, waging their infamous Crusader wars. They occupied the al-Aqsa Mosque, but after 90 years we regained our strength when we returned to our religion.[12] Thus, with the help of God, we regained the al-Aqsa Mosque at the hands of a wise leader who

10 Qur'an, 2:251.
11 Bilad al-Sham ("Land of the Sun/Dignity") was the Arab name for the region that corresponds to modern-day Syria, Jordan, Lebanon, Israel, and Palestine. For much of its history, Bilad al-Sham was closely integrated, sharing a common culture and economy; post-World War One colonialism, and the rise of individual states in the region, ended this unity.
12 Jerusalem fell to Christian soldiers of the First Crusade on July 15 1099; it was recaptured by the Kurdish Muslim general Saladin (1183–1193) at the Battle of Hattin on October 2 1187.

pursued a sound approach. The leader was Salah-al-Din, may God bestow his mercy on him, and the approach was Islam, whose pinnacle is *jihad* in the cause of God. This is what we need today, and should seek to do. Islamic countries in the past century were not liberated from the Crusaders' military occupation except through *jihad* in the cause of God. Under the pretext of fighting terrorism, the West today is doing its utmost to tarnish *jihad* and kill anyone seeking *jihad*. The West is supported in this endeavor by hypocrites. This is because they all know that *jihad* is the effective power to foil all their conspiracies. *Jihad* is the path, so seek it. This is because if we seek to deter them by any means other than Islam, we would be like the one who goes round in circles. We would also be like our forefathers, the Al-Ghasasinah. The concern of their elders was to be appointed officers for the Byzantines and to be named kings in order to safeguard the interests of the Byzantines by killing their brothers of the peninsula's Arabs.[13] Such is the case of the new Al-Ghasasinah; namely, Arab rulers.

Muslims, if you do not punish the Crusaders for their sins in Jerusalem and Iraq, they shall defeat you because of your failure. They will also rob you of the land of the Two Holy Sanctuaries. Today [they robbed you] of Baghdad, and tomorrow they will rob you of Riyadh and so forth unless God deems otherwise. Sufficient unto us is God.

What then is the way to stop this tremendous onslaught? As you may recall, the *umma* made several attempts in recent decades to resist the Zionist-Crusader alliance to liberate Palestine. The republics and kingdoms embraced several earthly religions in the region, like pan-Arabism, socialism, communism, democracy, and other doctrines.

These material forces have proved beyond any shadow of doubt that they surrendered to the US-led Zionist-Crusader alliance. The people followed these forces for a long time, only to find they are still where they were at the start. We have had enough of chasing mirages. Cease manipulating the minds of the people.

In such hard times, some reformers maintain that all popular and official forces should unite, and that all government forces should unite with all their peoples. Everyone would do what is needed from him in order to ward off this Zionist-Crusader onslaught. The question strongly raised is: Are the govern-

---

13 The Ghasasinah were an Arab tribe located in the northwest of the Persian empire (commensurate with modern-day Syria) in the centuries before the rise of Islam.

ments in the Islamic world capable of pursuing this duty of defending the faith and *umma* and renouncing allegiance to the USA? Let us have an objective look at these governments' history with regard to the *umma*'s crucial issues, in order to understand their policies, so that we will not be led into a dead end and so that we will not experience what we have endured for many decades.

1. Their [the Arab governments'] position on the Crusader aggression in World War One was as follows: When they [the Crusaders] attacked the Islamic world and sought to topple the Ottoman state, these rulers rose up against the Ottoman state, divided the Muslims, and made an effective contribution in terms of fighting this state, thus leading to its fall under the Crusader occupation and division into more than 50 countries. The prominent role in this treason was played by King Abd-al-Aziz al-Saud and Al-Sharif Hussain and his sons.[14]

2. The Palestine Question: The position of these rulers on this pivotal issue has for nine decades been based on pledging to the British to allow the Jews to establish a state on the land of Palestine, letting down the people of Palestine, and misleading them on several occasions into laying down their weapons. The most prominent of these attempts was made by King Abd-al-Aziz al-Saud. When the Zionist organization, or the so-called United Nations, issued its resolution on dividing Palestine and establishing a Jewish state in it, the Arab rulers stood idly by. Even today, the members of this organization remain. They have done nothing, except for shameful actions, to prevent this from happening. A fabricated war erupted after the Jewish state was established one year after the the resolution was passed to partition [Palestine].[15] Then, the Arab rulers agreed to sign a temporary truce in response to the request of the United States, which

14 For ibn Saud, see above, p. 197, n. 30. Hussain ibn Ali (d.1931) was the Sharif of Mecca (protector, or steward, of the holy cities of Mecca and Medina, and of pilgrims performing the *hajj*), and Emir of Mecca from 1908 to 1917. The last of the Hashemite rulers to be appointed by the Ottoman Empire, Hussain rebelled against Ottoman rule in 1916, allying himself with the British and proclaiming himself king of Hijaz. On the dissolution of the Ottoman Empire in 1924, he took the title of Caliph of Muslims. That year, he was defeated by the House of Saud, which eventually took Mecca, Medina, and Jeddah. The Sharifate came to an end shortly after Hussain's reign; the House of Saud has since exercised stewardship over the holy cities and the *hajj*, without claiming the title of Sharif of Mecca.

15 Following the proclamation of the state of Israel on May 14 1948, Jordanian, Egyptian, Syrian, Lebanese, and Iraqi forces began hostilities against it. In the ensuing war, an estimated 520,000 to 957,000 Palestinians fled the fighting or were expelled by Israeli forces.

asked them to sign a permanent truce after one year.[16] Thus, they almost buried Palestine and its people alive, but God protected them.

The conspiracies continued, including the Madrid conference and what came after it.[17] The efforts continued to abort the first *intifada*. In the Sharm al-Sheikh conference in 1416 Hegira, they supported the Jews and Christians against our oppressed people in Palestine.[18] In addition, the Beirut initiative recognized the Jews and a large part of the land they occupied in Palestine.[19] The most recent conspiracy is the road map. In the course of these conspiracies, they gave some money to the people of Palestine to throw dust in their eyes. History attests that they have restored nothing of Palestine during the past nine decades.

What is surprising, and disgusting as well, is the position of those rulers toward the families of the *mujahidin* who carried out martyrdom operations. While these families were expecting good deeds from them, the rulers responded with evil. Not only did they condemn the martyrdom operations, but they also came up with something that is more annoying and distressing. Look at the conditions of these families in Palestine as well as the conditions of our sisters the widows, whose husbands were killed by the Jews. Some of them sacrificed their sons for the sake of Islam and Islamic sanctuaries. After the possessors of thrones and armies abandoned them, the Jewish soldiers came to corrupt the land of Jerusalem, destroy the agricultural lands, and kill the people. They forced the Palestinian widow to leave her house, and destroyed its contents, not allowing her to take her precious possessions. She became homeless on roadsides, and tears filled her eyes, not knowing where to take her children and those of her son—whom we consider a martyr, but God knows best—as a result of her suffering and dire distress.

16 The 1949 Armistice Agreements were signed between Israel and Egypt, Jordan, Lebanon, and Syria.
17 The Madrid Conference (October 30–November 1 1991), co-sponsored by the USA and USSR, was designed to start a peace process in the Middle East. The conference was intended as a forum to inaugurate negotiation, and had no power to impose solutions or veto agreements. The subsequent Oslo accords of 1993 were based on terms that the Palestinian negotiators at the Madrid conference had essentially rejected. For Israel, a major benefit of the conference and process was the greatly increased number of countries that recognize and have diplomatic relations with it, such as Oman, Qatar, Tunisia, Morocco, and Mauritania, as well as China and India.
18 The "Summit of the Peacemakers" was held at Sharm el-Sheikh, Egypt, in March 1995, and was chaired by Mubarak and Clinton.
19 See above, p. 198, n. 35.

Thanks to God, some kindhearted people from Saudi Arabia and other countries were sending alms to the families of those widows and orphans to ease their suffering and distress. Unfortunately, the conceited, arrogant prince, Abdallah bin-Abd-al-Aziz, ordered that these well-doers be prevented from sending money to these families so that the martyrdom operations would stop.[20] What kind of heart is that to issue such an order? Is it a heart of a human being, or is it a heart made of stone? What kind of meanness is it to prevent small amounts of money from reaching a widow, an orphan, or a poor person? Can such cruel-hearted people bring us good or defend our countries and peoples? Those hypocrites, worshippers of money, claim that they are our leaders and will defend us.

I am surprised how those calling for reform say that the way to righteousness and defending our countries and peoples comes through these apostate leaders. I say to these people: If you have an excuse preventing you from *jihad*, it should not give you the right to stand beside those unjust leaders and thus be responsible for your sins and the sins of those whom you misled. Fear God for your sake and for your nation's sake. God does not need your flattery and praise for the tyrants for the sake of His religion. God Almighty says: "So do not yield to those who deny the truth—they want to compromise with them and then they will compromise with you".[21] It is better for a person to be at the bottom of right than to be at the peak of wrong.

3. The Gulf states proved their total inability to resist the Iraqi forces. As is well known, they sought help from the Crusaders, led by the United States. How can these states stand up to the United States and the Iraqi forces, which are being formed these days under American command?

The decision made by Jabir al-Sabah[22] and his comrades following the Iraqi invasion of Kuwait—when they fled the country—is the same decision that will be made by all the Gulf rulers, unless they reach an agreement with the United States to leave their thrones and be given other jobs to deceive the

20 In July 2003, Crown Prince Abdullah of Saudi Arabia announced the establishment of a Financial Intelligence Unit to oversee and account for charitable funding.

21 Qur'an, 68:8–9.

22 Jabir al-Sabah (1926–) is the Emir of Kuwait. He was briefly deposed following the 1990 Iraqi invasion of Kuwait, taking refuge in Bahrain and Saudi Arabia from August 2 1990 to March 14 1991, after which time he reassumed the throne.

people and protect US interests, pledging not to ask about oil revenues, as happened with their agents in the transitional Iraqi Governing Council.[23] What proves their defeatism and submission to the occupier is their acceptance to receive IGC members and cooperate with them.

In short, these states came to America's help and backed it in its attack against an Arab state which is bound to them by covenants of joint defense agreements. They reiterated these covenants at the Arab League just a few days before the US attack, only to violate them utterly.[24] This shows their positions on the *umma*'s basic causes.

4. These regimes wavered too much before taking a stand on using force and attacking Iraq. At times they totally rejected participation and at other times they fell into line with the UN. Then they went back to their first option— and in fact, the lack of participation [in the invasion of Iraq] was in line with domestic opinion in these states. However, they finally submitted and succumbed to US pressure, opening their air, land, and sea bases to contribute toward the US campaign, despite the immense repercussions of this move.[25] The most important of these repercussions is that this is a sin against one of the Islamic tenets and high treason against the *umma*. Such a move must also stir up popular anger and pave the way for bringing down these treacherous, apostate, and powerless regimes. The most significant danger in their view was the prospect that the door would be opened for armed forces from abroad to bring down dictatorial regimes, especially after they had seen the arrest of their former confederate in treason and collaboration with the United States, which ordered him to ignite the first Gulf war against Iran, which fought back.[26] The

23 The Iraqi Governing Council was the nominal authority elected by the US, under the occupation. In September 2003, it gained regional recognition from the Arab League; the council's representative was permitted to sit in Iraq's chair during meetings of the League. The Council was dissolved on June 1 2004, and replaced by the current Iraqi government.

24 In March 2003 the Arab League voted 21-1 in favor of a resolution demanding the immediate and unconditional removal of US and British soldiers from Iraq. Kuwait cast the only vote against.

25 Kuwait, Qatar, Bahrain, and Saudi Arabia all offered facilities for the US-led invasion of Iraq in March 2003, despite the resolution passed the same month.

26 The USA extended considerable support to Saddam Hussein in the 1980–88 Iran-Iraq war, supplying it with intelligence, and economic and military aid. It is now known that a vast network of companies, based in the US and elsewhere, fed Iraq's military capability up until August 1990, when Saddam Hussein invaded Kuwait. On May 25 1994, the US Senate Banking Committee released a report in which it was stated that pathogenic, toxigenic, and other biological research materials were

war consumed everything, plunging the region into a chaos from which it has not emerged to this day.[27] The wars that followed were repercussions of this war.

These states are aware that their turn will come. They do not have the will to make the difficult decision to confront [US] aggression, in addition to their belief that they do not possess the material resources for that. Indeed, they were prevented from establishing a large military force when they were forced to sign secret pledges and documents long ago.

5. What shows their position toward the *umma*'s causes is the support they provided to the United States by opening their bases for its crusader campaign against Afghanistan; this is obvious support for the infidels against an Islamic country, and a cardinal sin that renders one an infidel.

6. One of the obvious facts that showed what kind of position the Gulf rulers were ready to take when they came under US pressure to hand over oilfields to the United States was their collective support for Zayid's Initiative, which called on Saddam Hussein to hand over Iraq, its people, and its oil to the United States; to leave power; and to accept political asylum under the pretext of sparing Iraqi people bloodshed.[28]

Saud al-Faisal repeatedly and shamelessly underlined this principle. Ostensibly, and based on what has been said, this apparently shows that if they come under US pressure and face a US desire to occupy the oil regions, the Gulf rulers, including the ruler of Riyadh, will take the same stand.

---

exported to Iraq. They were not attenuated or weakened and were capable of reproduction. The report also detailed 70 shipments (including anthrax bacillus) from the US to Iraqi government agencies over three years, concluding that "these microorganisms exported by the United States were identical to those the UN inspectors found and recovered from the Iraqi biological warfare program." Donald Riegle, Chairman of the Senate Committee that produced the report, noted that "the executive branch of our government approved 771 different export licenses for sale of dual-use technology to Iraq. I think that is a devastating record."

27 1.5 million Iranians were killed in the Iran–Iraq war; Iran suffered financial losses amounting to $350 billion. An estimated 160,000–240,000 Iraqis were killed.

28 Sheikh Zayid bin Sultan al-Nahyan (1918–2004) was the ruler of Abu Dhabi and president of the UAE for over 30 years. In March 2003, he presented to the six-nation Gulf Cooperation Council a proposal to avert war in Iraq, requiring Saddam Hussein and his top advisers to leave Iraq, and the country to be turned over to the United Nations and Arab League for temporary administration.

7. The most obvious reflection of the rulers' attitude towards resistance to this aggression is the stance adopted by their leader when US tanks entered the Arabian peninsula and its waters were disturbed by the Crusader aircraft carriers that came carrying the most sophisticated ammunitions and weapons, to occupy the region. Their leader, who taught them submission, came out to address the public in order to instil into the nation submission, humiliation, and subjugation, and said: "these troop concentrations are not for war".[29] How shameful is this?

If you do not know, that is a calamity. If you do, the calamity is greater.

In short, the ruler who believes in some of the aforementioned deeds cannot defend the country. How can he do so if he believes in all of them and has done these things time and again? Those who believe in the principle of supporting the infidels against Muslims, leaving the blood, honor, and property of their brothers to be easy prey for their enemy in order to remain safe, claiming that they love their brothers but are being compelled to take such a path—this compulsion cannot of course be regarded as legitimate from the perspective of *sharia*—are in fact qualified to take the same course against one another in the Gulf states.

Indeed, this principle is liable to be embraced in the internal affairs of a state.

For example, the Riyadh ruler is capable of abandoning the eastern, central, and other provinces to the Americans. Likewise, he is capable of abandoning the northern province and part of the western province to Jews, in exchange for keeping Jazan, Samitah, and Abu Arish. Those who read and understood the histories of kings know that they are capable of committing more than these concessions, except those who enjoyed the mercy of God. Indeed, the rulers have practically started to sell out the sons of the land by pursuing and imprisoning them, and by unjustly and wrongly accusing them of becoming like the Al-Khawarij sect, who held Muslims to be infidels and went to excess in killing them.[30] We hold them to be martyrs. Sufficient unto them is God.

---

29 In a press briefing on February 26 2003, Saud al-Faisal, the Saudi Minister of Foreign Affairs, refuted the *Washington Post*'s claim that Saudi Arabia permitted US troops to use Prince Sultan air base in a war on Iraq, saying that "The newspaper reported something that we have not officially stated." He stressed that the troops' presence in the Kingdom's territories was aimed at implementation of the United Nations resolutions on monitoring the no-fly zones imposed on Iraq.

30 The al-Khawarij, or Kharijites, were an Islamic sect of the late 7th early 8th centuries, based in what is now southern Iraq. Distinct from both Sunni and Shia, Kharajite theology preached uncompromising observance of the Qur'an. Kharajites considered moderate Muslims to be hypocrites

All this happened before the Riyadh explosions in Rabi al-Awwal of this year [May 2003], which the regime cites as a pretext for its actions.[31] This campaign came as part of a drive to implement the US orders in the hope that they will win its approval, even though Saudi Arabia was the regime which provoked the youths by opening up the country for the Crusaders in violation of religion, in disregard for the Muslims' sentiments, and in defiance of the manliness of the men of Saudi Arabia. Consequently, it was the regime which really disturbed security. Because this statement cannot accommodate all my thoughts in this regard, I discussed this issue in a special message addressed to Saudi Arabia, which I hope will reach you soon.

What sums up the situation of the nation, the ferocious attacks of the enemies against it, the treason of the atheistic rulers, their betrayal of religion, their tyrannical treatment of their peoples, and the failure of Islamic groups to wage *jihad* are the following lines of poetry which are mostly written by Dr Yusuf Abu Hilala, who says:

The great nation has become a plaything in the hands of the priest and the rabbi.

It is like a nation that, in terms of standing [on its own two feet], it makes no difference regardless of whether it remains idle or stands up.

Now that calamities are eliminating it, its leaders are sitting on their thrones like dusty skeletons.

Jerusalem, woe unto Jerusalem, its chastity has been desecrated, and Muslims have chosen not to engage in *jihad*.

Baghdad, O house of the caliphate, woe unto you, why has your chastity been defiled by rabble?

Why did those who betrayed their religion yesterday choose to turn a blind eye to the raids on your sanctuaries?

---

or unbelievers, who could be killed with impunity. They deemed Ali, the fourth of the Rightly Guided Caliphs and cousin of Muhammad, to have betrayed Islam when he advocated arbitration over the question of who should succeed the third Caliph, Uthman. Ali was murdered by a Kharijite in 661. Kharijite sects survive today, particularly in Oman.

31 On May 12 2003, nine suicide bombers killed 26 people in attacks at three housing compounds for Westerners in Riyadh; more than 160 people were injured. After the attacks, Saudi Arabia arrested more than 600 suspects.

Are you ferocious lions when dealing with the people, and rabbits and ostriches when it comes to dealing with Jews?

I no longer have a home whose shelter I can seek, for my homeland has been desecrated and set on fire.

O my nation, I am a bird who has seen a thicket, may I sing? Will I be blamed if I do?

Am I to blame if I present you with a fact; namely, that the rulers are our mortal enemies?

They are unbelievers; yet, they are called the servants and imams of Muslims. They pretend to be our support, when, in point of fact, they are our disease and death.

The Crusaders' army has enveloped the universe; where are the pious, magnanimous, and audacious men?

Based on the above, the extent of the real danger, which the region in general and the Arabian peninsula in particular is being exposed to, is evident. It has become clear that the Gulf rulers are not qualified to apply religion and defend Muslims. In fact, they have provided evidence that they are implementing the schemes of the enemies of the *umma* and religion and that they are qualified to abandon its countries and peoples. Now, after we have become aware of the rulers' approach, we should examine the policy they have been pursuing. Anyone who examines the policy of those rulers will easily see that they follow their whims and desires, and their personal interests and Crusader loyalties.

Commitment to Islam is not one of the constants in their policies and religious practices. They believe in a part of the Book and reject the rest in conformity with their whims to keep their thrones, a grievous act of infidelity, as Almighty God demonstrates in the following Qur'anic verse: "So do you believe in some parts of scripture and not others? The punishment for those of you who do this will be nothing but disgrace in this life and on the Day of Resurrection they will be condemned to the harshest torment: God is not unaware of what you do do.[32]

32 Qur'an, 2:85.

To these rulers, the only major objective is remaining in power. Therefore, the flaw does not involve a secondary issue, such as personal corruption, which is confined to the palace of the ruler. The flaw is in their fundamental approach.

This [approach] came about when a malicious belief and destructive principle spread in most walks of life, so that absolute supremacy and obedience became due to the ruler, and not to the religion of God. This means that slavery is imposed by the ruler and not by Almighty God. This is the important reality that the rulers manipulate, even if they use Islam as a cover, particularly in some countries, where they assigned an army of *ulema*, preachers, writers, and the entire mass media for about a century to exaggerate the meaning of obedience to the ruler, deviating from the restrictions to this concept as stipulated in God's religion. Therefore, the ruler became an idol to be worshipped instead of God—this is the current situation in Saudi Arabia. If any of the *ulema* refuses to flatter the rulers, his fate will be prison until he is forced to flatter them. In other countries they use parliaments and democracy as a cover for this.

Thus, all Arab countries currently suffer from great deterioration in all walks of life, in both religious and worldly matters. It is enough to know that the economy of all Arab countries is weaker than the economy of one country that had once been part of our [Islamic] world when we used to truly adhere to Islam. That country is the lost al-Andalus.[33] Spain is an infidel country, but its economy is stronger than ours because the ruler there is accountable. In our countries, there is no accountability or punishment, but only obedience to the rulers and prayers of long life for them.

We have reached this miserable situation because many of us lack the correct and comprehensive understanding of the religion of Islam. Many of us understand Islam to mean performing some acts of worship, such as prayer and fasting. Despite the great importance of these rituals, the religion of Islam encompasses all the affairs of life, including the religious and the worldly, such as economic, military, and political affairs, as well as the scales by which we weigh the actions of men—rulers, *ulema*, and others—and how to deal with the ruler in line with the rules set by God for him, which the ruler should not violate. These rules also proscribe the enacting of legislation contrary to God's will, allegiance to infidels and supporting them against Muslims, or tampering

---

33 Al-Andalus was the name given to territories under Muslim rule (711–1492) on the Iberian peninsula.

with—or embezzling huge amounts of—the nation's money. Many people think that this is part of the ruler's authority, and do not know that these actions by the ruler are in fact some of the cardinal sins in our *sharia* that should not be tolerated. Furthermore, a ruler's enacting legislation contrary to God's will, and his allegiance to the infidels, constitute a greater atheism, which drives him away from faith, and necessitates a considered and planned uprising against him.

Had these rulers read the Qur'an and Prophet Muhammad's traditions, and had they learned lessons from them—which is what we should do—this would have become very clear to them in several texts. Among these texts is a tradition by Uday bin-Hatim, who converted to Christianity before Islam. He thought, as do many people, that following the leaders and *ulema* in allowing what has been forbidden by God, and banning what has been allowed by God, is not worship of these leaders and *ulema*, and is not atheism, because this does not mean praying or fasting for them. However, when bin-Hatim came to the Messenger of God, while he was reading this Qur'anic verse: "They take their rabbis and their monks as lords,"[34] he said that he told the Prophet: "They did not worship them." The Prophet answered: "Yes, but they forbade what is allowed and allowed what has been forbidden, and followed them. Therefore, this is what they worship."[35]

Be attentive to this verse, because both this verse and tradition clearly show that obedience to the ruler, a scholar, or anyone else in allowing what has been forbidden by God, and banning what God has allowed, is tantamount to worshipping them rather than God. This is a greater polytheism and drives the person away from faith: may God protect us and you from this.

This is what Almighty God disassociates himself from when he says: "Praise and glory to Him: He is far above whatever they set up as partners with Him;" he then says "But they were commanded to serve only One God: There is no god but Him."[36] This shows that issuing legislation concerning what is allowed and what is banned is a type of worship. This is one of the most important traits of God and one of the most important prerequisites for testifying that there is no god but God, the first and most important pillar of Islam. This is a serious warning to those who think that Islam consists of mere words uttered,

---

34 Qur'an, 9:31.
35 From the *hadith* collection of al-Tirmidhi.
36 Qur'an, 9:31.

in which one testifies that there is no god but God, but who do not know that these words have requirements that, if they do not heed them, they would not be properly committed to the testimony that there is no god but God. The gist here is that the absence of a comprehensive understanding of God's religion as a system for all walks of life, including Islam's way of holding the rulers accountable—because if they follow God's religion things become good for the country and its people—is one of the greatest flaws in the nation at present. We should be fully aware of this issue and start the march of reform today, in order to follow the right path. We should not continue in this deviant path for yet another century.

One of the beneficial books that explained the previous Qur'anic verse is *The Book of Faith* by Sheikh ibn Taymiyya, may God have mercy on his soul; and also the book titled *Fath al-Mujid* by Sheikh Abd-al-Rahman bin-Hasan al-Shaykh, may God have mercy on his soul; and the book entitled *Concepts that Should be Corrected*, by Sheikh Muhammad Qutb.[37] These showed that the rulers are incapable and treacherous, and that they have not followed the right path of Islam but followed their wishes and lusts—this is the reason for the setbacks in the nation's march during the past decades. Therefore, it is clear to us that the solution [to these problems] lies in adhering to the religion of God, by which God granted us pride in the past centuries, and installing a strong and faithful leadership that applies the Qur'an among us and raises the true banner of *jihad*.

The honest people who are concerned about this situation—such as the *ulema*, leaders who are obeyed among their people, dignitaries, notables, and merchants—should get together and meet in a safe place away from the shadow of these oppressive regimes and form a council for Ahl al-Hall wa al-Aqd[38] to fill the vacuum caused by these religiously invalid regimes and their mental deficiency. The people have the right to appoint an imam. The people

37 For ibn Taymiyya, see above, p. 5, n. 7. Here, bin Laden is probably referring to ibn Taymiyya's *The Concept of Worship in Islam* (*al-Ubudiyya fi al-Islam*), one of his most important expositions of faith. Muhammad Qutb, brother of the influential Islamic radical thinker and member of the Muslim Brotherhood Sayyid Qutb, was himself a well-known Egyptian writer.

38 According to Sunni doctrine, the leadership of Muslims is decided by either the consensus of the *umma* or by the oath of allegiance given by those among the Muslim community who possess the right to place or remove a ruler ("ahl al-hall wa al-aqd", literally, "those who loose and bind"). King Fahd of Saudi Arabia consulted with a group of this title, numbering between 100 and 150, comprising princes from the four principal al-Saud families and a number of leading *ulema*.

also have the right to make him correct his course if he deviates from it and to remove him if he does something that warrants this, such as apostasy and treason.

This temporary council should be made up of the minimum number of available personnel, who should be tough on the rest of the nation, except what the religion permits in case of necessity, until the situation improves and the number is increased, God willing. The council's policy should be based on the book of God and the tradition of his Prophet. It should start by directing Muslims to the important priorities at this critical stage, and lead them to a safe haven, provided that their top priority is uniting opinions under the word of monotheism and defending Islam, its people and countries, and urging Muslims to prepare for and carry out *jihad*.

The people should be given easy access to arms, particularly light weapons; anti-armored rockets, such as RPGs; and tank mines; as well as the declaration of a general mobilization in the nation to prepare for repulsing the raid of the Romans, which started in Iraq; no one knows where it will end. God suffices us and He is our best support.

My brothers in faith, we should be certain that our success and happiness in this world and in the hereafter lies in implementing Islam and carrying out *jihad*. Our pride and happiness lie in these things, based on the true Prophet's saying that was related by Abu Dawud citing ibn Umar.[39] The Prophet says: "If you practise Tabaiya al-Ainiya, followed the tails of cows, satisfied yourselves with agriculture, and abandoned *jihad*, God will cover you with humiliation and will not remove it until you return to your religion."[40]

Caliph Umar told Abu-Ubaydah: "We are a people whom God made powerful through Islam, and if we seek strength from other sources God will humiliate us." Therefore the advocates of reform should know that reforming and uniting the nation under Islam cannot be achieved through lectures and books only, but through a practical plan involving the entire nation, each according to his own capabilities, beginning with prayer to God and ending with fighting in the cause of God, for fighting in the cause of God is an indivisible part of our religion. In fact, it is the pinnacle of religion. So, how can religion survive without its apex? It is a pressing need for our nation's life,

39 For Abu Dawud, see above, p. 101, n. 4.
40 From the *hadith* collection of Abu Dawud, book 23, no. 3,455.

glory, and survival. Although our enemy lies, our religion tells the truth when it stipulates: You fight, so you exist. This is what they teach their children, but they tell us the contrary. Moreover, fighting comes about through the big powers' need for survival. Just read history if you want—including the history of America, which has ignited dozens of wars throughout only six decades. This is because this was one of its most pressing needs. When the United States makes a sincere decision to stop wars in the world, it knows before anyone else that that day will mark the beginning of its collapse and the disintegration of its states. This day is coming, God willing. So, beware of any call for laying down arms on the pretext of achieving peace. This is because this will be a call to humiliate us. Only a hypocrite or an ignorant person can promote such calls.

Before concluding, I urge the Muslim youths to carry out *jihad*, particularly in Palestine and Iraq. I also call on them to be patient and pious, and to weaken the enemy by inflicting wounds on it, along with protecting Muslims during these actions. They also should be careful not to expand on applying the law regarding the use of human shields, for this should be left to their honest *ulema* on a case-by-case basis. We beseech God to grant us victory through patience and piety. May God make us patient and pious.

Concluding, I would like to say a few words to Muslim youths, words which we heard from your grandfathers who had been tested by events throughout many years in Palestine, and who had been witness to many initiatives, con-spiracies, calamities, and calls for peace. I just want to remind you of these words, which are: My son, they will talk to you about peace; do not listen to such calls, because although I once believed them I am still living in a tent. "God always prevails in His purpose, though most people do not realize it."[41] "Our Lord, give us good in this world and in the Hereafter, and protect us from the torment of the Fire!"[42] O God, I beseech you to strengthen the *mujahidin* everywhere, particularly in Palestine, Iraq, Kashmir, Chechnya, and Afghanistan. We beseech God to grant them success, to strengthen them, to unite their ranks, and to grant them victory over their enemies, especially since no one grants them victory except Almighty God. O God, we beseech you to put this nation's feet firmly on the right path in order to strengthen those

41 Qur'an, 12:21.
42 Qur'an, 2:201.

who obey you and to humiliate those who disobey you. Praise be to God, Lord of the worlds.[43] May God's prayer and peace be on the last of the Prophets and messengers.

43 Qur'an, 1:2.

22

TO THE PEOPLES OF EUROPE

April 15 2004

On March 11 2004, simultaneous bombs planted on suburban trains in Madrid killed 191 people and wounded 1,460. Three days later, the Spanish Socialist Party, which had opposed Spain's participation in the war on Iraq, was elected the new government of the country. Against this background, a statement by bin Laden was broadcast a month later by both al-Jazeera and the UAE television network al-Arabiyya, addressed to "our neighbours north of the Mediterranean," the peoples of Europe. Remarking that "security is a vital necessity for every human being," but "we not let you monopolize it for yourselves," bin Laden pointed to the recent assassination of the wheelchair-bound leader of Hamas, Sheikh Ahmed Yassin, killed by an Israeli helicopter gunship. "In what creed are your dead considered innocent but ours worthless? By what logic does your blood count as real and ours as no more than water? Reciprocal treatment is part of justice, and he who commences hostilities is the unjust one." Muslims, he says, had respected this principle. "We only killed Russians after they invaded Afghanistan and Chechnya, we only killed Europeans after they invaded Afghanistan and Iraq, we only killed Americans in New York after they supported the Jews in Palestine and invaded the Arabian peninsula, and we only killed them in Somalia after they invaded it in Operation Restore Hope. We restored them to hopelessness, thank God."

In this cycle of bloodshed, observes bin Laden, European leaders have persisted in ignoring its roots in the occupation of Palestine. But the peoples of Europe and the Muslim world have a common interest in putting a stop to the mutual killing, and, to that end, bin Laden made a public offer to cease attacks against any European state that pledged not to attack Muslims or intervene in their affairs, including participation in "the American conspiracy against the great Islamic world." This peace proposal, he explained, would be on the table for three months from the date of the broadcast, and its terms would have to be renewed by successive governments. It did not extend to the United States, Israel, or the United Nations, all of which constitute "a fatal danger to the entire world." All European countries ruled out talks with bin Laden, but within another two weeks the government in Madrid had fulfilled its campaign promise to withdraw all Spanish troops from Iraq.

This is a letter to our neighbours north of the Mediterranean, incorporating a peace proposal in response to positive recent exchanges.

Evil kills its perpetrators and oppression's pastures are fatal.

There is a lesson in what is happening in occupied Palestine, and what happened on September 11 and March 11 are your goods returned to you. It is well known that security is a vital necessity for every human being. We will not let you monopolize it for yourselves, just as sensible people would not let their leaders compromise their security. On this basis, we warn you:

Since we have reacted in kind, your description of us as terrorists and of our actions as terrorism necessarily means that you and your actions must be defined likewise. Our actions are but a reaction to yours—your destruction and murder of our people, whether in Afghanistan, Iraq, or Palestine. Look, for example, at the event that terrorized the world, the murder of the wheel-chair-bound Sheikh Ahmed Yassin, God have mercy on his soul.[1] We give God our pledge that we will take revenge on America for his death, with God's will.

In what creed are your dead considered innocent but ours worthless? By what logic does your blood count as real and ours as no more than water? Reciprocal treatment is part of justice, and he who commences hostilities is the unjust one.

As for your leaders and their followers, who persistently ignore the real problem, which is the occupation of all Palestine, and indulge in lies and deceit about our right to self-defense, they have no self-respect. They show contempt for peoples' blood and minds through such deceit, but it only means that your blood will continue to be shed. If one looks at the murders that are still going on in our countries and yours, an important truth becomes clear, which is that we are both suffering injustice at the hands of your leaders, who send your sons to our countries, despite their objections, to kill and be killed. So it is in the interests of both sides to stop those who shed their own peoples' blood, both on behalf of narrow personal benefits and on behalf of the White House gang. This war is making billions of dollars for the big corporations, whether it be those who manufacture weapons or reconstruction firms like Halliburton and its offshoots and sister companies.[2]

---

1 For Sheikh Yassin, see above, p. 26, n. 12.

2 Halliburton Energy Services is a multinational corporation based in Houston, Texas. Its subsidiary, Kellogg, Brown and Root (KBR), an engineering and construction company, has contracts in Iraq worth up to $18 billion, including a single no-bid contract known as "Restore Iraqi Oil,"

It is all too clear, then, who benefits most from stirring up this war and blood-shed: the merchants of war, the bloodsuckers who direct world policy from behind the scenes. President Bush and other leaders like him, the big media institutions, the United Nations, which legislates between army leaders and the mighty General Assembly—all these are merely agents of deception and exploitation. These and others are groups who are a mortal danger to the entire world, the most dangerous and difficult of these being the Zionist lobby.

We are determined, with God's will, to continue our struggle and to build on what we have already done in order to stop the merchants of war. In response to the positive initiatives that have been reflected in recent events[3] and opinion polls showing that most people in Europe want peace, I call upon just men, especially scholars, media, and businessmen, to form a permanent com-mission to raise awareness among Europeans of the justice of our causes, primarily Palestine, making use of the enormous potential of the media.

So I present to them this peace proposal, which is essentially a commitment to cease operations against any state that pledges not to attack Muslims or intervene in their affairs, including the American conspiracy against the great Islamic world. This peace can be renewed at the end of a government's term and the beginning of a new one, with the consent of both sides. It will come into effect on the departure of its last soldier from our lands, and it is available for a period of three months from the day this statement is broadcast.

Whoever chooses war over peace will find us ready for the fight.

Whoever chooses peace can see that we have responded positively.

Therefore, stop spilling our blood in order to save your own. The solution to this equation, both easy and difficult, lies in your own hands. You know that

---

worth an estimated $7 billion. Halliburton's work in Iraq is diverse. As well as working to restore Iraqi oil infrastructure, it supplies troop support, air traffic control support, provides 74 million gallons of drinking water per month, and emergency services. Vice President Dick Cheney, a leading advocate of "regime change" in Iraq, was CEO of Halliburton from 1995 to 2000; his asso-ciation with the corporation continues to attract controversy, as do Halliburton's activities in Iraq. On June 27, a joint report by the US House Committee on Government Reform, Minority Staff, concluded that "New information from the Defense Contract Audit Agency reveals that Halliburton's questioned and unsupported costs now exceed $1.4 billion. Yet despite this record, Defense Department officials have repeatedly shown Halliburton special treatment by overruling the objections of career officials, waiving the requirements of the federal procurement obligations, and awarding Halliburton millions in lucrative fees."

things will only get worse the longer you take, but you will only have yourselves to blame. No sensible person would compromise his property, his security or his family just to please the liar in the White House. If Bush's call for peace was honest, why hasn't he spoken about the one who slit open the bellies of pregnant women in Sabra and Shatila or the planner of the surrender process,[3] the "man of peace" [Ariel Sharon]; why did he not just come out and say "we hate freedom and we kill for the sake of it"? Reality confirms we are right, and reveals him as a liar. For we only killed Russians after they invaded Afghanistan and Chechnya, we only killed Europeans after they invaded Afghanistan and Iraq, and we only killed Americans in New York after they supported the Jews in Palestine and invaded the Arabian peninsula, and we only killed them in Somalia after they invaded it in Operation Restore Hope. We restored them to hopelessness, thank God.

It has been said that a penny spent on prevention is better than a fortune on cure.

Happy is he who has warned others. Returning to truth is better than continuing the lie.

Peace be upon those who follow true guidance.

Osama bin Laden

---

3 Bin Laden is making a pun here. "peace process" is "amaliyat al-salam," but here he talks about "amaliyat al-istislam," the surrender process. The word for surrender is a cognate of the word for peace.

23

THE TOWERS OF LEBANON

October 29 2004

Bin Laden's address to the peoples of Europe in the spring of 2004 sought to capitalize on the Spanish elections that had just toppled one of the Bush Administration's allies in the occupation of Iraq. This videotape, made available in the autumn of 2004 to al-Jazeera by the al-Sahab Institute for Media Production—by now the major conduit for al-Qaeda's video messages—was designed as an intervention in the US Presidential elections.[1] The timing of its broadcast, a few days before voters went to the polls on November 3, made it one of the most dramatic of bin Laden's statements. Possibly under American pressure, al-Jazeera initially broadcast only an edited five-minute extract. But its impact may not have been inconsequential, if the Democratic contender for the White House is to be believed. In an interview given in January 2005, John Kerry attributed the failure of his campaign not only to 9/11, but to this eve-of-poll message from bin Laden: "We were rising in the polls up until the last day when the tape appeared. We flat-lined the day the tape appeared, and went down on Monday."[2]

The aim of the message, crafted for its non-Muslim audience, is to isolate the Bush administration, and beyond it the American political establishment as whole, from American popular feeling—as well as European opinion. Bin Laden repeats that he well understands that "security is one of the pillars of human life," whose value no free people underestimate. The cause he represents is not hostile to freedom or the West as such. Al-Qaeda has not attacked Sweden, which has never been an aggressor in Muslim world. If the American people wish to avoid another Manhattan, they must understand the causes and consequences of US policies in the Middle East. For the first time claiming direct responsibility for the attacks of 9/11, bin Laden links them with

1 A link to the video was posted on the Islamist al-Islah message forum (http://www.islahi.net/ vboard/showthread.php?t=116671), which has since been closed down. The videotape was also posted on http://www2.vh–p.net/su/img/257.zip.

2 Interview with NBC's "Meet the Press" on January 30 2005. For a full transcript, go to http://www.msnbc.msn.com/id/6886726/

the American-backed Israeli invasion of Lebanon in June 1982. He recalls the horrific images of the siege of Beirut, and the repeated attacks on West Beirut's high-rise apartment blocks: "As I looked at those destroyed towers in Lebanon, it occurred to me to punish the aggressor in kind by destroying towers in America." He then lists the occasions when he repeatedly warned America that an assault like 9/11 would happen, both in interviews with Western journalists in the late 1990s, and in attacks on US military and diplomatic outposts in the Middle East.

Pouring scorn on the Bush family—the father, visiting kings and dictators in the Middle East, sought to emulate them in the US; the son failed to react to the first news of 9/11—bin Laden says the current administration has played into al-Qaeda's hands by plunging into a war on Iraq against which American thinkers and intellectuals themselves had warned it. Bush had every opportunity to remove weapons of mass destruction peacefully, if Saddam had possessed them in the first place. But oil seduced him into an adventure in which the profits of vast corporations connected to his administration, which have won enormous contracts for the reconstruction of Iraq, were put ahead of American public interest. The result has been heavy casualties on both sides, and a mounting federal deficit, requiring emergency budgets. "This shows the success of our plan to bleed America to the point of bankruptcy, with God's will." The security of the American people, bin Laden concludes, lies not in the hands of Bush, or Kerry, or al-Qaeda, "but in your own hands"—for "whichever state does not encroach upon our security ensures its own."

Peace be upon those who are rightly guided.

People of America,

I speak to you today about the best way to avoid another Manhattan, about the war, its causes, and its consequences. First of all, I tell you that security is one of the pillars of human life. Free men do not underestimate the value of their security, despite Bush's claim that we hate freedom.[3] Perhaps he can tell us why we did not attack Sweden, for example?

It is well known that those who despise freedom do not possess proud souls, unlike the nineteen [the 9/11 attackers], may God bless them. We have been fighting you because we are free men who cannot acquiesce in injustice. We want to restore security to our *umma*. Just as you violate our security, so we violate yours. Whoever encroaches upon the security of others and imagines that he will himself remain safe is but a foolish criminal. When disasters happen,

3 On September 18 2001, at a photocall with President Chirac of France, President Bush stated that "we have entered a new type of war. It's a war against people who hate freedom."

intelligent people look for the reasons behind them, so that they can avoid them in the future.

But I am amazed at you. Although we are now into the fourth year since the events of September 11, Bush is still practicing his deception, misleading you about the real reason behind it. As a result, there are still motives for a repeat [attack]. I will explain to you the reasons behind these events, and I will tell you the truth about the moments when this decision was taken, so that you can reflect on it. God knows that the plan of striking the towers had not occurred to us, but the idea came to me when things went just too far with the American-Israeli alliance's oppression and atrocities against our people in Palestine and Lebanon.

The events that made a direct impression on me were during and after 1982, when America allowed the Israelis to invade Lebanon with the help of its third fleet.[4] They started bombing, killing, and wounding many, while others fled in terror. I still remember those distressing scenes: blood, torn limbs, women and children massacred. All over the place, houses were being destroyed and tower blocks were collapsing, crushing their residents, while bombs rained down mercilessly on our homes. It was like a crocodile devouring a child, who could do nothing but scream. Does a crocodile understand anything other than weapons? The whole world heard and saw what happened, but did nothing. In those critical moments, many ideas raged inside me, ideas difficult to describe, but they unleashed a powerful urge to reject injustice and a strong determination to punish the oppressors.

As I looked at those destroyed towers in Lebanon, it occurred to me to punish the oppressor in kind by destroying towers in America, so that it would have a taste of its own medicine and would be prevented from killing our

4 On June 6 1982, Israel invaded Lebanon in Operation Peace for Galilee, under the direction of Defense Minister (now Prime Minister) Ariel Sharon. The stated aim of the invasion was to prevent Palestinian militia from firing rockets at civilian targets in Galilee (the first such attack for ten months had been provoked by an Israeli air raid on refugee camps and other PLO targets in Lebanon, killing 45 and wounding 150); its real aim was the destruction of the PLO. Israeli forces reached Beirut, where they encountered strong opposition from Palestinian militia; in the ensuing siege, nearly 20,000 people died, at least half of them civilians. Later that year, the Israeli military allowed Lebanese Christian Phalange militia to massacre Palestinians in the Sabra and Chatila refugee camps (see above, Statement 163, n. 5). Here bin Laden recalls the repeated Israeli bombardments of West Beirut's high-rise apartment blocks. US opposition to the Israeli invasion was muted at best; in the Arab world it was widely believed to have endorsed the invasion. See Paul Rogers, "Iraq, al-Qaeda and a Renewed Caliphate," International Security Monthly Briefing, October 2004.

women and children. On that day I became sure that the oppression and intentional murder of innocent women and children is a deliberate American policy. It seemed then that "freedom" and "democracy" are actually just terror, just as resistance is labelled "terrorism" and "reaction." Imposing lethal sanctions on millions of people, as Bush Sr did, and carrying out the mass butchering of children, is the worst thing that humanity has ever known. So is dropping millions of pounds of bombs and explosives on millions of children in Iraq, as Bush Junior did, to remove a former collaborator, and install a new one who will help steal Iraq's oil, as well as commit other atrocities.[5]

Against the background of these and similar images, the events of September 11 came as a response to these great injustices. Can you blame someone for protecting his own? Self-defense and punishing the oppressor in kind: is this shameful terrorism? Even if it is, we have no other option. This is the message that we have repeatedly tried to convey to you in words and deeds, years before September 11. You could see this, if you were so inclined, in the interview with Scott MacLeod in *Time* magazine in 1996, as well as the one with Peter Arnett on CNN in 1997, and with John Weiner in 1998. You could see it in the events in Nairobi, Tanzania, and Aden; you could see it in my interviews with Abdel Bari Atwan and with Robert Fisk, who is a fellow [Westerner] and a co-religionist of yours, but one whom I consider unbiased.[6]

Would those in the White House, and the TV channels who answer to those who claim to stand for freedom, dare to interview him [Fisk], so that he could explain to the American people everything he has learned from us about the reasons for our struggle? For if you could avoid perpetrating these injustices, you Americans would be on the right path towards the security you enjoyed before September 11. This is what I can say about war and its reasons.

As for the consequences of 9/11, they are, thanks to God Almighty, very positive. They surpassed all expectations and measures. This was so for many

---

5 On March 21 2003 the US launched 1,700 bombing sorties, 504 using cruise missiles, against Iraq. Eighteen months later, a detailed analysis in *The Lancet* concluded that the civilian death toll for the conflict might be as high as 100,000.

6 Abdel Bari Atwan, editor of the Arabic-language London newspaper *Al-Quds Al-Arabi*, interviewed bin Laden in Afghanistan in August 1996. The British journalist Robert Fisk has covered events in the Middle East for London's *Independent* newspaper for over 23 years; he interviewed bin Laden in 1993 and 1996.

reasons, the most important of which are as follows: we found no difficulty in leading Bush and his administration on, in light of the similarity between them and the regimes in our countries, half of whom we would describe as being ruled by the military, and the other half by sons of kings and presidents. We have long experience of them. There are many of both types who are well known for their arrogance, conceit, and illegal theft of funds.

This similarity goes back to the visits of Bush Senior to the region. While some of our people were dazzled by America and hoped that these visits would make an impression on our countries, in fact it was he who was impressed by these monarchic and military regimes. He envied the fact that they could remain in power for decades, embezzling the nation's funds with neither account nor regulation. So he brought tyranny and the suppression of liberties to his own country and called it the Patriot Act, implemented under the pretext of fighting terrorism.

Bush Sr saw the benefits of making his sons state governors. Nor did he forget to import into Florida from our region's leaders the idea of falsifying elections, so that he could use this plan at tricky moments.[7] As we mentioned previously, it was easy for us to provoke this administration and lure it into perdition. All we had to do was send two *mujahidin* to the Far East to raise up a rag on which "al-Qaeda" was written, and the generals came running. This inflicted human, financial, and political losses on America without them even achieving anything worth mentioning, apart from providing business for their private corporations. In addition, we gained expertise in guerrilla and attritional warfare in our struggle against the great oppressive superpower, Russia, in which we and the *mujahidin* ground it down for ten years until it went bankrupt, and decided to withdraw in defeat, praise and thanks be to God. We are continuing to make America bleed to the point of bankruptcy, by God's will. For God is able to do that. It would not be accurate to say that al-Qaeda has defeated the White House administration, or that the White House administration has lost this war, for on closer inspection it cannot be said that al-Qaeda is the sole reason for these amazing gains. The White House leadership, which is so keen to open up war fronts for its various corporations,

7 George W Bush became Governor of Texas in 1994; he won re-election in 1998. John Ellis ("Jeb") Bush was appointed Governor of Florida in 1998. The role of Jeb Bush, and his Secretary of State Katherine Harris, in the Florida elections of the 2000 US presidential election attracted considerable controversy.

468

whether in the field of arms, oil, or construction, has also contributed to these remarkable results for al-Qaeda. To some analysts and diplomats, it seems as if we and the White House are on the same team shooting at the United States' own goal, despite our different intentions.

These and other such ideas were referred to by a British diplomat at the Royal Institute for International Affairs. For example, al-Qaeda spent $500,000 on the September 11 attacks, while America lost more than $500 billion, at the lowest estimate, in the event and its aftermath. That makes a million American dollars for every al-Qaeda dollar, by the grace of God Almighty.

This is in addition to the fact that it lost an enormous number of jobs—and as for the federal deficit, it made record losses, estimated at over a trillion dollars.

Still more serious for America was the fact that the *mujahidin* forced Bush to resort to an emergency budget in order to continue fighting in Afghanistan and Iraq.[8] This shows the success of our plan to bleed America to the point of bankruptcy, with God's will.

It truly shows that al-Qaeda has made gains, but on the other hand it also shows that the Bush administration has likewise profited. Anyone seeing the enormity of the contracts won by dubious large corporations, like Halliburton and others connected to Bush and his administration, can be certain of that. But the reality is that it is you, the American people and your economy, who are losing.

For your information, we agreed with the general commander Muhammed Atta,[9] may God bless his soul, to carry out all operations within twenty minutes, before Bush and his administration could be aware of them, and it did not occur to us that the Commander-in-Chief of the American armed forces would leave fifty thousand of his citizens in the two towers to face this great horror on their own, just when they needed him most. It seems that a little girl's story about a goat and its butting was more important than dealing with aeroplanes and their butting into skyscrapers.[10] This gave us three times the amount of required time to carry out the operations, praise be to God.

8 On October 25 2004, Pentagon and Congressional figures announced that the Bush administration intended to seek around $70 billion in emergency funding for the wars in Iraq and Afghanistan, pushing total spending to $225 billion since the 2003 invasion of Iraq.

9 The Egyptian Mohammed Atta al-Sayed (1968–2001) was named as the pilot of the first plane to crash into the World Trade Center on 9/11, and was, as bin Laden indicates, the leader of the attacks.

10 A play on words in Arabic: "skyscrapers" are literally "cloud-butters".

It should also be clear to you that American thinkers and intellectuals warned Bush before the war that everything he needed to guarantee America's security by removing weapons of mass destruction—assuming they existed—was at his disposal, that all countries were with him when it came to inspection, and that America's interest did not require him to launch into a groundless war with unknown repercussions. But the black gold blinded him and he put his own private interests ahead of the American public interest. The war went ahead and many were killed. The American economy bled and Bush became embroiled in the quagmires of Iraq, which now threaten his future. He is like the grumpy goat who dug out of the ground the very knife with which he would be killed.

I tell you, fifteen thousand of our people have been killed, and tens of thousands injured, while you have had over a thousand killed and more than ten thousand wounded.[11] Bush's hands are covered with the blood of all these casualties, from both sides, all in the name of oil and more business for his private companies.

You should know that you act like the nation that punishes the weak man who has profited from the death of one of its sons, but absolves someone from a more privileged background who has profited from the deaths of a thousand of its sons—just like your allies in Palestine who terrorize women and children, and kill and imprison men.

You should remember that every action has a reaction. Finally, you would do well to consider the wills of the thousands who left you on September 11, waving desperately for help. These are inspiring testaments, worthy of being published and studied. One of the most significant things I have read about their torments before falling was that they said: "We were wrong when we let the White House inflict unchecked its aggressive foreign policy on the poor people." They were saying to you: "People of America, call those who caused our murder to account." Happy is he who learns from the experiences of others. Their desperate signals also remind me of a verse of poetry I once read:

Evil kills its perpetrators and oppression's pastures are fatal.[12]

11 At end October 2004 a total of 1,155 US service personnel had died in Iraq, with 8,235 wounded. See http://www.globalsecurity.org/military/ops/iraq_casualties.htm
12 Also quoted above, p. 234.

It has been said that a penny spent on prevention is better than a fortune on cure. You should know that returning to truth is better than continuing to lie, and that any sensible person would never underestimate the value of his security, his property, or his home for the sake of the liar in the White House.

In conclusion, I say to you in truth that your security lies not in the hands of Kerry, Bush, or al-Qaeda. It lies in your own hands, and whichever state does not encroach upon our security thereby ensures its own. God is our master; you have none.

Peace be upon those who follow true guidance.

24

DEPOSE THE TYRANTS

December 16 2004

This message returns to bin Laden's first preoccupation: the fate of Saudi Arabia, his homeland. Posted on the website of the Global Islamic Media Front, and circulated widely in English translation, it also addresses Muslims at large, all of whom are concerned by developments in the kingdom. But now bin Laden speaks with utter clarity, abandoning the caution or ambiguity of his original letters to bin Baz and the Muslim scholars, for a blistering indictment of the House of Saud and the calamity it has historically represented for the peninsula. He states that the Saudi dynasty betrayed any covenant with its people from the outset, was a collaborator with Britain, and then became a client of America. Its rule, he continues, has brought misery, corruption, and oppression to the land—mass unemployment and grotesque palaces, a gaga king and bloated princes, inability to defend the Holy sanctuaries and treachery towards neighbors and believers. Now finally "naming names" with a vengeance, bin Laden details the poisonous relations between Fahd's heir Abdallah, and his relatives, Sultan and Nayef, Ministers of Defense and the Interior; the damaging revelations of his son Talal and of his nephew Bandar, Bush's intimate in Washington; the continual interference by the US in Saudi affairs and appointments; the depression of oil prices in the interests of America; the collaboration with the Pentagon in the invasion and occupation of Iraq. Nor, he says, are matters better elsewhere in the Arab world: the Hashemite dynasty in Jordan is fully as treacherous and subordinate as its Saudi rival, while secular tyrants like Nasser, Sadat and Qadhafi were greeted as believers in Riyadh as soon as made they peace with the Saudi regime. Elections in Egypt, Jordan, or Yemen are as much a comedy as what "passes for rule in Saudi Arabia" today. The leaders of these countries offer no hope of improvement for the people, only disaster.

In this situation, bin Laden says that there is only one solution, made clear by God's law— to depose these rulers by force of arms. There is no distinction to be drawn between Paul Bremer, head of the CPA in Iraq, and Iyad Allawi, the local premier imposed by the US; both equally simply implement American policies like all the other regimes in the region, who have themselves rejected every consensual solution for what they have done to their countries. Dialogue with them is now possible only with the sword and the gun. "How can any sane person, seeing the apostate ruler and his soldiers armed to the teeth, claim he wants a solution through peaceful reform?". If the dynasty in Riyadh refuses to restore trusteeship of the land to the people, it will meet the fate of such hated despots as the Shah of Iran or Ceauşescu in Romania—"for things are descending with extraordinary speed towards an explosion." The struggle against such tyrants within the region is, states bin Laden, a manifestation of a far wider conflict "between global unbelief, with the apostates today under the leadership of America, on one side, and the Islamic umma and its brigades of mujahidin on the other". In this confrontation, the current battles in Iraq "are merely an extension of the struggle against the Zionist-Crusader alliance, who fight us everywhere, just as we fight them everywhere, including Saudi Arabia, from which we are trying to expel them, with God's will." The struggle will continue in every arena of jihad: "Lord, make the mujahidin stand firm everywhere, in Palestine, Iraq, Kashmir, Chechnya, Afghanistan, and Saudi Arabia. Lord, guide their weapons and make their hearts firm, give them support and assistance against Your enemies and theirs, for neither we nor they have anyone to help us, but You, the strong and beloved one."

The battle lines between faith and unbelief, which bin Laden has been defining throughout his statements, have now been fully drawn.

To Muslims in Saudi Arabia in particular and Muslims elsewhere generally: This is a letter concerning the conflict and dispute among the rulers of Riyadh, and the way to solve them.

There has been much talk in Saudi Arabia about the need for safety and security, about the sanctity of Muslim blood and those who have been granted safe passage, about the importance of social harmony and cohesion, and about the dangers of division and conflict. Some have claimed that the *mujahidin* have brought about the current predicament in Saudi Arabia, but the clear truth of the matter is that responsibility falls on the shoulders of the regime, which has neglected the necessary conditions to maintain security, life, social harmony, and cohesion. This is because it disobeyed God Almighty and committed sins that exposed the country to His warning and punishment. God has told us the stories of the disobedient and their punishment so that we could take heed.

God Almighty said: "God presents the example of a town that was secure and at ease, with provisions coming to it abundantly from all places. Then it became ungrateful for God's blessings, so He afflicted it with the garment of famine and fear for what its people had done."[1] And He said: "All of them committed excesses in their lands, and spread corruption there: your Lord let a scourge of punishment loose on them. Your Lord is always watchful."[2]

It is the supporters and sycophants of the regime, as well as those who refrain from denouncing evil, who are also responsible for this predicament. For God Almighty said:

> Those children of Israel who defied [God] were rejected through the words of David and Jesus, son of Mary, because they disobeyed, they persistently over-stepped the limits, they did not forbid each other to do wrong—how vile their deeds were![3]

And the Prophet is reputed to have said, as related by al-Hakim:[4] "Their leaders have not ruled in accordance with the book of God Almighty, nor have they paid attention to what God has revealed. May God keep the harm they intend amongst themselves." And he also said, as related by ibn Dawud: "When people see an oppressor but do nothing about it, God will let him punish them all."[5]

A line of wisdom:

> If you have a blessing then take care of it, for sins eradicate blessings.

The Saudi regime has committed very serious acts of disobedience—worse than the sins and offenses that are contrary to Islam, worse than oppressing slaves, depriving them of their rights and insulting their dignity, intelligence, and feelings, worse than squandering the general wealth of the nation. Millions of people suffer every day from poverty and deprivation, while millions of riyals flow into the bank accounts of the royals who wield executive power. At

---

1 Qur'an, 16:112.
2 Qur'an, 89:11–14.
3 Qur'an, 5:78–79.
4 Quoted in Abu Naim al-Isbahawi, *Halia-al-Ulia*, p. 1,513. Imam-Caliph al-Hakim (985–1021) was the 6th Fatimid Caliph in Egypt. In 1005 he founded the Dar al-Ilm ("House of Knowledge") and completed the al-Hakim mosque in 1013. In 1009 he destroyed the Chruch of the Holy Sepulchre in Jerusalem, an act that was later cited in support of the First Crusade in 1096.
5 From the *hadith* collection of Abu Dawud, book 37, no. 4,324.

the same time, public services are being reduced, our lands are being violated, and people are imposing themselves forcibly through business, without compensation. It has got to the point where the regime has gone so far as to be clearly beyond the pale of Islam, allying itself with infidel America and aiding it against Muslims, and making itself an equal to God by legislating on what is or is not permissible without consulting God.

It is well known that these are among the ten acts contrary to Islam, and we have referred to some of the injustices committed by the regime in matters of religion and worldly life in some detail in Communiqué 17. Whoever wishes to go back to it will find that these are the most important reasons behind the dispute between Muslims and the rulers of Riyadh, and that the solution to these issues is easy and well known in the religion of God Almighty, so long as the ruler is truthful and honest in his desire for reform, or even has any desire for it at all. As for us, God knows that we want the reform that we strive for; we left our country out of our desire for it, for we did not need any worldly goods, all thanks and praise to God.

I miss my country greatly, and have been long absent from it; but this is easy to endure because it is for the sake of God.

Love for the Hijaz is deep in my heart, but its rulers are wolves. In Afghanistan I have a home and friends, and God gives great provision.

And it has been said: True friends are rare, but he who is inexperienced thinks they are many.

Everyone loves beautiful things, and everywhere that pride grows is good.[6]

Whoever relies on God will find Him sufficient, and He will reward those who are not distracted by worldly pleasures. There is no meaning to this life except to be judged obedient to God, so I ask God for steadfastness and a good outcome. The solution to this problem is reform, and commitment to the straight path at the command of God Almighty and his Prophet.

God Almighty said: "So keep to the right course as you have been commanded, together with those who have turned to God with you. Do not overstep the limits, for He sees everything you do."[7]

And God's Prophet said: "Say, 'I believe in God' and keep to the right course."

---

6 A line of poetry by Al-Mutawahbi, a celebrated medieval Arab poet.
7 Qur'an, 11:112.

The prosperity of this nation will be achieved in the same way as it was originally. For the Arabian peninsula was beset by crashing waves of murder and oppression, drowning in ignorance, but when God sent our Prophet Muhammad and revealed the Qur'an, and people joined him in Islam, their condition prospered and their lives were improved. God made them proud after they had been humble and made them harmonious after they had been enemies. He brought them together after they had been split, He fed them when they were hungry, and comforted them when they were afraid. God Almighty said:

> If they intend to deceive you, God is enough for you: it was He who strengthend you with His help, and with the believers, and brought their hearts together in friendship. Even if you had given away everything in the earth you could not have done this, but God brought them together: God is mighty and wise.[8]

And he said:

> If the people of those towns had believed and had been mindful of God, we would have showered them with blessings from the heaven and earth, but they rejected the truth and so we punished them for their misdeeds.[9]

The solution to the dispute between ruler and ruled is the plan proposed by the first Caliph to the second: "Be upstanding, and so will your subjects."[10] These are the words of the rightly guided Caliphs, who shine with clear light. If a commander is upright in obeying God's law, then his subjects will be likewise, for it is their duty to obey him absolutely, as commanded by God Almighty. If however he becomes an apostate and abandons God's law, then it is also their duty to abandon him, as commanded by God Almighty. For obedience is not absolute, but conditional on the ruler's integrity, and the men of knowledge have insisted upon unity and harmony in obeying God Almighty. The Sheikh of Islam, ibn Taymiyya, said: "If the reason for unity and

---

8 Qur'an, 8:62–63.
9 Qur'an, 7:96.
10 In the Sunni tradition of Islam, Abu Bakr (c.573–634) was the first of the Four Rightly Guided Caliphs, succeeding Muhammed in 632; his words here are spoken to his successor Umar ibn al-Khattab, who became Caliph in 634.

harmony is religion and working for it, then the reason for division is abandonment of what God has ordered of His servant." He also said that the restrictions and limitations imposed on the *umma* by its scholars, sheikhs, rulers, and noblemen are what allowed the enemy to gain control over it, and that was a result of the people's abandonment of obedience to God Almighty and His Messenger. Here ended his words, prayers and peace be upon Him.

Society should be as the first community of God's Messenger and his companions, the group who are saved, who are in the right—[you should strive for this] even if you are on your own in doing so, as ibn Mas'ud showed when people abandoned some of what God had commanded and enmity and hatred rose up among them, and their enemies gained power over them.[11] That is what has happened to us, and there is no strength or power save in God.

Can the rulers follow God's commands in the right way so that their subjects can too, and so that people will be happy in their lives, both in worldly and religious matters?

Some people say they can. They began with the National Center for Dialogue [Majlis al-Hiwar al-Watani],[12] as well as with municipal elections, but that has not alleviated the basic disease one bit. They claim it has improved things by letting people play the game of elections, as in Yemen, Jordan, or Egypt, and spinning around for years in a vicious circle, regardless of the fact that it is forbidden to abide by polytheistic laws.

So if we want a proper solution, both theoretical and practical, to this dispute, we need to know the truth of the matter in all its different dimensions, and we need to know all its root causes. This struggle is partly an internal regional struggle, but in other respects it is a struggle between global unbelief, with the apostates today under the leadership of America on one side, and the Islamic *umma* and its brigades of *mujahidin*, on the other. These oppressive, traitorous ruling families in the region today, who persecute every reform movement and impose upon their peoples policies that are against their

11 Abdullah ibn Mas'ud was one of the companions of the Prophet Muhammad, and was renowned for his skill in reading the Qur'an. Bin Laden is referring here to a time when Mas'ud went to recite the Qur'an to the non-receptive citizens of Mecca, who severely beat him for doing so.

12 On August 3 2003, Crown Prince Abdallah of Saudi Arabia announced on behalf of King Fahd, that a National Center for Dialogue would be formed to increase citizens' participation in government, as part of a package of reforms to make the Saudi government more open to its citizens. The Center has no power in the government other than making recommendations to the king.

religion and their worldly interests, are the very same families who helped the Crusaders against the Muslims a century ago. And they are doing this in collaboration with America and its allies. This represents a continuation of the previous Crusader wars against the Islamic world. The extent to which the Zionist-Crusader alliance controls the internal policies of our countries has become all too clear to us. For when it comes to American intervention in internal affairs, where do we start?

No appointment of a king or representative can take place without the agreement of America, something which goes back to the agreements between previous kings and the American government.

The comedy that passes for rule in Saudi Arabia today is likewise a product of American agreement, in order to forestall deterioration of the situation and further disagreements among the royal family, particularly in the last few difficult years. The state of government in Saudi Arabia is unprecedented in history. After the ruler's death, the people may be ruled for some hours or days in his name, as in the case of Shajarat al-Durr.[13] But the idea that the entire length and breadth of the land is ruled in the name of a king who for a decade has no longer known what is going on, is incredible![14]

His authority has diminished not just because he has committed acts that contradict Islam, but because of his general incapacity and the loss of his mental capacity to do even the smallest of tasks, let alone govern a country and people. His brothers should not make him do what he is not equipped to do. But they insist on keeping him, because of their refusal to let Abdallah become king, since this would reduce their own power and he would exercise power without them.

---

13 A slave in the harem of the Caliph of Baghdad, Shajar al-Durr, or "String of Pearls" (d.1257) was presented to the Ayyubid Sultan of Egypt and Syria, whose favourite she became. When the Sultan died unexpectedly, Shajar al-Durr concealed his death, assuming control until his son and heir could be recalled from Syria; consequently, she became de facto ruler of Egypt for nearly a year. On his return, the Sultan's heir, Turanshah, set her aside, giving her neither position nor authority. Shajar al-Durr subsequently married a Mameluk officer, Aybak, initiating the Mameluk Dynasty of Egypt and Syria, which would go on to defeat the Mongols, expel the Crusaders from the Holy Land, and remain the most powerful political force in the Middle East until the coming of the Ottomans.

14 In 1995 King Fahd suffered a stroke, after which he became noticeably frail, and handed over government of Saudi Arabia to his half-brother, Crown Prince Abdallah, after which he was mostly inactive. On King Fahd's death, on August 1 2005, Abdallah succeeded him as King of Saudi Arabia.

And for his part, he cannot overcome them, because they control the reins of power, in particular the Ministry of Defense and the Ministry of the Interior, as well as the Intelligence Services. More importantly, they control the Royal Court, which enables them to issue a royal edict in the name of the nominal ruler to remove him or appoint someone else as heir.[15]

This acute struggle within the royal family, besides their oppression of the people, has allowed America to continue blackmailing the competing princes, especially Abdallah, into meeting its demands. He knows for sure that if he does not respond to their orders then at the very best he will be removed by his brothers, as they previously removed his brother Saud,[16] for he is aware that his brothers have experience in such things, and that they are prepared to do more than remove him, if that is what it takes. Anyone wanting a living example of America's role in such things need look no further than Prince Hassan bin Talal of Jordan. After he had been the king's deputy for a number of decades, his brother Hussein returned from America a few days before his death and decided to remove him, which he did. Hassan submitted to the decision and became politically isolated.[17] This is what scares Prince Abdallah if he disobeys his protector America. Therefore it is no secret that the decision makers in important matters are in America.

The proof of the depth of Crusader control over our country lies in the way these collaborators carry out the changes their superior imposes on them, even in things like educational curricula, with the aim of distorting the character of the *umma* and alienating its sons. This is an old project that started decades ago in the curricula of al-Azhar in Egypt.

Then America asked the rest of the collaborationist countries to change their educational curricula, to dry up what it called the sources of [religious] awakening.

15 On his accession to the Saudi throne, Abdallah appointed the Defense Minister Prince Sultan (1928–) as Crown Prince. Along with Prince Sultan, Prince Nayef (1934–) is one of the most powerful members of the House of Saud; on the death of King Fahd, he became the third most influential man in Saudi Arabia, and is more active in government than King Abdallah. Nayef controls all the media in the kingdom.

16 In 1964, King Saud (1902–69) was deposed in a family coup, with the backing of the *ulema*, after Saud's half-brothers feared that he would select his own son as his successor.

17 Brother to King Hussein of Jordan (1935–99), Prince Hassan bin Talal (1947–) was Crown Prince of Jordan from 1965–99. On his deathbed, King Hussein reverted the succession back to his son Abdullah, wanting his direct descendants on the throne rather than his brother's.

For instance, it asked Yemen to close its religious institutes more than two decades ago, and asked the rulers of Riyadh to change the religious curricula, which they did in deference to its wishes. All this was more than a decade and a half before the raids on New York and Washington [9/11]. Besides that, there are also the new additional changes intended by the regime, as well as the removal of imams and preachers. This Crusader interference in changing curricula is categorically one of the most dangerous kinds of interference in our affairs, because—to put it bluntly—it amounts to changing our religion, which is an indivisible whole.

Whoever believes in some of the book and doesn't believe in other parts of it is an infidel indeed.

The polytheists are the ones whose hearts resembled each other. God Almighty said:

> When Our clear revelations are recited to them, those who do not expect to meet with Us say: "Bring [us] a different Qur'an, or change it." [Prophet], say "It is not for me to change it of my own accord; I follow only what is revealed to me, for I fear the torment of an awesome day.[18]

But the rulers of Riyadh were afraid of America and changed the curricula. It is no secret that the consequence of changing the religious curricula is the loss of religion, in both its religious and its everyday dimensions. As far as the religious dimension is concerned, as you know, this represents wilful apostasy. As far as the day-to-day issues are concerned, these curricula will produce in our country educated slaves who will be loyal to America, and who will sell the interests of the country and smile in the face of America while it occupies our land and corrupts our honor under the pretext of liberty, equality, and the laws of the United Nations. This is just one example of American interference in our domestic politics.

As for foreign policy, the ruling families have responded to America's wishes, leading the way in treachery. King Hussein of Jordan, for example, continued the policy of betrayal started against Palestine by his grandfather Abdallah bin al-Sharif Hussein, as well as his father.[19]

---

18 Qur'an, 10:15.
19 Abdallah bin al-Sharif Hussein (1882–1951) was Emir of Transjordan under the British Mandate. He negotiated with the British to gain independence for Transjordan, which was proclaimed

And his son Abdallah II has continued the same course, while Muhammad VI in Morocco is following the same path of treachery pursued by his father and grandfather before him.[20] Their implementation of Crusader plots is still going on today. Since there isn't scope here to cover them completely, we will just mention some of the most significant ones.

This government in Riyadh has entered into a global alliance with Crusader unbelief, under the leadership of Bush, against Islam and its people, as happened in Afghanistan, and the conspiracies in Iraq, which have not yet ended. They opened up their bases to the American forces so that they could conquer Iraq, which helped the Americans and facilitated their occupation. Then the Saudi Minister of Defense got up one day and scorned the religion, the blood, and the minds of Muslims by admitting that his government had opened its airports to the Americans for their allegedly humanistic objectives.

And now here they are today showing us a new link in their chain of conspiracies with America. This one they have described as the initiative to send Arab and Muslim forces to maintain security in Iraq.

This is an enormous act of treachery. They weren't satisfied with helping the infidels to occupy the lands of Islam, but they also had to come up with this initiative to confer legitimacy on the American occupation. "We rely on God, for He is our protector."

What made this disaster even more offensive to people was the fact that many of them thought that when Prince Abdallah bin Abd al-Aziz [now King Abdallah of Saudi Arabia], took over management of the country he would save it from the mires of religious disobedience, and administrative, financial, and

on May 25 1923, before becoming King of Jordan in 1949. His aim of a Greater Syria (comprising Jordan, Syria, and Iraq under a Hashemite dynasty) and moderate outlook towards Israel, led many Arab countries, in particular the Saud dynasty, to distrust him. He was assassinated in Jerusalem's al-Aqsa mosque on July 20 1952. In 1915–16, his father, Hussein ibn Ali (see above, p. 219, n. 14), was involved in an exchange of letters with the British High Commissioner of Egypt, Sir Henry McMahon, concerning the future political status of the Middle East, where the United Kingdom was seeking to bring about armed revolt against the Ottoman Empire. McMahon promised immediate Arab independence, an agreement Arab nationalists believe was violated by the secret 1916 Sykes-Picot agreement (see above, p. 187, n. 5).

20 Abdallah ibn al-Hussein (1962–) became King Abdallah II of Jordan on February 7 1999. Abdallah's mother is the British-born Antoinette Avril Gardiner (Muna al-Hussein); many Jordanians considered it unfitting that he should assume the Hashemite throne, which traces its descent directly to the Prophet Muhammad. King Muhammad VI of Morocco (1963–) was enthroned on July 23 1999; he established a reputation as a modernizer, and brought about a constitutional monarchy in Morocco.

media corruption, as well as other kinds of corruption, and that he would save it from its subservience to America. But although people were expecting good to come from him, he brought them evil. For while America was sending its armies to the Gulf to invade Iraq, the Riyadh regime was deceiving the *umma* with its statements, saying that it refused to let America use force against Iraq.

Shortly before the invasion, Prince Abdallah presented a plan which he claimed was humanitarian. This was that Saddam should go into exile in order to spare our blood, as he put it—which was a clear statement that Iraq should surrender to America, with all the spoils and booty that it contains.

Such a person is like a criminal who ambushes you and gives you one of his slaves as a sincere peacemaker, who tells you: "I advise you to leave your family and property, and escape on your own." This is how the thief takes people's property in Iraq, attacking their land and honor without caring about the support or advice of the Bedouin Prince.

It is true that Saddam is a thief and an apostate, but the solution is not to be found in moving the government of Iraq from a local thief to a foreign one. Helping the infidel to take the land of Muslims and control them is one of the ten acts contradictory to Islam.

Before the invasion Prince Abdallah also came out in public to make the sly, deceptive statement that the American troops were not gathering for war. Those who gave him the benefit of the doubt thought that this was merely an example of his negligence and nothing more, but no more than a year, or even a few months, had passed before God Almighty shamed him in front of everyone and revealed his lies, deceit, treason, and treachery against the *umma*, the like of which has never before been seen, with clear and irrefutable evidence.

Prince Talal bin Abd al-Aziz[21] also stated publicly that his father had received money from the English, thereby affirming the facts and documents that prove that his father was a collaborator with the English.

And today too you have his nephew and ambassador in America, Prince Bandar bin Sultan, admitting in public that he met with the American Vice-

21 Talal bin Abdul Aziz al-Saud (1935–) is a brother of King Fahd. In 1958 he wrote a proposed constitution for Saudi Arabia, which would have created a constitutional monarchy and expanded political rights. His proposals were rejected by King Fahd, and the Saudi *ulema* issued a *fatwa* that declared them to be contrary to Islamic law. When his passport was revoked in 1961, he left for Egypt, declaring himself a socialist. He returned to Saudi Arabia in 1964 after agreeing to temper his criticisms.

President and his Defense Minister and the Chief of Staff, who informed him of their secret plans to invade Iraq and everything else. This came in the midst of his comments following the publication of a book shaming Prince Abdallah, in which he pledged support for America and encouraged it to invade Iraq.[22]

Other statements like this were issued before the invasion, including his pronouncement that he felt that the American forces that had arrived in the Gulf were not there for war. In this instance he was lying to the *umma* in full knowledge in order to deceive it and spread false ideas within it. As such he undertook the first part of the psychological war, acting as America's proxy, against Iraq and its people, so that they would surrender and not be hostile to the war, and so that the ideas of submissiveness and surrender to the enemy would spread amongst us, and so that the American forces would not meet with any significant resistance. Oh what shame and ignominy! What unbelief and treachery! What treason and betrayal! People still remember the presence of the Iraqi delegation at the Beirut conference and the announcement of a settlement between the two countries. Then Abdallah betrays them, going in the middle of the night to make an agreement with America over the invasion of Iraq and pledging to pay a billion dollars towards it to support this war.

Is this the extent to which the rulers of Riyadh have sunk? The hypocrites claim that they are responsible rulers. They are lying to the *umma* and deceiving it for a few pennies that they don't deserve.

Here, sensible people should make a stand with each other and consider the conduct of their rulers. The disorder is great indeed. No Muslim can be content to be ruled by such men. Sensible people who want to see reform achieved through these rulers should think: how could such people undertake reform when they are swimming in such a stormy sea of disgusting characteristics? It is impossible, because drowning awaits them. No sane person could be satisfied to have anyone with such characteristics as a partner in anything at all. How could he, when we are talking about such important issues as the fate

---

22 Bandar bin Sultan (1949–) is son of Crown Prince Sultan, the Deputy Prime Minister of Saudi Arabia. He was Saudi ambassador to America from 1983 to 2005, and formed close relationships with President George W Bush and Vice-President Dick Cheney. Prince Bandar attracted controversy over allegations in Bob Woodward's book *Plan of Attack*, to the effect that President Bush informed him in advance of the decision to invade Iraq, ahead of Secretary of State Colin Powell. The book also alleged that a deal had been struck to reduce oil prices before the November 2004 US election, in which Bandar publicly endorsed Bush.

of the *umma*, and the efforts and conversations of advisers, the results of which are evidently very far from the realms of reality. The rulers' conduct varies between procrastination and lying, enticement and temptation, or prison and exile. But the one certain aim of this ruler in his dialogue with every reformist movement is to abort that movement, even if this takes some time. I have experienced this myself, when two decades ago I offered advice to the government through senior scholars, but the situation did not change.

Then a decade and a half ago, I directed my advice straight to the deputy Minister of Defense, informing him of the great sins from which the state should desist, and of the danger of persisting with them, but to no avail. Then I met the deputy director of the ministry for security affairs, who strongly reproached me for advising the deputy Minister of Defense and began haranguing me about exactly the same sins that I had mentioned to the minister. Then he said: "This is well known—we don't need anyone to tell us about it." And these sins that I advised you about have been going on for decades, and the rulers have been advised about them by many people before me, but these evils are still present today, the rulers are defending them and committed to them because their royal status has supposedly rendered them legitimate. The result is that people are not committed to God's law. This means that absolute sovereignty and obedience are due to the king and his laws, not to the religion of God Almighty. This is the dangerous reality, and this is the belief of the people as expressed by the deputy director with his statement "that this is well known—we don't need anyone to tell us about it". They know that the grave sins that I mentioned to them are prohibited in God's religion, but they do not want anyone to forbid them for one simple reason, which is that they are not prohibited in the religion of the king. So they wonder how we can forbid them, and they even ask us not to tell them that they are prohibited. The king issued edicts and laws permitting and protecting them. The word of religion has a say only when the king or ruler considers it legitimate. God Almighty said: "[Joseph] began by searching their bags, then his brother's, and he pulled it out from under his brother's bag."[23]

Whoever has been given insight by God and ponders the regime's conduct will find this reality being played out in front of his eyes, both in domestic and foreign affairs: dominion and obedience apply to the order of the king and not

---

23 Qur'an, 12:76.

to God Almighty—what the king declares lawful becomes lawful, what he prohibits is forbidden, for in his eyes it is his true right as king to legalize or prohibit whatever he wants.

I'll give you some examples: it is well known in religion that usury is strictly forbidden, for God Almighty has said: "God has allowed trade and forbidden usury."[24] But the regime has issued edicts and laws making usury legal and establishing it, and punishing anyone who prevents it or avoids paying what they illegally call profit. It is well known that all usury is a grave sin, and that legislation without reference to God is one of the acts contradictory to Islam.

As for the second example, this involves taking the infidels as allies. For instance, the Jordanian regime is an infidel regime. If a preacher or writer described King Hussein as a collaborator with the Jews, he would be subjected to punishment at the hands of the Riyadh regime through laws that have been made specifically for this purpose. But when King Hussein entered into alliance with Saddam, when he invaded Kuwait, King Fahd washed his hands of his former ally.[25] The Riyadh newspapers were filled with documents and pictures proving Hussein bin Talal to be a collaborator with the Jews, which is true—he is. By contrast, the newspapers of Jordan were filled with documents and pictures proving that the rulers of Riyadh collaborated with the English and then with America, which is true—they did. So, despite the great disaster for us that the rulers of the region are collaborators, there is a greater disaster in that most of the leaders of the Islamic world insist on describing these tyrants as responsible leaders. Some people think they are a lifeboat, when in fact all they are is a sinking ship.

Honest people in these Islamic associations should ensure that Islamic works have nothing to do with such mendacious regimes, especially after these conclusive documents showed that King Fahd had been received by King Hussein, forgetting about the past, and then when King Hussein died the Princes of the Saud family attended his funeral, along with the Israeli and American delegations and others, and then the prayer of the absent was performed for him in the Haram Mosque.

Devotion to God has confirmed the bonds of faith with which we ally ourselves with the allies of God and His Messenger, and that we are enemies of

---

24 Qur'an, 2:276.
25 King Hussein sided with Saddam Hussein in the Gulf War of 1990–91.

their enemies too. But the hypocrites are slaves to money and follow the king whatever he does. They blow with the winds, and are enemies of his enemies. Is a person still a human being even if he changes his mind in such a humiliating and insulting way? Is a Muslim supposed to rid himself of his religion and trample his own brain underfoot to become a good citizen?

The same goes for the regimes of Abdel Nasser, Sadat, Qadhafi, Saddam.

Abdel Nasser was in conflict with the Saudi regime, so they declared him an infidel from the pulpit of the Haram Mosque in Mecca. And that's what he is. But when he made peace with the Saudis, he became a Muslim again.

The same thing happened with that atheist Qadhafi. For over three decades he was an infidel when he insulted them, and then when they made peace with the Saudi government he became a Muslim and they brought him into the Noble Ka'ba.

As for Sadat, when he signed the capitulation initiative with the Jews, the rulers of Riyadh and the rest of the Arab states accused him of being a traitor and a collaborator, which he was. Their newspapers were filled with insults and abuse against him. Then when Prince Abdallah also committed the same treachery and collaboration in the Beirut initiative the hypocrites praised him and supported him. The scholars of evil and writers-for-rent said whatever the ruler wanted them to, and went wherever he went, all for money. And then they claim to have religious knowledge, guidance, and rectitude.

The above shows clearly that the ruler has another religion and that he is trading with the religion of Islam and deceiving the people in regard to it. After the general behavior we have seen from all the rulers of the region, and the rulers of Riyadh in particular, who besides their other bad characteristics, are apostate collaborators, it is clear that the dispute is one between two paths, and a profound struggle between two beliefs: a struggle between the divine, perfect belief, which has submitted to God's authority in all matters—the way of "Say, my prayer, my piety, my life and death are for God, lord of the two worlds, who has no partner. So I have been instructed and I am the first of Muslims,"[26] the way of "There is no god but God and Muhammad is His Messenger",[27] in all its meanings and with all its requirements—and the

---

26 Qur'an, 6:162–3.
27 The *shahada*, the Muslim declaration of belief in the unity of God and the prophethood of Muhammad.

crudely secular way, the way of "those who deceive God and those who believe, although they only deceive themselves even if they do not realise it,"[28] the way of "those who take each other as lords instead of God,"[29] they way of those about whom God said: "When they are told, 'Turn to God's revelations and the Messenger [for judgment],' you see the hypocrites turn away from you [Prophet]."[30]

Now that this is clear, the solution to improve the situation is what has been made clear by God's law, and that is to remove the ruler. Even if he refuses to go, it is obligatory to depose him through force of arms. This is the ruling of God's law, which maintains people's religious and material interests. The regime, for its part, has proposed a similar solution in its maintenance of its own laws and worldly interests—it proposed that the [Islamic] reformers should submit unconditionally to the laws and edicts of royal power.

And if the dialogue has to be done through the sword and the gun, as the Minister of Defense put it, it is well known that every master, whether he is royal or not, needs a weapon. So how can any sane person, seeing the apostate ruler and his soldiers armed to the teeth, claim that he wants reform through a peaceful solution? This is complete nonsense. It is reducing the establishment of the truth, for we are not talking merely of a debauched and depraved ruler, but one who is an apostate and a collaborator with the infidels.

In the same way, there is no difference between [Paul] Bremer, the former American ruler in Baghdad, and [Iyad] Allawi, the current ruler, in terms of implementing American policies in Iraq. For there is no difference between Bremer and the rest of the regimes in the region when it comes to implementing America's policies.

The scholars of Islam have agreed that authority cannot be given to an infidel, so if he becomes one his authority is thereby revoked and it is obligatory to remove him by force. Ayad Qadi[31] said: "Scholars are agreed that leadership of the religious community cannot be given to an infidel, and that if he becomes one, he must be deposed."

28 Qur'an, 2:9.
29 Qur'an, 3:64.
30 Qur'an, 4:61.
31 Qadi Ayad (1118–66), from Ceuta, Morocco, was an imam and jurist. His greatest work was *As-Shifa*, an account of the life of the Prophet Muhammad.

He also said: "If he becomes an infidel, changes God's law or indulges in innovation, he has stepped outside of the judgment of authority and he is not due allegiance. It is then incumbent upon Muslims to rise up against him and remove him and to appoint a just imam, if they can do so—even if there is only one group of Muslims, they are obliged to depose the infidel."

Therefore, it is not we who say that the infidel leader has overstepped the bounds of his authority; it is the consensus of the imams who say so. This is the judgment of God's law in a case such as ours, so it is obligatory for all Muslims to strive for reform, taking into consideration[32] the size and dimension of the dispute and the fact that these regimes are nothing but a part of the organization of global unbelief.

Reform should be carried out according to God's law, or else it is a deviation from it and a waste of time and effort, whether it be well-intentioned or deceitful.

Our countrymen who reject armed confrontation with the governments in order to restore their rights are engaging in a huge fraud. You can't get rights restored by a regime whose ruler is an apostate and who rejects everything except the force of arms, who knows that he has on his side these purveyors of blatant error, as well as those who have called directly for acts contradictory to Islam. They have helped the infidels to occupy the lands of Islam, as some of them have stated, under the deceitful cover of helping to get rulers to respect human rights, or the others who mix truth and falsehood and cooperate with the infidels to occupy our lands. It's true, with their refusal to remove these apostate rulers by force, their approach can only bring one outcome.

The approach of these people is extremely dangerous for two reasons:

Firstly, they are a great danger because they have let their wishes and desires compete with God's law, which as everyone knows is a grave sin. God Almighty said: "When God and his Messenger have decided on a matter that concerns them, it is not fitting for any believing man or woman to claim a freedom of choice in that matter: whoever disobeys God and his Messenger is far astray."[33]

32 This phrase "taking into consideration" ("akhidin bil i'tibar") appears to be a clear example of Western phraseology in bin Laden's speech. It has no basis in classical Arabic, and is an example of a neologism translated into Arabic from Western speech; other such phrases include "the lion's share" ("nasib al-asad") and "gave the green light" ("a'ta al-dau al-akhdar").

33 Qur'an, 33:36.

He also said: "By your Lord, they will not be true believers until they let you decide between them in all matters of dispute, and find no resistance in their souls to your decisions, accepting them totally."[34]

Secondly, these people are participating in barring people from the way of God, and sowing strife in their religion, in that they are preventing them from assuming their rights in the ways that God made lawful, which is what makes hypocrites and ignorant people think of taking the course of the Northern Alliance in Afghanistan, and others like them such as Allawi and his companions. This is in no way allowed.

Before finishing, we should respond to some of the regime's allegations, whose repetition has upset people both day and night throughout the past two years. It has accused the *mujahidin* of following the path of the Kharijites, but they know that we have nothing to do with such a school of thought.[35] Our messages and conduct attest to that.

Did our own people attack us with weapons in Sudan to kill everyone except Kharijites? We believe that no sin besides that of unbelief makes a believer step outside his faith, even if it is a serious sin, like murder or drinking alcohol. Even if the culprit died without repenting of his sins, his fate is with God, whether He wishes to forgive him or to punish him. His destiny will be to go to Heaven. We do not anathematize[36] people in general, nor do we permit the shedding of Muslim blood. If some Muslims have been killed during the operations of the *mujahidin* then we pray to God to take mercy on them; this is a case of accidental manslaughter, and we beg God's forgiveness for it and we take responsibility for it.

But I say to the ruler of Riyadh, I will tell you about who has been killing Muslims, for he has killed them before, whole groups of them.

I can tell you about those who declare people in general unbelievers, and who permit the shedding of Muslim blood: your father, Abd al-Aziz [ibn Saud]. He is the one who came out and helped the English against the Ottoman state and their deputy, ibn Rashid, at Ha'il.[37] You yourselves came

34 Qur'an, 4:65.
35 See above, p. 224, n. 30. Bin Laden has been labeled in some quarters as a "neo-Kharijite," somebody who emphasizes the practice of *takfir*, or declares individual or groups of Muslims to be apostate.
36 The Arabic term is *mukaffir*, the step before *takfir*.
37 Ha'il is an oasis town in northwest Saudi Arabia, and was the center for the Rashid family, enemies of the Saud. In 1921, it was the location of the Rashidi army's surrender to ibn Saud's forces.

out with force of arms against your brother King Saud, and you would have massacred each other had it not been for God Almighty. Your scholars did not call you and your father Kharijites, and if we open the file on the horrifying massacre of Taif we learn who it was that declared everyone else infidels.[38] That was the massacre in which your father deceived his own soldiers, telling them that the people of the Hijaz were infidels and that killing them was *jihad* for the sake of God. In saying this he was lying to them. If we discuss all the terrible things that happened at Taif, all the other disasters of the regime pale by comparison. Adversaries are supposed to stick to the code of conduct of conflict and fighting by not lying. It is much better to abide by such rules. And if you weren't so sure that we would not lie on your behalf, since we have been lied to for so long, then you would ask me about a Muslim man who has gone into hiding with me and whom you unjustly want to oppress or kill. To lie in such circumstances would be a duty, just as the men of knowledge have mentioned that the ruler must be a Muslim, and just as you accuse Al-Sabbab of ignorance in issues that all Muslims know about. Al-Nawawi said: "As for the idea that he only orders and forbids what he knows about, this is something else entirely; every Muslim knows about obvious duties like the forbidden months, praying, fasting, adultery, drinking alcohol, and the like."[39]

Is there any Muslim alive who is unaware that it is forbidden to help the infidels against a Muslim, or to make usury legal? This is well known to be part of the religion, just as knowledge of the prohibition of wine or adultery is well known. Is anyone unaware of this, or of the fact that you want to make a priesthood in Islam! For you are making a council of elder scholars of the sultan like some Christians do.[40] By doing so you are despising the religion and declaring legal what God prohibited, and prohibiting what He has authorized. You issue pardons to whoever you like, and describe the youth as having erroneous and corrupt ideas—but who is it that really has the erroneous ideas?

Are the ones with the corrupt and erroneous ideas those who follow the words of God's Messenger about the duty of expelling the Jews and Christians

38 In September 1924, ibn Saud's forces sacked the western Saudi city of Taif, massacring most of its male inhabitants.
39 From the *hadith* collection of Muslim. The Syrian Al-Nawawi (1233–78), was a Muslim theologian and writer, producing many collections of *hadith* and commentaries.
40 There are no priests in Islam, and this would therefore represent *kufr* (unbelief).

from the Arabian peninsula? As the Prophet said, according to al-Bukhari: "Banish the polytheists from the Arabian peninsula"[41] and "There can be no two religions in the Arabian peninsula".[42] He also said: "Fight the Jews and Christians, take their sons' graves as places of worship—there can be no two religions on Arab land"[43] and "I am banishing the Jews and Christians from the Arabian peninsula so that I preach only to Muslims."[44]

Or are they the ones who scorn the sayings of the Prophet and act treacherously towards them, like the Jews? Like Prince Abdallah did when he said that our arguments were groundless, and then turned to serve foreigners. However, our arguments are simply the clear and correct sayings of the Prophet concerning the duty of banishing the polytheists, with no exception, regardless of whether they come to serve or be served.

Are we the ones with erroneous ideas? Or is it those who have betrayed the *umma* and allowed Muhammad's peninsula to be occupied by the Jews and Christians, letting them take control and giving them military bases. This is besides their [the Saudi regime's] betrayal of Iraq, even though betrayal is forbidden, even betrayal of infidels.

Our Prophet said, as related by Muslim: "Every traitor will have agony on the Day of Judgment in accordance with his treachery, and the greatest betrayal is that of a commander of his people."[45]

So who are the ones with the corrupt and erroneous ideas? Is it those who enjoin what is good and forbid evil, and who believe in God? Or is it those who betray Muslims with their policies and propaganda, even in the sacred land and in the forbidden months and around the mosque of the Haram?[46]

God Almighty said: "As you the disbelievers, who bar others from God's path and from the Sacred Mosque—which He made for all people, residents and vistors alike—and who try to violate it with wrongdoing, we shall inflict upon them a painful punishment."[47] He also said: "She said, 'Whenever kings

41 From the *hadith* collection of al-Bukhari, vol. 4, book 52, no. 288. This was one of three requests Muhamad made on his deathbed.
42 From the *hadith* collection of ibn Malik, book 45, no. 45.5.18.
43 From the *hadith* collection of ibn Malik, book 45, no. 45.5.17.
44 From the *hadith* collection of ibn Muslim, book 19, no. 4,366.
45 From the *hadith* collection of ibn Muslim, book 13, no. 3,272.
46 By highlighting these sacrosanct issues, bin Laden accentuates the misdeeds of the Saudi rulers. First, the land of the holy sanctuaries, then the holiest months of the year, and finally the holiest site in Islam, are mentioned.
47 Qur'an, 22:25.

go into a city, they ruin it and humiliate its leaders—that is what they do—but I am going to send them a gift, and see what my envoy brings back.'"[48]

Who are the ones with the corrupt and erroneous ideas? Is it those who defend Muslims and their honor and property in Iraq, Palestine, Afghanistan, Kashmir, and Chechnya?

Or it is those who have entered into the alliance of global unbelief against the Muslims, as well as plundering the *umma*'s public funds?

All we need to do to clean up this issue is to point to the huge arms deal, or what you might call the huge theft—for they amount to the same thing—which is known as the al-Yamama contract,[49] which comes to more than $30 billion—this was a humiliation five years before the Gulf War. But when the war actually started there was no positive effect from this deal to be seen, nor from any of the hundreds of other deals that have been made. When I emigrated from my country to defend you, the unemployment rate was low. If we estimate the number of unemployed at 100,000, then we can divide the value of the deal, $30 billion, into 100,000, which comes to 1,125,000 riyals per head. If these funds were put into publicly owned companies in a legitimate way and into generating work for the unemployed, and if they were spent on their own people, like the poor, the miserable, and those in debt, then the people's condition would improve.

As for the violation of our peoples' lands and the greed of the rulers of Riyadh in building palaces, King Fahd has commissioned the building of the Salam Palace, on which he has spent 4 billion riyals.

As for the palace of Dhahban, where do we start? It is 40km down the Jeddah-Medina road on the Red Sea coast, but to get an idea of the land it has greedily used up, if the Kingdom of Bahrain were put in its back courtyard, those in the palace wouldn't even notice it. And Bahrain has nearly a million inhabitants and an area of more than a million square metres! Even if the whole

---

48 Qur'an, 27:34–35.

49 The UK-Saudi "al-Yamamah" ("the Dove") air defense contract was signed on February 9 1986. It was valued at £5 billion ($8 billion), thus far the biggest contract in the history of the UK arms trade. The terms of the contract were not disclosed, but it was understood that most, if not, all of the payment would be in oil. The contract attracted considerable controversy, involving allegations of corruption and the value of the deal. Despite these issues, a second contract, "al-Yamamah II" was signed between the UK and Saudi Arabia. The initial list of orders valued at £10 billion ($16 billion); higher sums of up to $50 billion, were predicted for the long term.

world came into the palaces of these kings and presidents, or into this palace in Dhahban, they would be dwarfed. Has history ever seen such foolishness?

And then the hypocrites describe them as reliable, sensible, and wise. God Almighty said of such people: "The boat belonged to some needy people who made their living from the sea and I damaged it because I knew that coming after them was a king who was seizing every serviceable boat by force."[50]

Who are the ones with the corrupt and erroneous ideas? Is it those who allowed the land of the Haram to be occupied and who kill Muslims in the holy city of Mecca? Is it Khaled al-Mihdar and Nawaf al-Hazimi and his brother Salem, who came from Mecca to strike America right on its own territory, in defense of Islam in and around Mecca?[51]

Is it Fahd bin Abd al-Aziz, who has defiled the honor of the Haram? He could have solved this crisis without a shot being fired, as all sensible people agreed at the time. What the situation needed was some time, especially since those present inside the Haram were only a few dozen. They had only light weapons, mostly hunting rifles, they had few provisions and they were surrounded, but the enemy of God, Fahd, did what not even al-Hajjaj[52] presumed to do: he stubbornly fought with them and put bulldozers and armored cars inside the Haram. I still remember the bulldozer's tracks on the paving stones of the Haram. There is no strength or power save in God. People still remember the minarets covered in black after they had been pounded by tanks—we are God's creation and to Him we return. Who was it who defiled the honor of the country of the Haram and the blood of Muslims? Was it the youth? Or was it the security forces who killed poor people in the Rasifa district of Mecca, who forced those who were still alive out of their houses or their tiny tin-roofed shacks to greet their prince in the Ministry of the Interior? The scholars and preachers of the Haram knew about these things but did not say a word about the illegality of shedding Muslim blood in the land of the Haram, because the people who had been attacked there were only the poor and defenseless.

Who are the ones with the corrupt and erroneous ideas? Is it the *mujahidin*? Or is it the ones who helped America to kill more than a million children in

50 Qur'an, 18:79.
51 A reference to the November 1979 occupation of the Grand Mosque at Mecca; after the occupation, all the surviving males were executed. Khaled al-Midhar and Nawaf al-Hazimi, both Meccans, were identified as having been involved in the 9/11 attack.
52 See above, p. 5, n. 5.

just a few years in the greatest slaughter of children that mankind has known, your wicked embargo on Iraq?

The Prophet said: "A women went to Hell because she had a cat whom she tied up so that it could not eat, not even the crumbs on the floor, and so it died."[53]

Those who are allying themselves with the regime and supporting it are partners in this great crime. There is another Prophetic saying: "If the people of the heavens and earth agree to kill a Muslim man, then God will throw them into the Fire."[54] God Almighty said: "If anyone kills deliberately, the punishment for him is Hell, and there he will remain: God is angry with him, and rejects him, and has prepared a tremendous torment for him."[55]

The Prophet also said: "The end of the world is not as bad as the murder of a Muslim."

Ibn Abbas reports that the Prophet said: "On the Day of Judgment, the killer and the victim will come face to face, and the victim will be holding his head in his hands, and his veins will spill forth blood. He will ask: 'Oh Lord, ask this man why he killed me.' And God will bring the victim closer to the throne.'"[56]

This is just one victim talking about his murderer, so what about a million murdered children, each of them holding up his head and his hand and saying, "Oh Lord, ask these men why they have killed us, the greatest massacre of children in the history of mankind." This is a huge injustice and a great crime. Muslims have a duty to repent themselves of it and wash their hands of these oppressive, debauched, infidel governments that they have been allying themselves with and supporting. They should free themselves of those who support murder. God Almighty said: "Abraham asked forgiveness for his father because he had made a to promise to him, but once he realized that his father was an enemy of God, he washed his hands of him. Abraham was tender-hearted and forbearing."[57]

He also said: "You have a good example in Abraham and his companions, when they said to their people: 'We disown you and what you worship beside

53 From the *hadith* collection of al-Bukhari, vol. 3. book 40, no. 553.
54 From the *hadith* collection of al-Nisai, book 17, ch. 2, no. 3,922.
55 Qur'an, 4:93.
56 From the *hadith* collection of al-Tirmidhi, vol. 47, book 5, no. 2,955. Abdullah ibn Abbas was a cousin of the Prophet Muhammad. An expert on the Qur'an and authority on the *hadith* of Muhammad, he is revered by both Sunni and Shia for his great knowledge.
57 Qur'an, 9:114.

God! We renounce you! Until you believe in God alone, the enmity and hatred that has arisen between us will endure!'—except when Abraham said to his father, 'I will pray for forgiveness for you though I cannot protect you from God' [they prayed]."[58]

Despite this terrible massacre that went on for a number of years in Iraq, we did not hear a single word or decree from your supposedly brilliant scholars, or from your preachers who talk about the illegality of spilling Muslim blood. But when the young men killed that American warmonger, these scholars finally raised their voices, and the hacks didn't stop talking night and day about the illegality of spilling the blood of those in your trust. But according to the laws of the king's religion, and that of his companions, the murder of a million Muslims and the murder of a million children is merely a matter to be looked into, whilst the killing of a single Crusader is an unforgivable crime![59]

God is sufficient for me against you all.

It is unbelievable—and a lie—that the regime should accuse the youth of the very sins that it commits itself, such as its claim that the Zionists are supporting the *mujahidin*! What deceit, what duplicity, what utter contempt for people's basic intelligence!

Everyone, Muslims or infidels, knows that the youth of *jihad* are Zionism's worst enemy, yet still the regime accuses us of its own crimes.

God Almighty said: "And anyone who commits an offence or a sin, and then throws the blame on to some innocent person, has burdened himself with deceit as well as flagrant sin."[60]

And here I ask the rulers of Riyadh: who was it that supported Arafat with hundreds of millions of dollars to suppress the first *intifada* of the *mujahidin*? Who was it that helped the Jews against the poor people in Sharm al-Sheikh in 1996?

Who opened up their military bases to help the invasion of Iraq? Who pays the costs of training the Iraqi police to fight against the *mujahidin* in Iraq? Is it not you, the mastermind behind the Beirut initiative which recognized the

58 Qur'an, 60:4.
59 Possibly a reference to the explosion in Riyadh on November 13 1995, which killed five Americans.
60 Qur'an, 4:112.

Zionists and their occupation of the land of Palestine. You are the head of the National Guard—where is your mind? Have you lost all self-respect?[61]

How dare you make these vile, baseless accusations against the *mujahidin*? God's Prophet said: "The three kinds of people whom God will not speak to, praise or even look at, on the Day of Judgment, and who will have a painful torment, are the sheikh who defames people, the king who lies, and the one who fails to support those in his charge."[62]

So, you banned imams from preaching to the *mujahidin* in Chechnya, and ordered them instead to preach to the youth of *jihad* in Saudi Arabia, whom you dishonestly and deliberately accuse of being Zionist collaborators. And the preachers and poets who support your slanderous claims are also liars— they know you are a liar and a traitor; how similar are these years to the years that the Prophet told us about.

The Prophet said, as related by Imam Ahmad: "People will suffer years of deception in which lies will be deemed the truth and the truth lies, and in which a traitor will come and faithful people will betray, and the foolish will speak." "And who are the foolish?" the Prophet said: "The stupid man who discusses public matters."[63]

I call on all Muslims to curse the Zionists and their collaborators, and I call on you, if you are an honest man, and those in your command, to make the following prayer in the Two Holy Sanctuaries and all other mosques in the land: "Oh Lord, abandon the Zionist-American alliance and their supporters and collaborators, oh Lord, destroy them and break their backs, take away their power and shatter their unity, make their wives widows, turn them against each other, look for their weak points just as You do to the *mujahidin*, shame them before the whole world, rid us of them however you wish."

And to my *mujahidin* brothers in particular, I say: you have made a stand to help your religion when all around you have failed, you have waged *jihad* when others have only talked about it, you have spoken the truth when the timid and the greedy were silent. "When the sorcerers came to Pharaoh, they said: 'Shall we be rewarded if we win?' and he said, 'Yes, and you will join my inner court.'"[64]

61 These questions are directed specifically to Crown Prince Abdullah of Saudi Arabia.
62 From the *hadith* collection of al-Bukhari, vol. 3, book 48, no. 838.
63 From the *hadith* collection of ibn Hanbal, vol. 6, book 1, no. 7,571.
64 Qur'an, 26:41–42.

As for you, who hope to be rewarded and to be close to the Merciful, you have tasted the sweetness of faith, and you have not been led astray by the sweetness of this world. This is how I consider you, but God is your reckoner. There is no one purer than you in God's eyes and He will give you the best rewards.

You have made a stand, and death brings no doubt to those who do so. You have smashed all delusions and fantasies, and they were shattered.

You have plunged into the sea of death, utterly fearless. And he who does not fear death cannot be scared of anything.

You have smashed the haloes that have been unjustly around the heads of the tyrants for decades now, and to your credit you have lit up the way with your blood to the millions in the coming generations to remain on the straight path and avoid the way of these criminal tyrants.

There is a Prophetic saying, related by al-Bukhari: "By God, for one man to be guided by God's path by you is better for you than all the blessings in the world.[65]

God have mercy on our brothers the martyrs everywhere: in Palestine, in Iraq, in Saudi Arabia, in Morocco, in Kashmir, in Afghanistan, in Chechnya, in Nigeria, in Indonesia, in the Philippines, and in Thailand.

God have mercy on Sheikh Yusuf al-Airi, Abu Ali al-Harithi, Khaled al-Hajj, Abd al-Aziz al-Muqrin, Isa al-Aushin and all their brothers ...[66]

We pray to God Almighty to have mercy on the *mujahidin* who attacked the American consulate in Jeddah.[67]

How can they hope to be blessed with security while they are dishing out destruction, devastation, and murder on our people in Palestine and Iraq?

These people do not deserve security in any part of the world. As for their presence in Saudi Arabia, and indeed in all of the Arabian peninsula, that is

65 From the *hadith* collection of al-Bukhari, vol. 4, book 52, no. 192.

66 Yusuf al-Airi (d.2003) is alleged to have been involved in the planning of the Madrid train bombings of March 15 2004. Abu Ali al-Harithi, a Yemeni, is alleged to have been involved in the USS *Cole* bombing in October 2000; he was killed by a CIA missile attack east of Sana'a on November 3 2002. Khaled al-Hajj, a Palestinian from Jenin, is a political spokesman for Hamas, was imprisoned without charge on May 28 2002 by the Israeli authorities, and remains in detention without trial or charge. Abs al-Aziz al-Muqrin (1972–2004) is alleged to have been involved in attacks against Westerners in Saudi Arabia; on June 18 2004 he was killed in Riyadh during a government-sponsored raid.

67 On December 6 2004, an attack on the US Consulate in Jeddah left eight dead, including three of the five attackers.

forbidden under God's law, as we have demonstrated. And we pray to God that He will accept our brothers who have been killed as martyrs.

I say to our brothers and our people, it is God who gives and God who takes away. Nothing lasts for ever, so be patient and think of the rewards of the hereafter.

I remind you of God's words: "No misfortune can happen, either in the earth or in yourselves, that was not set down in writing before We brought it into being—that is easy for God."[68]

How can a Muslim who believes in God's truth not be patient, for He is our Master, the Creator, who said to the leader of the path that we are on: "Wait patiently [Prophet] for your Lord's judgment: you are under Our watchful eye. Celebrate the praise of your Lord when you rise."[69]

After the invasion of the joint forces and all its horrors, God Almighty also said:

> The Messenger of God is an excellent model for those of you who put your hope in God and the Last Day and remember Him often. When the believers saw the joint forces, they said, "This is what God and His Messenger promised us; the promise of God and His Messenger is true," and this only served to increase their faith and submission to God.[70]

And God's Messenger said: "The size of your reward will be in proportion to your bravery, and if God loves a people He puts them to the test, and whoever pleases Him will be rewarded in kind and whoever angers Him will be rewarded in kind."[71] So do as the speaker said.

I suffer what afflicts me with patience—you should remember that God has praised patience.

I am not on the side of the wealthy, if exaltedness is on the side of the poor.

So continue on the path, don't be afraid of any difficulty, and be sure to cleanse the Arabian peninsula of polytheists, atheists, and heretics.

---

68 Qur'an, 57:22.
69 Qur'an, 52:48.
70 Qur'an, 33:21–22. The "joint forces" refer to the confederation of tribes that comprised the Meccan army in the Battle of the Trench (627).
71 From the *hadith* collection of al-Tirmidhi, vol. 36, book 49, no. 2,320.

God Almighty said: "Do not be faint-hearted in pursuing the enemy: if you are suffering hardship, so are they, but you hope to receive something from God for which they cannot hope. God is all-knowing and wise."[72]

Don't be fooled by the number of deserters and defectors, for God's Messenger said: "There is still a group in my *umma* who fight at God's command, conquering their enemies. Those who differ with them can do them no harm, until their Hour comes."[73]

So we say to the tyrants what the believers said before: "They said, 'We shall never prefer you to the clear sign that has come to us, nor to Him who has created us. So decide whatever you will: you only can decide matters of this present life.'"[74]

Mujahidin, be patient and think of the hereafter, for this path in life requires sacrifices, maybe with your life. You scare the enemy but they do not scare you, and you are well aware that the burning issues of the *umma* today are the *jihads* in Palestine and in Iraq. So be very sure to help them, be sure to know that there is a rare and golden opportunity today to make American bleed in Iraq, in economic, human, and psychological terms. So don't waste this opportunity and regret it afterwards. Remember too that the biggest reason for our enemies' control over our lands is to steal our oil, so give everything you can to stop the greatest theft of oil in history from the current and future generations in collusion with the agents and foreigners. They are taking this oil for a paltry price in the knowledge that the prices of all commodities have multiplied many times. But oil, which is the basis of all industry, has gone down in price many times. After it was going for $40 a barrel two decades ago, in the last decade it went for as little as $9, while its price today should be $100 at the very least. So keep on struggling, do not make it easy for them, and focus your operations on it, especially in Iraq and the Gulf, for that will be the death of them.

In conclusion, I address a short message to the rulers of Riyadh, and others in power. I say to you:

Leadership is a covenant between the leader and his subjects in which both parties have rights and duties. That covenant is broken if the leader takes it

---

72 Qur'an, 4:104.
73 From the *hadith* collection of Muslim, book 20, no. 4,721.
74 Qur'an, 20:72.

upon himself to betray his community and his nation. This is what you have done. Even if this covenant of the last century was right, which it is not, you have still trampled all over the people, neither satisfying them nor consulting them, with the support of the English, in total disregard of the interests of the country and its citizens. You can hardly be unaware that the people have woken up from their apathy and realized the sheer scale of the tyranny and corruption that you recklessly commit against their rights and property, and that Muslims in Saudi Arabia are now insisting that their rights be restored, no matter what that costs.

You therefore now have a choice between two paths.

One: to restore to the people their trusteeship in a peaceful way and to let the people of the country choose a Muslim ruler who will rule according to God's book and the *hadith* of His Prophet.

Two: to refuse to give people their rights back, to continue oppressing them and depriving them of their rights, to exploit certain people by paying them money out of the nation's public funds so that they beat and kill their brothers and cousins who have rejected your authority. But you should know that things have gone far enough already, and that when people rise up to demand their rights no security apparatus can stop them. Don't forget what happened to the Shah of Iran despite the reputation, strength, and experience of his security apparatus, or what happened to Ceauşescu in Romania[75] and the terrible fate that he and his family met for what he did to his people. So clearly you would be better off if you restore to the people their rights.

You know that we in the al-Qaeda organization are not competing with you over worldly affairs. What offends us is that you commit acts contrary to religion, such as failing to rule in accordance with what God revealed, and making alliances with the infidels.

I also address the following statement to those righteous scholars, leaders, dignitaries, notables, and business leaders:

You must take the necessary steps before it is too late, for things are descending with extraordinary speed towards an explosion. Do whatever is in your

75 Mohammed Reza Pahlavi (1919–80) was the last reigning Shah of Iran. On January 16 1979 he was forced to flee Iran following a year of public protest that presaged the Iranian revolution. The regime of the Romanian leader Nicolae Ceauşescu (1918–89) was overthrown in December 1989. On December 25, Ceauşescu and his wife Elena were condemned to death by a military kangaroo court and executed by firing squad.

power to defuse the crisis, in the knowledge that the *mujahidin* in Saudi Arabia have not yet started their fight against the regime. If they had really done so, then getting rid of the local leaders of unbelief, namely those in Riyadh, would be at the top of the list. However, current events are merely an extension of the struggle against the Crusader-American alliance who fight us everywhere, just as we fight them everywhere, including Saudi Arabia, from which we are trying to expel them, with God's will.

So, you men of influence, fear God for your sake and for the sake of your *umma*. Those of you who can do so should emigrate and in so doing liberate yourselves from the shackles of illusion and from all the psychological pressure the regime imposes on you, so that you can take up your duty of guiding the *umma* and sorting out the important priorities. If you hesitate any longer things will get even more complicated and problems will only become deeper and more entangled. This will encourage the youth to think for themselves at your expense and to take up arms against the ruler, if they think that they have prepared what is necessary in order to do so, and that they deem themselves ready to remove the apostate ruler, despite the fact that what should really happen is that we unite the efforts of the righteous people to undertake this great deed. Even if some of them have abandoned the task, the duty of standing up to the ruler still remains, as I have said many times before. Things have not been put right, so do your duty and be quick to put the situation right. The rulers of Riyadh very nearly came to blows with each other some decades ago at the time of ibn Saud, but there was mediation between them and the king was convinced to step down. That was how the conflict was resolved then, and this is your role today: to convince these tyrants who trample all over people to restore trusteeship to the people to whom it belongs. For that is their right—they have not asked for falsehood. This is their right. As they say, a penny of protection is worth a fortune of cure.

And I address my prayers to God, saying: Lord, give us good in this world and in the next, save us from the torment of the Fire. Lord, give us truth and provide for us, protect us from falsehood, Lord, spread harmony amongst the hearts of Muslims and unite their ranks, show mercy on their weakness and help them recover from setbacks.

Lord, establish true guidance for the *umma* in which those who obey can be proud and those who disobey can be humiliated, in which good is enjoined and evil forbidden. Lord, make faith dear to us and adorn it in our hearts, and make unbelief, depravity, and disobedience hateful to us.

Lord, lay open the hearts of our young men and women to commitment to Your religion, and provide us with guidance, piety, virtue, and wealth.

Lord, make us stand firm when we slip up, and make the *mujahidin* stand firm everywhere, in Palestine, Iraq, Kashmir, Chechnya, Afghanistan, and Saudi Arabia. Lord, guide their weapons and make their hearts firm, give them support and assistance against your enemies and theirs, for neither we nor they have anyone to help us but You, the strong and beloved one.

God has power over everything, although most people do not know. Praise to God and blessings on Muhammad, and all his family and companions. Our final prayer is praise be to God, lord of the worlds.

FURTHER READING

Ali, Tariq, *Bush in Babylon: The Recolonization of Iraq* (Verso, 2004)

Bergen, Peter, *Holy War Inc: Inside the Secret World of Osama bin Laden* (Free Press, 2002)

Burke, Jason, *Al-Qaeda: The True Story of Radical Islam* (Penguin, 2004)

Fisk, Robert, *Pity the Nation: Lebanon at War* (OUP, 2001)

Gunaratna, Rohan, *Inside Al Qaeda: Global Network of Terror* (Berkeley, 2003)

Jacquard, Roland, *In the Name of Osama bin Laden: Global Terrorism & the bin Laden Brotherhood* (Duke University Press, 2002).

Kepel, Gilles, *The War for Muslim Minds: Islam and the West* (Belknap Press, 2004)

Khosrokhavar, Farhad, *Suicide Bombers: Allah's New Martyrs* (Pluto, 2005)

Lawrence, Bruce, *Shattering the Myth: Islam Beyond Violence* (Princeton, 1998)

Lewis, Bernard, *The Crisis of Islam: Holy War and Unholy Terror* (Modern Library, 2003)

Lincoln, Bruce, *Holy Terrors: Thinking about Religion after September 11* (University of Chicago Press (2003)

Mann, Michael, *Incoherent Empire* (Verso, 2003)

Miles, Hugh, *Al-Jazeera: How Arab TV News Challenged the World* (Abacus, 2005)

The Qur'an, translated by MAS Abdel Haleem (OUP, 2005)

Rashid, Ahmed, *Taliban: The Story of the Afghan Warlords* (Pan, 2001)

Roy, Olivier, *Globalized Islam: The Search for a New Ummah* (Columbia University Press, 2004)

Ruthven, Malise, *A Fury for God: The Islamist Attack on America* (Granta Books, 2004)

Sageman, Marc, *Understanding Terror Networks* (University of Pennsylvania Press, 2004)

Scheuer, Michael, *Imperial Hubris: Why the West is Losing the War on Terror* (Potomac, 2005)

Townshend, Charles, *Terrorism: A Very Short Introduction* (OUP, 2002)

The 9/11 Commission Report: Final Report of the National Commission on Terrorist Attacks Upon the United States (Authorized Edition) (Norton, 2004)

INDEX

in Afghanistan 23, 41, 48
assassination attempts 55–6
assets frozen 78
biographical information 31
children 144, 159
claims responsibility for 9/11 attacks
237–8, 239–40
denials of involvement 27
emigration 19
expulsion from Saudi Arabia 49
expulsion from Sudan 23, 50
family pressure on 55
genius of 46
goals 89–91, 120
health 70–1, 139, 144
marital alliance with Mullah Omar
144
message 92–4
migrations 26–7
outlook 32
plagiarism 157
poetry 16, 205–6
radicalization 31
relationship with the Taliban 73,
83–5
reward for 65
Saudi citizenship withdrawn 4, 33
wealth 39
Western phraseology 261
wives 144
bin Malik, Ka'b 81
bin Salih al-Uthaimain, Muhammad 91
bin Sultan al-Saud, Bandar 255
bin Talal, Hassan 252
bin Zu'air, Sa'id 206
Blair, Tony 59, 112, 114

Blix, Hans 214
Book of Faith (Ibn Taymiyya) 229
Bosnia 15, 17, 48–9, 136, 142, 153
Bosnia-Herzegovina 25, 40
Bremer, Paul 245, 260
Buddhists 76
al-Bukhari, Muhammad 13, 30, 81, 96,
97, 115, 125, 181, 184, 187, 191, 196,
199, 200, 264, 269
Burke, Jason 78, 88
Burma 25
Bush-Blair axis 188
Bush, George HW 56, 148, 181, 240,
241
Bush, George W 101
7th November 2001 speech 142
and the 9/11 attacks 242
air strikes on Iraq 149
arms control policy 142
benefit from war 235
blinded by oil 243
call for peace 236
"Crusade attack" speech 121, 135,
143–4, 215
deception 239
election 241
emergency war funding 242
environment policy 168
global head of unbelief 105
image 122
and the invasion of Iraq 240, 243, 256
kinds of people 113
Middle East policy 114, 174
Muslim policy 139
new type of war speech 238
re-election 237

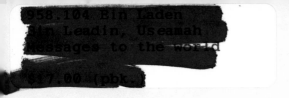